INSIGHT CITY GUIDE

RIO DE JANEIRO

APA PUBLICATIONS

Part of the Langenscheidt Publishing Group

✳ INSIGHT GUIDE
RIO DE JANEIRO

Editor
Pam Barrett
Managing Editor
Dorothy Stannard
Art Director
Klaus Geisler
Picture Editor
Hilary Genin
Production
Kenneth Chan
Cartography Editor
Zoë Goodwin
Editorial Director
Brian Bell

Distribution

UK & Ireland
GeoCenter International Ltd
Meridian House, Churchill Way West
Basingstoke, Hampshire RG21 6YR
Fax: (44) 1256-817988

United States
Langenscheidt Publishers, Inc.
36–36 33rd Street 4th Floor
Long Island City, NY 11106
Fax: (1) 718 784-0640

Australia
Universal Publishers
1 Waterloo Road
Macquarie Park, NSW 2113
Fax: (61) 2 9888 9074

New Zealand
Hema Maps New Zealand Ltd (HNZ)
Unit D, 24 Ra ORA Drive
East Tamaki, Auckland
Fax: (64) 9 273 6479

Worldwide
Apa Publications GmbH & Co.
Verlag KG (Singapore branch)
38 Joo Koon Road, Singapore 628990
Tel: (65) 6865-1600. Fax: (65) 6861-6438

Printing

Insight Print Services (Pte) Ltd
38 Joo Koon Road, Singapore 628990
Tel: (65) 6865-1600. Fax: (65) 6861-6438

©2006 Apa Publications GmbH & Co.
Verlag KG (Singapore branch)
All Rights Reserved

First Edition 1988
Second Edition 2001
Third Edition 2006

ABOUT THIS BOOK

The first Insight Guide pioneered the use of creative full-color photography in travel guides in 1970. Since then, we have expanded our range to cater for our readers' need not only for reliable information about their chosen destination but also for a real understanding of the culture and workings of that destination. Now, when the internet can supply inexhaustible (but not always reliable) facts, our books marry text and pictures to provide those much more elusive qualities: knowledge and discernment. To achieve this, they rely heavily on the authority of locally based writers and photographers.

How to use this book

The book is carefully structured both to convey an understanding of the city and its culture and to guide readers through its sights and activities:

◆ To understand Rio today, you need to know something of its past. The first section covers the city's history and culture in lively, authoritative essays written by specialists.

◆ The main Places section provides a full rundown of all the attractions worth seeing. The main places of interest are coordinated by number with full-color maps.

◆ The Travel Tips listings section provides a point of reference for information on travel, hotels, shops and festivals. Information may be located quickly by using the index printed on the back-cover flap – and the flaps are designed to serve as bookmarks.

◆ Photographs are chosen not only to illustrate geography and buildings but also to convey the moods of the city and the life of its people.

Other Insight Guides available:

Alaska
Amazon Wildlife
American Southwest
Amsterdam
Argentina
Arizona & Grand Canyon
Asia, East
Asia, Southeast
Asia's Best Hotels
  and Resorts
Australia
Austria
Bahamas
Bali & Lombok
Baltic States
Bangkok
Barbados
Belgium
Belize
Berlin
Bermuda
Brazil
Brittany
Buenos Aires
Burgundy
Burma (Myanmar)
Cairo
California
California, Southern
Canada
Caribbean
Caribbean Cruises
Channel Islands
Chicago
Chile
China
Colorado
Continental Europe
Corsica
Costa Rica
Crete
Cuba
Cyprus
Czech & Slovak Republic
Delhi, Jaipur & Agra
Denmark
Dominican Rep. & Haiti
Dublin
East African Wildlife
Eastern Europe
Ecuador
Edinburgh
Egypt
England
Finland
Florida
France
France, Southwest
French Riviera
Gambia & Senegal
Germany
Glasgow
Gran Canaria
Great Britain

Great Railway Journeys
  of Europe
Great River Cruises
  of Europe
Greece
Greek Islands
Guatemala, Belize
  & Yucatán
Hawaii
Hungary
Iceland
India
India, South
Indonesia
Ireland
Israel
Istanbul
Italy
Italy, Northern
Italy, Southern
Jamaica
Japan
Jerusalem
Jordan
Kenya
Korea
Laos & Cambodia
Lisbon
Madeira
Malaysia
Mallorca & Ibiza
Malta
Mauritius Réunion
  & Seychelles
Melbourne
Mexico
Miami
Montreal
Morocco
Namibia
Nepal
Netherlands
New England
New Mexico
New Orleans
New York State
New Zealand
Nile
Normandy
North American and
  Alaskan Cruises
Norway
Oman & The UAE
Oxford
Pacific Northwest
Pakistan
Peru
Philadelphia
Philippines
Poland
Portugal
Provence
Puerto Rico
Rajasthan

Rio de Janeiro
Russia
Sardinia
Scandinavia
Scotland
Seattle
Sicily
South Africa
South America
Spain
Spain, Northern
Spain, Southern
Sri Lanka
Sweden
Switzerland
Syria & Lebanon
Taiwan
Tenerife
Texas
Thailand
Trinidad & Tobago
Tunisia
Turkey
Tuscany
Umbria
USA: On The Road
USA: Western States
US National Parks: West
Utah
Venezuela
Vienna
Vietnam
Wales

INSIGHT CITY GUIDES
(with free restaurant map)

Barcelona
Beijing
Boston
Bruges, Ghent & Antwerp
Brussels
Cape Town
Florence
Hong Kong
Las Vegas
London
Los Angeles
Madrid
Moscow
New York
Paris
Prague
Rome
St Petersburg
San Francisco
Singapore
Sydney
Taipei
Tokyo
Toronto
Venice
Walt Disney World/Orlando
Washington, DC

Pocket Guide: Rio de Janeiro and has contributed to earlier Insight Guides. She hopes you will share her passion for the vibrant city of Rio as you get to know its many moods and faces. She is a founding director of the Margaret Mee Foundation, which honors the English painter who fell in love with the natural wonders of Brazil on a visit that was to last a lifetime.

The features on Contemporary Rio, Music and the Movie Industry were contributed by **Christopher Pickard**, a consultant on Brazil who set up the Brazilian Tourist Office in London and is a board member of the Latin American Travel Association. As well as writing on travel and tourism he has written extensively about the media and entertainment industries, and for more than 20 years covered these topics for *Moving Pictures*, *Pulse*, *Screen International* and *Variety*, among others. Pickard also contributed to the *Berlitz Pocket Guide: Rio de Janeiro*.

Most of the pictures in this book are by by Rio resident **Eric Carl Font** and by the **Campos & Davis** photographic team, who have worked extensively in Latin America.

Under the guidance of in-house managing editor **Dorothy Stannard**, this new edition was edited by **Pam Barrett**, who also updated the feature on Rio's Residents.

The book was proof-read by **Neil Titman** and indexed by **Helen Peters**.

The contributors

This new edition of *City Guide: Rio de Janeiro* builds on foundations laid by contributors to the original *Insight Guide: Rio de Janeiro*, among them **Moyra Ashford**, **Jenny Byers**, **Kristen Christensen**, **Harold Emert**, **Ricardo Librach Buckup**, **Tom Murphy** and **Edwin Taylor**.

The chapters in the Places section were updated and in some cases completely rewritten by **Liz Wynn-Jones**, who also wrote all the picture stories and the feature Beauty and the Beach, as well as compiling the fact-packed Travel Tips section at the end of the book. Wynn-Jones, a native Brazilian, is a journalist and travel writer who has been involved in the guidebook business for many years. She also wrote the *Insight*

CONTACTING THE EDITORS

We would appreciate it if readers alerted us to errors or outdated information by writing to:

Insight Guides, P.O. Box 7910, London SE1 1WE, England. Fax: (44) 20 7403 0290. e-mail: insight@apaguide.co.uk

NO part of this book may be reproduced, stored in a retrieval system or transmitted in any form or means electronic, mechanical, photocopying, recording or otherwise, without prior written permission of Apa Publications. Brief text quotations with use of photographs are exempted for book review purposes only. Information has been obtained from sources believed to be reliable, but its accuracy and completeness, and the opinions based thereon, are not guaranteed.

www.insightguides.com
In North America:
www.insighttravelguides.com

Travel Tips

THE BEST OF RIO DE JANEIRO

Setting priorities, saving money, unique attractions...
here, at a glance, are our recommendations, plus some
tips and tricks even *cariocas* won't always know

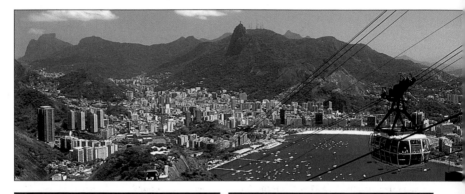

BEST VIEWS

- **Corcovado**. The mountain pedestal of Rio's famed Cristo Redentor statue offers stunning views over the city and beyond. A little cog train will take you most of the way up. *See page 141*.
- **Pão de Açúcar**. The panorama from the top of Sugar Loaf Mountain, reached via cable car, is breathtaking. It's all laid out before you – the vast curve of Copacabana Beach, the perfect curl of Botafogo, and the Rio–Niterói Bridge. *See page 142*.
- **The Soberbo Belvedere**. The belvedere, on the Rio–Teresópolis highway, provides an unforgettable vista over the Serra dos Orgãos mountain range, with the city and the bay spread out below. *See page 180*.

BEST FOR FAMILIES

- **Maracanã Stadium**. The boys, and the increasing number of girls who are soccer mad, won't want to miss a match at Maracanã Stadium. Don't go if there's no match on: they'll probably find it boring. *See page 119*.
- **Floresta da Tijuca Safari**. Hang on tight, as you go deep into the woods. There are no teddy bears' picnics, but lots of excitement on a real forest safari. *See page 162*.
- **Corcovado train**. All aboard the Jungle Express: take the train to Corcovado, and experience the thrill of a steep ride through lush vegetation in an open-sided train. *See page 141*.
- **Museu Casa do Pontal**. Push all the buttons and watch those people move! Brazilian life in action can be viewed through the animated exhibits in this fascinating museum of popular art. *See page 158*.
- **Santa Teresa trolley**. Ride the rattling old yellow trolleys round the narrow streets, but hang on tight and don't let the kids emulate local schoolchildren who like to jump on and off as the vehicle trundles along. *See page 104*.

ABOVE: view of Botafogo Bay from Sugar Loaf Mountain.
LEFT: clinging onto the Santa Teresa trolley.

BEST MUSEUMS

● **Museu de Arte Moderna**. One of Rio's outstanding exhibition sites, with works by notable Latin American and European artists. *See page 89.*

● **Museu Nacional de Belas Artes**. Includes works by Cândido Portinari, one of Brazil's greatest 20th-century painters. *See page 91.*

● **Chácara do Céu**. The Little House in the Sky exhibits work by some of the greatest 19th- and 20th-century European artists: Braque, Degas, Matisse, Modigliani, Monet and Picasso as well as fine examples of Brazilian art. *See page 104.*

● **Espaço Cultural da Marinha**. The Marine Museum charts the history of Brazil's colorful maritime past, but the highlights are the detailed model ships. *See page 98.*

● **Museu da República**. Housed in the Palácio do Catete, you can visit what were the private quarters of the country's presidents, their elegant reception rooms and extensive gardens, and there's a fascinating display of presidential memorabilia. *See page 87.*

● **Museu de Arte Contemporânea**. Enjoy Niemeyer's swooping architecture, as well as the fine collection. *See page 111.*

● **Museu Internacional de Arte Naïf**. Estimated to hold the world's largest collection of naïve art, with 8,000 works from around Brazil, and many other countries. *See page 142.*

ABOVE RIGHT: settling down for a day on the beach.
BELOW: the stunning Museu de Arte Contemporânea de Niterói.

BEST BEACHES

● **Praia de Copacabana**. A long stretch, enlarged in the 1960s by imported sand. It offers every form of life and entertainment, as bars and restaurants line the shore and the kiosks are favorite gathering places. Volleyball, beach soccer, and paddle-ball are all played on this wide, sandy stretch. *See page 125.*

● **Praia de Leblon**. This is a family beach. At the corner of Rua General Venâncio Flores is the famous Baixo Bebê, the kiosk where the babies of Rio are taken by their mothers or nannies for their early-morning airing. *See page 147.*

● **Praia de Ipanema**. The continuation of Leblon Beach, and the most famous of all. In the morning, joggers and cyclists throng the promenade, while others exercise on the sands. Later, it is packed with sunbathers. *See page 133.*

● **Praia de Barra**. This is Rio's longest beach, at 18 km (11 miles). Some parts are built up, with bars and restaurants, others are deserted, as they form part of a nature reserve. The beach is extremely busy at weekends, but fairly quiet during the week. *See page 157.*

● **Praia do São Conrado**. At the farthest end is the famous Praia do Pepino. This is the landing strip for hang-gliders, who love it here, but not so good for swimmers. *See page 155.*

● **Praia do Arpoador**. A beach that has pedestrian-only access and is very popular with surfers. *See page 133.*

BEST EATING AND DRINKING TIPS

● **Coffee**. The best coffee in Rio can be sampled at **Armazém do Café**, with branches all over town. Simple snacks partner some of the best brews around. *See page 136.*

● **Juice bars**. Fruit as you have never tasted it: refreshing, filling, and good for you. Any of Rio's numerous juice bars can serve up a natural cocktail you'll never forget. Try *açaí*, made from the fruit of an Amazonian palm. Or mango and melon... the choice is endless.

● **Burgers**. For Rio's best burgers, you can't beat **Joe and Leo's**. Sporting souvenirs garnish the walls; tasty sauces garnish the burgers. *See page 161.*

● **Grazing**. If you are a grazer, **Celeiro** is the place to sample salads. Get there soon after noon, or you'll have to wait for a table. *See page 152.*

● **Ice cream**. Brazilian imagination runs riot when it comes to ice cream, and full advantage is taken of the huge variety of fruits available. **Mil Frutas café** is a prize-winner. *See page 136.*

● **Barbecue**. Local people all have their favorite *rodízio* barbecue, but **Porção Rio's** really is the slickest. Not cheap, but well worth it. *See page 113.*

● **Breakfast**. Rio's favorite upmarket bakery is in the food emporium **Garcia & Rodrigues**. Crusty croissants and buttery brioches make this a great place for a stylish breakfast. *See page 152.*

● **Cocktails**. If you're going to have one expensive, glamorous cocktail experience, make sure it is a *caipirinha* by the pool at the **Copacabana Palace**. Unforgettable, like the stars who've done the same before you. *See page 122.*

ABOVE: treat youself to some sophisticated and distinctive jewelry while you're in Rio.

BEST SHOPPING OPPORTUNITIES

● **Swimwear**. No surprise that swimwear is a great buy in Rio. Two leaders in this field are **Lenny**, who has shops in the São Conrado Fashion Mall and Ipanema (www.lenny.com.br), and the so aptly named **Bum Bum**, with shops in Barrashopping and Ipanema (www.bumbum.com.br). *See page 222.*

● **Leather goods**. A favorite with Rio visitors. Select designer handbags can be found in any of the malls, but the Sunday Ipanema Hippie Fair has a wide range of modestly priced leather goods, too. *See page 222.*

● **Jewelry**. The range is huge. **Pepe Torras** uses Brazilian hardwood to create sophisticated, stylish and wearable pieces. **Tereza Xavier** is a trail-blazer in the use of indigenous materials. **Flavio Guidi** combines craftsmanship with the classics of the gem spectrum to produce unique pieces of top-of-the range jewelry. *See page 221.*

● **Brazilian music**. **Modern Sound** in Copacabana is a temple to rhythm, and the selection of Brazilian music here is unbeatable. *See page 124.*

● **Thongs**. Thongs, or flip-flops, the ubiquitous rubber-soled sandals, are a steal in Rio, and they're for sale on every corner. *See page 222.*

BEST EXCURSIONS

- **Petrópolis**. Rio de Janeiro state's leading mountain getaway, ideal when the weather is very hot. The premier attraction is the Museu Imperial, housed in the 19th-century palace built for the monarchy, who spent their summers here. *See page 171.*

- **Búzios**. Once a fishing village, Búzios has endless unspoiled beaches, palm trees and coconuts, beautiful people and a relaxing lifestyle beneath a perpetual tropical sun. *See page 183.*

- **Ilha Grande**. A pristine island, much of it a protected area, with with some spectacular fauna and flora, waterfalls and limpid pools, and some of Brazil's most beautiful tropical beaches. *See page 196.*

- **Paraty**. The star of the Costa Verde, Paraty is an attractive colonial town of cobbled streets and brightly painted houses, that has been designated a UNESCO monument of international interest. *See page 201.*

ABOVE: taking the plunge at Búzios.
BELOW: São Conrado Beach is a top place for hang-gliding.

CITY SURPRISES

- **Pista Claudio Coutinho**. An early-morning walk along the Pista Claudio Coutinho at the foot of Sugar Loaf Mountain will introduce you to countless numbers of birds as well as the very sociable marmoset colony, all so close to the city centre. *See page 144.*

- **Hang-gliding**. Feel the urge to fly? Hang-gliding is big in Rio. The place for those who want to emulate Santos Dumont is São Conrado Beach. *See page 156.*

- **Helicopter trips**. Take a helicopter trip from the landing pad at Morro da Urca. It's not cheap, of course, but the views are unforgettable and it's an experience you will never forget. *See page 223.*

BIGGEST EVENT

- **Carnival**. Rio's flamboyant Carnival, in February or early March, is undoubtedly the biggest and best-known event in the calendar. If you want to attend, book well in advance and be aware that flights and accommodation will be expensive. *See page 65.*

- **New Year's Eve**. Next in line are the celebrations for New Year, and homage to Iemanjá, a revered goddess of the Umbanda religion. The whole city, it seems, and many from outside, flock to Copacabana beach. *See page 61.*

MONEY-SAVING TIPS

Kilo restaurants Pile your plate up high in one of Rio's kilo restaurants, or self-service eateries, which provide excellent value for money. As the name suggests, your food is priced by weight rather than by content. They also make things easy for picky or cautious eaters: if you don't like it, don't pick it!

Ferry trips Take the ferry boat from Praça Quinze to Niterói or Paquetá. No marks for luxury, but you can't beat the price, or the views.

Events Listings The daily newspaper *O Globo* produces a *Rio Show* magazine insert on Friday, a useful source of information and listings. *Veja* is a national glossy weekly news magazine that also publishes a Friday entertainment insert, called *Vejinha*.

Taxis Taxis are reasonably priced, as long as you avoid those lined up outside the elegant hotels, as they have very different rates. Otherwise, a ride from Copacabana to Central Rio should not cost more than US$10, and is well worth taking.

CIDADE MARAVILHOSA

For the beautiful people of a beautiful city, hedonism coexists harmoniously with urban chaos, and there are few visitors who do not respond to Rio's vibrant appeal

Sprawling in majestic disarray across a narrow strip of land between granite peaks and the South Atlantic, Rio de Janeiro lives up to the name bestowed on it by its residents – the *cidade maravilhosa* or "marvelous city." Each day, Rio's streets and sidewalks support some 6½ million people, transported by more than a million cars, trucks, buses, motorcycles, scooters, and bikes, as well as on foot, all competing for room in a space designed for one-third their number. This spectacular chaos does nothing to dampen the enthusiasm of the *cariocas*, as Rio's imperturbable residents are known.

The *carioca* lifestyle is a mixture of hedonism and irreverence. They appear to respect nothing and no one, and are constantly on the lookout for something to provide them with a new diversion or pleasure. They are, of course, conscious of their national identity as Brazilians, but above all each is a *carioca*, and their overwhelming loyalty is to their city. They see themselves as individuals of immense resourcefulness, of keen wit, of engaging conversation, of stunning beauty, and of worldly knowledge. The *cariocas'* unflagging optimism, boundless confidence and utter self-absorption might be seen as egotism, but few can resist their charm.

There are around 6.4 million residents in Rio itself, but an additional 5 million live in suburbs ringing the city. As many as 70 percent are poor by American or European standards, and the divide between the haves and the have-nots inevitably leads to tension and conflict. But Rio's citizens cope surprisingly well with inequality, perhaps because there is always the beach and the sunshine, the samba and Carnival, and the exhilarating presence of Rio's extraordinary beauty. The beach is their playground, samba is their music and Carnival is their party, where the poor parade as if they were the rich and the rich mingle with the poor.

Cariocas love their "marvelous city," and visitors soon understand why. Romantics lose their hearts in Rio; reasonable people lose touch with reality. This is a city where anything seems possible. ❑

PRECEDING PAGES: the ultimate party city; a new day on Copacabana; everyone flocks to the beach. **LEFT:** Rio doing what it does best – a samba show at a Leblon nightclub.

CAPITAL OF AN EMPIRE

Rio went from colonial outpost to capital of the Portuguese
Empire, the most advanced and sophisticated city in
Latin America, with a history and reputation
as sparkling as its natural setting

The first Europeans arrived in Rio de Janeiro on January 1, 1502, as part of a Portuguese voyage of exploration, one of a series launched by ambitious Portuguese explorers in the 15th and early 16th centuries. Pedro Álvares Cabral, who was blown off course on a voyage to India, had discovered the east coast of Brazil in 1500, and at first believed it was an island, which he called Ilha de Vera Cruz.

There was further confusion when the 1502 expedition entered what was thought to be the mouth of a river, hence the name Rio de Janeiro – January River. It was, in fact, a 380-sq. km (147-sq. mile) bay, which the explorers originally called Santa Luzia, in honor of the favorite saint of the navigator Amerigo Vespucci, who had sailed along the coast, liberally bestowing saints' names as he went.

Portugal laid claim to the whole of the coastal territory, which it initially divided into 15 captaincies, but concentrated its colonization in the northeast, where sugar plantations were established, making it the economic powerhouse of the new colony. Seeing no immediate economic value in Rio, the Portuguese delayed any settlement, leaving the way open for the the French to move in.

French colony

In 1555, a French fleet arrived, intending to found the first French colony in the southern half of the continent. By then, the bay was

widely known by the Indian name Guanabara (Arm of the Sea), which it is still called today. Under Admiral Nicolas de Villegaignon, some 500 French settlers disembarked on an island in the bay that now bears the admiral's name. A fort was built, and the French proceeded with their grand scheme to found Antarctic France, which was to be settled by European Calvinists.

Another 1,000 settlers arrived, but problems arose when the Calvinists discovered that the religious freedom they sought in the New World was less than they had expected. Rumors of religious persecution in the colony reached Europe, bringing further immigration

---

LEFT: funeral cortège of the dethroned Pedro II, 1891.
RIGHT: Pedro Álvares Cabral entered the bay in 1502.

to a halt. Meanwhile, Portugal began to take an interest in the southern part of its colony, resolving to drive out the French.

In 1560, a Portuguese fleet entered Guanabara Bay, and after a week of fighting the French were defeated. But the Portuguese left almost immediately, apparently believing that the territory was secure, and the French returned. A second expedition was mounted five years later. This time, the Portuguese seemed to have learned from their earlier careless mistakes and were determined to gain lasting control of Rio de Janeiro. It took two years of intermittent fighting, but ultimately they were successful.

BUILDING RIO

Missionaries always followed conquerors to the New World, and in 1608 a number of different religious Orders, who had already converted many of the indigenous people to Christianity, began building in Rio. The Franciscans established a monastery on Morro Santo Antonio, the Carmelites in Praça XV, the Benedictines on the Morro do São Bento, and the Jesuits on the Morro do Castello. All the Orders had great political and economic power.

In 1673 an important piece of secular building began when work started on the Arcos da Lapa aqueduct, designed to bring water into the city from the Rio Carioca in Santa Teresa. It was completed in 1724.

Foundation of the city

From then on, Rio received increasing attention from the Portuguese colonizers. In 1567, the fortified city of São Sebastião do Rio de Janeiro was founded. It was named in honor of St Sebastian, on whose feast day (January 20) the French were finally vanquished, but the name soon became simplified to Rio de Janeiro. Initially confined to the Morro do Castello, the area facing the bay, close to where the present domestic airport now stands, Rio's growth was determined by the importance of its port to the colony. By the end of the 16th century, it had become one of the four main population centers of Brazil. But its port remained secondary to those of the sugar-growing northeastern provinces, particularly the colony's capital of Salvador in the province of Bahia.

The slave trade

During these years, Rio's port was extremely important, however, for the import of slaves from Africa – many of them dead on arrival, others destined for the *casas de engordo*, where the young men, weak from their long sea voyages, were fed and fattened up before being dispatched to the sugar plantations. The story of Brazilian slavery is inevitably harrowing. Historians believe 12 million Africans were captured and shipped to Brazil between 1549 and the outlawing of the Brazilian slave trade in 1853. Of that number, about 2 million died on the slave boats before they reached Brazilian shores.

Once in Brazil, white masters – like those in other countries – treated their slaves as a cheap and expendable investment. An African youth enslaved by the owner of a sugar plantation or gold mine could expect to live only eight years. Slaves' lives were unimportant to their masters, who regarded them as barely human. It was cheaper to buy new replacements for their labor force than preserve the health of existing members.

Gold rush

When gold was discovered towards the end of the 17th century in the neighboring province of Minas Gerais, thousands of prospectors and fortune hunters, many of them from Portugal, flocked to Minas to participate in the largest gold rush of its time. Rio, the only port city close to the mines, benefited immediately. A road was built to link Rio to the mines, while in the city's port, gold-seekers disembarked daily. Minas made Portugal the world's largest producer of gold in the 18th century, generating enormous wealth – although most of the riches went straight to Portugal, a source of dissatisfaction to the resident settlers. Gold became the colony's main export item, and it all went through Rio de Janeiro, thus shifting Brazil's economic center from the northeast.

Boom days also brought problems. Twice, in 1710 and 1711, the French attacked Rio. On their second try, they broke through its

capital of a European empire, when the Portuguese royal family fled to Rio in 1808, during the Napoleonic Wars, after refusing an ultimatum to declare war on England. With Brazil's independence in 1822, Rio became capital of the Brazilian Empire, and in 1889, capital of the Republic of Brazil. Throughout these years, it was the economic, cultural and political center of Brazil, home to the pomp of monarchy and intrigue of the republic.

Flight from Europe

The flight of Emperor Dom João VI from Portugal, with an entourage of more than 15,000 noblemen, created the unprecedented situa-

defenses and sacked the city. Thanks to the seemingly unending flow of gold from Minas, however, the city was soon rebuilt. In 1763, Portugal finally recognized Rio's status as the colony's leading city and transferred the capital there from Salvador.

Brazil's capital

For the next 200 years, Rio would reign supreme. Among the events that shaped the city during these years, the most remarkable was its sudden and unexpected elevation to

tion of a colony becoming the seat of government for the mother country. The arrival of the emperor thrust Rio into a world of courtly manners and elegance which hardly fitted its backwoods character. More incongruous still was the insistence of the transplanted nobles on maintaining their European court dress in a fetid port city in the tropics.

Determined to make the best of the situation, the emperor set about upgrading his new capital. Over the next decade, Rio became more Europeanized than any other New World capital. Schools (including a school of medicine), newspapers, banks, and various imperial government organizations sprouted. The

LEFT: a mid-19th-century slave market.
ABOVE: French ships attack Rio in 1711.

Imperial Palace and formal gardens at Quinta da Boa Vista were established, as was the Jardim Botânico, which Dom João created to nuture imported plants *(see page 148)*. Trade, which previously had been conducted only with Portugal, was opened up. By engaging in trade with Napoleon's enemies, principally England, Portugal gave a giant boost to Rio's economy and ended its previous isolation, making it an important trading center.

Tumultuous times

During Dom João's 13-year residence, Rio's population tripled to 100,000. When he was forced to return to Portugal in 1821, he left his son, Dom Pedro, behind as prince regent. The following year, Pedro was also summoned to return to Lisbon, but he refused to do so, believing that both Brazil and Portugal would benefit if he remained. "Considering that my presence here pleases the people and makes the nation happy, I am ready: let them know that I will stay *(Diga ao povo que fico)*," was the official statement he made on January 9, 1822, which is now known as the Dia do Fico (The Day of Commitment).

This was a time of upheaval throughout the Latin American colonies, with the emergence of vociferous and charismatic nationalist leaders rejecting their European rulers and

VISITORS TO THE COURT

The presence of the Portuguese court in Rio encouraged artistic and adventurous Europeans to visit the city. One was Maria Graham, Lady Calcott, whose watercolors, now hanging in the National Library of Brazil in Rio, depict the lives of the people of Brazil, particularly the slaves in Bahia state. Ms Graham (1785–1842), who was for a while a guest at the Imperial Palace, was a remarkable woman who had set up home in Valparaíso, Chile, after her sea-captain husband had died on their journey to the city.

Her *Journal of a Residence in Chile* and *Journal of a Voyage to Brazil*, published in 1824, give fascinating glimpses into life in both countries, as well as a first-hand account of the 1822 earthquake in Chile.

Another eminent European visitor was the French artist Jean-Baptiste Debret (1768–1848). His beautifully illustrated *Voyage pittoresque et historique au Brésil (A Picturesque and Historical Trip to Brazil)* (1834) can also be found in the National Library of Brazil.

Nicolas-Antoine Taunay (1755–1830) was another visiting artist from France, who painted a graphic depiction of a Rio de Janeiro slave market – a subject that seemed both to horrify and to fascinate many European visitors to the city.

demanding independence. Pedro came under the influence of the nationalists, and on September 7, 1822, the colony's declaration of independence from Portugal was signed. Rio then became the capital of the independent nation of Brazil, which was formally entitled the Brazilian Empire, although it had no territorial possessions, and Brazilian noblemen replaced the Portuguese.

In 1825 a treaty was signed with Britain, who agreed to recognize the independence of the Brazilian Empire in exchange for a guarantee that her trading privileges in Brazil would continue. In 1826 the first parliament was instituted, and in the same year (when the literacy rate was just 3 percent) the country's first universities were founded, but not in Rio – one in Olinda, to serve the north, and one in São Paulo, to cater for the south.

But the capital, and the empire itself, were about to go through their most tumultuous period. For the next 20 years, Brazil was nearly torn asunder by constant revolts and regional challenges to the central authority in Rio. The first disappointment to emerge from independence was the emperor himself, who had initially been so popular. Rather than adopting the liberal policies his subjects wanted and had expected of him, Pedro I insisted on maintaining the privileges and power of an absolute monarch.

The extraordinary Dom Pedro II

Bowing to pressure, after a confrontation with liberal members of Congress, Pedro abdicated and turned the empire over to his five-year-old son, Dom Pedro II. For 10 years the country was ruled by a regency. Finally, in 1840, the country's political leadership agreed to declare Pedro prematurely of age and hand over the reigns to this 15-year-old boy. But the decision proved to be sound, for Pedro was able to silence the squabbling separatist movements and unite the nation.

For the next 48 years, Pedro II reigned as emperor, using his extraordinary talents to create domestic peace and giving Brazil its longest continuous period of political stability. A surprisingly humble man, Pedro was

blessed with enormous personal authority which he used to direct the nation. During the American Civil War, Abraham Lincoln remarked that the only man he would trust to arbitrate between north and south was Pedro II. Under his wise guidance, regional rivalries were kept in check and Pedro's own popularity reinforced the control of central government over the nation.

Peace and progress

The four decades of domestic peace which followed were marked by steady progress and increasing contact with the outside world. A coffee boom further enhanced Brazil's econ-

omy and the status of its capital. Pedro II, a scholarly, well-traveled man, made Rio a South American showcase for the latest marvels of modern science. Between 1845 and 1851, regular passenger services were established to London and Paris. The city was lit by gas in 1854 (by which time, with a population of a quarter of a million, it was Latin America's largest metropolis), and was linked to London by telegraph in 1874.

Pedro's greatest coup was the construction of the first telephone line outside of the United States of America, between Rio and his imperial retreat, Petrópolis, where he had built a sumptuous summer palace in the

LEFT: Jean-Baptiste Debret pictured ladies on their way to church. **RIGHT:** Pedro II, the wise ruler.

mountains outside the capital, as an escape from the heat of the city.

End of an era

An ugly feature of the country's history finally came to an end on May 13, 1888, when the princess regent, Isabel de Orleans e Bragança, signed the Lei Áurea (Golden Law) abolishing the institution of slavery. This law immediately freed an estimated 800,000 slaves, but it was long overdue: Brazil was the last country in the western hemisphere to abolish the system. The European nations had earlier put pressure on Brazil to end the trade in slaves, and the Aberdeen Law of 1845 had allowed British ships to attack, in international waters, any Brazilian ship involved in such trading. The trade officially ended in 1853, but the institution continued. There were still thousands of slaves, and their descendants, in the country, and international pressure for their freedom continued.

Not all critics of slavery were outsiders, however – there was a vocal abolitionist movement within Brazil. Castro Alves (1847–71) wrote a passionate critique of the institution, *Navio Negreiro (Black Slave Ship)*, but died young, too soon to see abolition. Joaquim Nabuco de Araujo (1849–1910), a writer and diplomat, was a respected leader of

NAMING NAMES

Place names in Rio have some interesting antecedents. Copacabana, for example, comes from the indigenous Quechua language: *copa* means "luminous place," and *caguana* means "blue beach." It was originally the name of a little settlement on Lake Titicaca, where the Spanish erected a chapel and placed an image of the Virgin Mary. When a copy of the image was taken to Rio by an itinerant silver merchant, and placed on a remote beach called Sacopenapā, it became an object of pilgrimage, and the name, now corrupted into Copacabana, went with it, and soon became accepted.

Ipanema also has indigenous origins, but less of a story: it is a Tamoio word meaning "dangerous waters."

Carioca – the name given to Rio's residents – also comes from the Tamoio language, and is believed to mean "the house of the white man." Because some of the early settlers built huts near a river, this became known as the Rio Carioca.

Leblon, on the other hand, is named after the area's first important landowner, Frenchman Charles Le Blon; while Flamengo got its name after a war with the Dutch in 1654. Prisoners of war, most of them Flemings – *Flamengos* in Portuguese – were brought to prison camps which became known as Campos dos Flamengos.

the struggle. He founded the Brazilian Anti-Slavery Society in 1880, and wrote extensively about the subject.

Manumission (freedom from bondage), when it came, was a pragmatic move rather than a humanitarian one, brought about largely by the beginning of industrialization. Once sugar production began to move away from the labor-intensive plantations towards the factory system, slavery made less economic sense. However, freed slaves discovered that liberty did not really improve their way of life. Indeed, in some ways they were worse off: factory owners preferred the new immigrants who were flooding in from Europe and Japan

nobility and bringing to a halt Rio's days of titled elegance. The 1891 Constitution created a situation of permanent conflict, and the capital of the newly formed Republic of Brazil became the battleground of civilian politicians as Brazil embarked on the first of several attempts at democracy.

In reality, however, the republic amounted to little more than an exchange of elites. In place of Rio's nobles were the wealthy landowners of the states of São Paulo and Minas Gerais. These new power brokers quickly became the nation's political establishment, deciding among themselves the vital issues of the day, including the choice of the

and were regarded as more reliable. The ex-slaves were relegated either to performing the most menial of tasks, or being unemployed and destitute, and their living conditions were often appalling.

Revolution

The tranquil and prosperous reign of Pedro II came to an abrupt end in 1889 when the military, expressing growing republican sentiments, overthrew the monarchy in a bloodless coup, and sent Pedro into exile, scattering the

LEFT: a contemporary depiction of Rio, around 1900.
ABOVE: an imperial banknote from the 1870s.

THE WAR OF CANUDOS

The so-called War of Canudos, an uprising in a remote settlement in Bahia, began as a religious conflict, led by the fanatical Antônio Conselheiro and opposed by the Catholic Church. It developed into an early experiment in socialism, then became seen as a threat to the republic. It was brutally suppressed by federal troops in 1897 and inspired one of the classics of Brazilian literature, *Os Sertões (Rebellion in the Backlands)*, by Euclides da Cunha, as well as Peruvian writer Mario Vargas Llosa's *La Guerra del Fin del Mundo (The War of the End of the World)*, and a 1997 film, *Guerra de Canudos (The War of Canudos)* by Sergio Rezende.

president. Rio was soon caught up in the urban turmoil that marked Brazil's industrialization.

During these years, the city underwent rapid urbanization. Its swelling population, fuelled by European immigrants and by migrants from the northeast of the country, where sugar and coffee plantations were declining, forced the government to find creative solutions to overcome the chronic lack of space. By 1890, the city's population numbered a little over one million (the population of the country as a whole had by then reached 14.3 million, due to the government's encouragement of foreign immigration, as a substitute for slave labor).

Establishing a trend that continued throughout the 20th century, city planners looked south. Starting in 1892, tunnels were drilled through the granite mountains to open up the beachside neighborhood of Copacabana and prepare the way for the later development of Ipanema, the Rodrigo de Freitas area, and the beaches further south. The first beachfront boulevard was built, running along the bay to Sugar Loaf.

Dramatic facelift

The downtown area itself was given a dramatic facelift with the construction of Rio's most elegant avenue. Inaugurated in 1905,

RIO BRANCO

Rio Branco actually means White River in Portuguese, but the Avenida Central was renamed (as was the town of the same name in the province of Acre) to honor José Maria da Silva Paranhos, Baron of Rio Branco (1845–1912), one of Brazil's most eminent statesmen. Born in Rio de Janeiro, the son of a prominent diplomat, he was Consul-General in Liverpool, in the UK, at the end of the 19th century, and became Brazil's foreign minister in 1902. He is recognized as having established a close relationship with Argentina and Chile, and for setting up the first Brazilian embassy in the United States.

Avenida Central was built in response to President Rodrigues Alves's vision of "a tropical Paris." Unfortunately, Alves overlooked the fact that downtown Rio, unlike Paris, had no room to grow other than vertically. Later in the century (especially through the 1960s), the elegant three- and five-story buildings of Avenida Central, the Champs-Élysées of Rio, were replaced by 30-story skyscrapers, and the avenue underwent a name change, becoming Avenida Rio Branco. Of the 115 buildings that flanked Avenida Central in 1905, Rio Branco has preserved only a handful.

Construction booms were important for the modernization of Rio, but the city paid a heavy price in the loss of its architectural heritage. With space severely limited by topography, the wrecking ball did away with much of old Rio. Modern-day landmarks such as the wide Copacabana Beach and the giant Flamengo Park that flanks the bay were only made possible by landfill from downtown hills, as was the Santos Dumos airport; and Ilha de Villegaignon in Guanabara Bay was joined to the mainland by landfill in 1929. The saddest example of this destruction was in 1922, when the Morro do Castello, site of the original city, was carted off for landfill purposes, together with most of the remaining 16th- and 17th-century structures.

such as Maurice Chevalier, Tommy Dorsey and Josephine Baker performed on stage, and the city became synonymous with gambling, glamor and high living. In 1931, the statue of Christ the Redeemer (Cristo Redentor) was inaugurated on the peak of Corcovado, from where it presided over this hedonistic city.

City rivalry

In 1930, a coup brought to power Getúlio Vargas, who enjoyed mixing with the stars at the Copacabana, but was also a defender of the urban working class. Vargas brought in a social security system and introduced a minimum wage. Populism and nationalism became

Holiday highspot

In the period between the late 1920s and the end of the 1950s, Rio's reputation was at its height. It was the favorite holiday spot for international stars and celebrities, many of whom stayed at the splendid Copacabana Palace Hotel, which, when it opened in 1923, was one of the few luxury hotels in Latin America. Some came to the Copa mainly for the casino, where gambling – black tie only – was permitted from the early 1920s until 1946 (although with a nine-year hiatus). Big names

the dominant political themes, with the nation's politicians fighting for influence over the masses.

Meanwhile, as Rio struggled to find room to expand, its rival to the south, São Paulo, was enjoying a surge of economic and population growth. By 1950, the city of São Paulo had surpassed Rio in population and economic importance, a lead that it has never relinquished. In 1960, as we shall see in the next chapter, Rio suffered the final humiliation when President Juscelino Kubitschek formally moved the nation's capital to Brasília, the brand-new city he had created in the geographical center of the country. ❑

LEFT: the elegant Avenida Central was built in 1905.
ABOVE: Getúlio Vargas *(left)* enjoyed the good life.

Decisive Dates

The Colonial Era (1500–1822)

1494 The Treaty of Tordesillas divides the non-European world between Portugal and Spain. Portugal gets present-day Brazil.

1500 Portuguese explorer Pedro Álvares Cabral lands near Pôrto Seguro, and becomes the first European to set foot in Brazil. He names the country Ilha de Vera Cruz, but it eventually takes the name Brazil, after *pau brasil*, a wood from which the Europeans extracted red dye.

1502 On January 1, Álvares Cabral's expedition enters what was believed to be the mouth of a

river, hence the city's name, Rio de Janeiro – January River. It was actually the bay now known by its Indian name, Guanabara.

1533 The colony of Brazil is divided into 15 *capitanias* (captaincies), each governed by a Portuguese courtier.

1549 A central administration, based in Salvador and directed by a governor general, is put in place to oversee the *capitanias*.

1555 A French fleet under Admiral Nicolas de Villegaignon arrives in the Bay of Guanabara. A fort is built, and the French proceed with their grand scheme to found Antarctic France, which was to be settled by European Calvinists.

1560–7 The Portuguese resolve to drive out

the French. After some years of intermittent fighting, they gain lasting control of Rio.

1567 The fortified city of São Sebastião do Rio de Janeiro is founded, named in honor of St Sebastian, on whose feast day (January 20) the French were finally vanquished. Initially confined to the Morro do Castello, the area facing the bay, Rio's growth is determined by the importance of its port to the colony.

1695 Discovery of gold in Minas Gerais leads to rapid growth of gold-rush towns. Rio, the only port city close to Minas, benefits immediately. Minas makes Portugal the world's largest producer of gold in the 18th century. Brazil's economic center shifts from the northeast to Rio.

1710–11 The French attack Rio, break through its defenses and sack the city. Thanks to the seemingly unending flow of gold from Minas, the city is soon rebuilt.

1763 Portugal at last recognizes Rio's status as the colony's leading city and transfers the capital there from Salvador.

1808 João VI of Portugal flees from Napoleon and establishes his court in Rio, which becomes the capital of the Portuguese Empire. The population of the city triples to 100,000 during João's 13-year residence.

1821 João returns to Portugal and names his son, Pedro, as prince regent and governor.

The Empire (1822–89)

1822 Pedro I proclaims independence from Portugal, and establishes the Brazilian Empire.

1831 The autocratic and unpopular Pedro I abdicates in favor of his five-year-old son, also named Pedro, who rules through a regency.

1840–89 Pedro II becomes king at the age of 15. He creates peace and stability during his long reign. The population of Brazil increases from 4 million to 14 million. A coffee boom enhances Brazil's economy and Rio's status.

1853 The slave trade is outlawed.

1860 Rio becomes South America's largest city, with a population of 250,000.

1874 Rio is linked to London by telegraph.

1888 The last slaves are freed.

Republican Brazil (1889–1963)

1889 Pedro II is overthrown by the military and exiled. Rio remains capital of the Republic of Brazil and undergoes rapid urbanization throughout the 1890s, years of political turmoil.

1892 Tunnels are drilled through the mountains to Copacabana and later to Ipanema.

1894 Prudente de Morais becomes the first elected civilian president.

1905 President Rodrigues Alves's vision of a "tropical Paris" results in the *belle-époque* period and the construction of Avenida Central.

1920s Beginning of Rio's heyday, which lasts until the late 1950s. Rich and famous from all over the world flock here to dance and gamble.

1923 The Copacabana Palace Hotel is built.

1931 The statue of Christ the Redeemer is inaugurated on Corcovado.

1930–45 The military installs Getúlio Vargas as president. Vargas gives himself absolute power, and brings in a social security system and a minimum wage.

1942 Brazil declares war on Germany – the only Latin American country to take an active part in World War II.

1946 Gambling is outlawed.

1950 Rio is surpassed by São Paulo in population and economic importance. The Maracanã Stadium is completed in time for the first postwar World Cup. Brazil loses to Uruguay.

1951–4 Vargas again made president – this time through a democratic election. In 1954, on the brink of a coup, he commits suicide.

1958 Brazil – with Pelé in the team – wins the World Cup in Stockholm.

1960 President Kubitschek's new capital city, Brasília, is inaugurated.

1964 Foundation stone laid for Rio's new cathedral.

Military Dictatorship (1964–84)

1964–7 General Humberto de Alencar Castelo Branco rules as president after a military putsch.

1969–74 Under General Emílio Garrastazu Medici, state terrorism is used against guerrilla insurgents, but the economy soars.

1974 The Rio–Niterói bridge opens.

1975 Rio made capital of a new, unified Rio state.

1974–79 General Ernesto Geisel begins a gradual relaxation of the military regime.

1979 João Baptista Figueiredo becomes president. Political rights restored to the opposition.

1982 Latin American debt crisis – Brazil has largest national debt in the Developing World.

1985–Present

1985 Tancredo Neves becomes president, but dies six weeks later. José Sarney takes over.

1985 Rock in Rio, one of the world's largest rock festivals, takes place in Rio. Further festivals follow in 1991 and 2001.

1988 A new constitution is introduced, but without the long-hoped-for land reform. Indigenous Indians are granted full civil rights.

1989 Fernando Collor de Mello becomes the new president.

1992 UN Earth Summit (Rio 92) is held in Rio.

1994 Brazil wins the World Cup for a record fourth time, defeating Italy in Los Angeles.

1994 Formula 1 motor-racing champion Ayrton Senna killed at the San Marino Grand Prix.

1995 Fernando Henrique Cardoso is elected president. His *Plano Real* brings inflation under control.

1998 Fernando Henrique Cardoso is re-elected as president for a second term.

2000 Brazil celebrates its 500th anniversary as a country.

2002 Luís Inácio da Silva ("Lula"), a former union leader, is elected president.

2007 Rio de Janeiro to host the Pan American Games. ❑

LEFT: coffee plantations demanded slave labor.

RIGHT: "Lula," who was elected president in 2002.

CONTEMPORARY RIO

Although Rio relinquished its role as the nation's capital, the loss of status was compensated for by a series of bold architectural projects. Most importantly, it retained its position as Brazil's capital of culture and fun

The shot that killed President Getúlio Vargas on August 24, 1954, did not reverberate around the world in quite the same way as would the shot that killed President John F. Kennedy, but it was to have a profound impact on Brazil. The bullet that killed Vargas did not come from an assassin's gun: the author of the shot was the president himself, who chose to commit suicide in the presidential palace, rather than resign or be forced from office by a military coup.

At the time of his death, Vargas had been the leading figure in Brazilian politics for nearly 25 years. He ruled as dictator from 1930–4, as the congressionally elected president from 1934–7, and again as dictator from 1937–45. He also served as a senator from 1946–51 and as the popularly elected president from 1951 until his death three years later.

The immediate impact of Vargas's suicide was an outpouring of popular grief for the "father of the poor." As a result of this public reaction, his political rivals were unable to assume power, and the threatened military coup and introduction of an authoritarian regime were delayed until 1964. The vice-president, Café Filho, replaced Vargas immediately after his death, and the presidential election, scheduled for 1955, went ahead.

Kubitschek comes to power

The winner was Juscelino Kubitschek, who had campaigned on a promise of "50 years of

progress in five." This progress included the building, in record time, of Brasília, which would take over from Rio as the country's capital. Kubitschek's plan to move the capital to the central plateau was nothing new. It had been enshrined in the Constitution of 1891, but had always been delayed or overlooked, as most politicians, as well as large sections of the Brazilian population, had seen it as a costly utopian ideal. There was also the fact that many of those who worked for the government did not relish the idea of giving up Rio in order to be shipped more than 1,000 km (620 miles) inland, away from the sea, the beaches and the city's many other attractions.

LEFT: contemporary Rio is a thriving modern city.
RIGHT: Juscelino Kubitschek – a man of vision.

But Kubitschek had no such doubts, and in his first year in office submitted to Congress the project for the new capital. For the president, Brasília would be the symbol of a new, modern Brazil. Kubitschek also believed that the building of Brasília would unlock the country's vast interior, and the new roads to the city would open up agricultural frontiers.

Downgrading Rio

After nearly 200 years as capital of Brazil, the clock was counting down for Rio, and at a far more rapid pace than anyone could ever have imagined. Vargas was the last of 18 Brazilian presidents to use the presidential palace in Rua

do Catete. Many employees of the federal government had to choose whether they should up roots and move to Brasília, or stay and look for other work in Rio.

The curtain for Rio, as the political capital, came down on April 21, 1960, with the dedication of Brasília as the new capital of the republic. While politicians and most civil servants had to move immediately, many, including a good number of foreign ambassadors and the diplomatic corps, hung on to life in Rio for as long as possible, and it was not until the early 1970s that everyone who should have moved to Brasília finally did so.

Stripped of the title of Federal District, Rio de Janeiro became the State of Guanabara, a situation that continued until 1974, when Rio became a municipality again in its own right. The following year, it assumed from Niterói the mantle of capital of the new State of Rio de Janeiro.

Appeasing the *cariocas*

Perhaps to appease the *cariocas* – as Rio's residents are known – for their loss of status, the federal government supported a number of major projects to benefit the city. Most impressive was Brazil's biggest landscaping project, which reclaimed from the bay what is now Flamengo Park, the largest urban park in the world. Completed in 1960, it included a number of expressways that helped alleviate congestion for traffic entering the center from the fast-growing residential areas of Copacabana and Ipanema.

A further landfill project involved Copacabana and resulted in the beach we see today, which is considerably longer and wider than it was in the 1960s. The mid-1960s also saw the opening of the Santa Barbara and Rebouças tunnels, both of which greatly helped the flow of traffic around the city.

In 1964 the foundation stone was laid for a new cathedral, dedicated to the city's patron, São Sebastião. Standing close to the Arcos de Lapa, this towering building (inaugurated in 1978) is reminiscent of a space capsule.

Another key construction to get under way in the 1960s was that of the Rio–Niterói bridge, which would finally link the two cities on either side of the bay. In the process it opened up the coast to the northeast of Rio,

---

LEAVING THE TRAPPINGS BEHIND

Although the political base shifted from Rio to Brasília, the infrastructure and trappings of power could not be moved. This included buildings such as the presidential palace in Catete (now home to the Museum of the Republic); the Itamaraty Palace in Centro, which had housed the Brazilian foreign service from 1889 until its move to Brasília in 1970; the Maracanã Stadium, where the finals of the World Cup had been played in 1950; and many other buildings, including the impressive structures that were the foreign embassies. Britain sold its splendid embassy building in Botafogo to the mayor of Rio, and it is still used for city functions.

which included the weekend playground of Búzios, and the economically important town of Macaé, which is the heart of Brazil's offshore oil industry, of key importance to Rio and to the country as a whole.

Construction on the bridge began, symbolically at least, in August 1968, in the presence of Queen Elizabeth and the Duke of Edinburgh, as British banks had financed the project and a British company was responsible for the work that would get under way in January 1969. The bridge, which is more than 13 km (9 miles) long, nearly 9 km (5.5 miles) of which is over water, was inaugurated on March 4, 1974, and officially named the President Costa e Silva Bridge, in honor of the man who had ordered its construction.

The inauguration in 1979 of the first line of the city's metro system was another major transport project, although it was not until the 1990s that the red and the yellow lines were completed. In terms of public works, the early years of the 21st century will be best remembered for the investments and improvements to the infrastructure that will host the 2007 Pan American Games.

The military takes control

Rio may have been thankful that responsibility for running the country moved in 1960 to Brasília, because democracy was to be short-lived. Despite the success of Brasília, Kubitschek was unable to choose his successor, and the electorate voted in Jânio Quadros, who was to discover the real cost to the country not only of building Brasília but of Kubitschek's economic programs, paid for by massive overseas borrowing. Quadros took over a country with massive bills to pay and no money to do so, and his only option was to introduce unpopular legislation that gave ammunition to the opposition in Congress. After just seven months, Quadros resigned. His successor, the vice-president, João Goulart, was unpopular with the military, who viewed him as a communist sympathiser. As he moved further to the left to try and shore up popular support, it was only a question of time before the army stepped in.

On April 1, 1964, troops moved into Rio from Minas Gerais, and quickly took control of the city. President Goulart, who was visiting Rio at the time, was so concerned for his safety that he departed for Brasília, only to find that it, too, was under military control. He headed to his power base of Porto Alegre, from where he hoped to contain and suppress the uprising, but civil support for the coup was growing, and in Goulart's absence from Brasília, Congress passed a vote to impeach him. By April 11, the military had appointed one of their own, Humberto de Alencar Castelo Branco, as president. The armed forces moved quickly to crush any civil or

THE SKY'S THE LIMIT

Air transport was not overlooked during the years of expansion, and 1977 saw the inauguration of a new terminal at the international airport on Ilha do Governador. This would be the country's main airport until the second half of the 1990s, when sheer pressure of demand saw many airlines give priority to flights to São Paulo rather than Rio. As the main gateway to Brazil, Rio was honoured in 1976 by Air France choosing Paris–Dakar–Rio as its first Concorde service, and for a number of years Concorde was to be a common sight in the sky above Rio. In June 1999 a second, even more modern, terminal began operation.

LEFT: the space-age cathedral in central Rio.
RIGHT: an engineering triumph: the Rio–Niterói bridge.

political opposition by removing the political rights of individuals, even from some politicians, like Kubitschek, who had supported the coup. What started out as a popular movement soon fell from favour, and when – surprisingly – the junta held elections in 1965 for the governorship of 11 states, they struggled to win eight. Crucially, they lost in Rio de Janeiro, and this was seen as the country's rejection of their performance.

Partly because of this, the military rulers introduced an act (AI-2) that basically made Brazil a two-party state, where a politician or individual was either pro-government or pro-opposition. It was a brave politician who

chose the latter, but some did. The right of the people to choose their own president was also removed by AI-2, and Congress, controlled by the ruling junta, had to elect the president from an approved list of military candidates. The military were to rule Brazil for the next two decades, during which time Rio, for the most part, stood in opposition as one of the most vocal cities in its criticism of the authoritarian regime, often using the arts as its mouthpiece.

Rio finds a new role

Having being stripped of political power, Rio was able to reinvent and re-position itself. The early 1960s saw the beginnings of bossa nova, which reinforced the city's position as Brazil's cultural capital, as did the birth and huge popularity of television *(see box opposite)*. The 1960s also saw the birth of the Tropicalia movement. Founded by musicians Gilberto Gil and Caetano Veloso *(see page 74)*, and inspired by Jimi Hendrix and other musical icons of the time, it was an echo of the protest movements taking place in Europe and the US, and a challenge to the military authorities that has since been described as Brazil's cultural revolution. It was to be short-lived, however: in 1968 Veloso and Gil were arrested. After their release from jail they went into exile in London, where they remained until the mid-1970s. In 2003, Gil became Brazil's Minister of Culture.

Culture would turn out to be a trump card for Rio and would help build its reputation worldwide as Brazil's best-known and most iconic city. When foreign artists and celebrities came to Brazil, they all wanted to visit and perform in Rio with their Brazilian counterparts. International jazz, dance, and film festivals sprang up and prospered, and resulted in 1985 in the first Rock in Rio, one of the largest music festivals the world had ever seen. Top Brazilian acts shared the stage with the leading international names of the day, including Queen, Rod Stewart, Iron Maiden, Ozzy Osbourne, and AC/DC. The festival took place again in 1991 and 2001. On April 21, 1990, Paul McCartney attracted a crowd in excess of 180,000 to the Maracanã Stadium, and set a world record for the largest paying public for a single act. Maracanã became the venue for a number of other memorable events, including a Mass by Pope John Paul II, who visited the city in 1980, 1982 and 1997.

On February 18, 2006, the Rolling Stones gave a free concert on Copacabana Beach as part of the Bigger Bang world tour. The stage was set up in front of the Copacabana Palace, and the crowd, estimated at around 1.5 million, stretched down the beach as far as Leme.

Part of Rio's cultural heritage is Carnival, another event that was completely unaffected by the city losing its role as capital. In fact, the samba schools found it gave them more freedom, as they could be more critical of, and satirical about, the political classes than they had in the past.

Return to democracy

While the military regime worked its economic miracle – at a price Brazil will still be paying for many years to come – the popularity of the government was in no way harmed by Brazil winning its third World Cup, in spectacular style, in Mexico in 1970.

However, it was not until the second half of the 1970s that Ernesto Geisel, the fourth military president, began a gradual relaxation of the authoritarian regime. In 1979, a political amnesty was granted to all those who had been persecuted by the military regimes.

In January 1985, as a result of massive popular demonstrations throughout the country, a trade union leader who had been a candidate in every presidential election since 1989.

In 1992 Rio returned briefly to the political spotlight when it hosted the United Nations' Conference on Environment and Development, known as the Earth Summit. The conference, based in Riocentro in Barra, witnessed the greatest global gathering of world leaders ever assembled up to that point.

Rio remains a vibrant city, both politically and socially. It will next take center stage when it hosts the Pan American Games in 2007, proof that while no longer Brazil's political capital, it still remains the country's most recognizable, desirable and iconic destination. ❏

member of the opposition assumed the presidency. That man was Tancredo Neves, who, due to ill health, never actually became president, but returned the country to democracy.

In 1989 Fernando Collor de Mello won 53 percent of the vote in the first direct presidential election in 29 years, but was forced to resign in 1992 after a major corruption scandal. He was followed, in 1995, by Fernando Henrique Cardoso, who served two terms, and in 2003 by Luís Inácio "Lula" da Silva, an ex-

LEFT: Gilberto Gil, Minister of Culture, with Lula.
ABOVE: *cariocas* flocked to the funeral of Roberto Marinho, founder of the Globo empire, in 2003.

TV GLOBO

TV Globo was launched in 1965 and became a national power house. When its founder, Roberto Marinho, died at the age of 98 in 2003, the president declared three days of official mourning. The Globo empire – television, print, internet, music, and radio – is synonymous with Rio's success. It is Brazil's largest media group, and among the most respected in the world. Despite the advent of cable, pay-TV and the internet, Globo's principal terrestrial channel still dominates the airwaves of one of the world's largest television markets. As long as Globo remains anchored to Rio, the city will remain Brazil's cultural capital.

RIO'S RESIDENTS

This is a wonderfully diverse city. Its residents are hugely
proud of it, and have a stoicism and sense of fun that help
them overcome difficulties, but it is undoubtedly a city
deeply divided by social and economic factors

The Latin American continent is one of great diversity, but Brazil is, perhaps, more diverse than most of the other nations. Its people share a common language, but they worship several different gods and their ancestors came from all over the globe.

Melting pot

This melting pot is, of course, a legacy of Brazil's colonial past. Among the countries of the New World, its history is unique. Where the Spanish-American colonies were ruled by rigid bureaucracies, and the future United States by a negligent England, Brazil's colonial society followed a flexible middle course.

The Portuguese colonists were not outcasts from their native land, seeking religious freedom, like the Puritans of New England. Nor were they like the Spanish courtiers, fulfilling a brief colonial service, and enriching themselves if possible, before returning home. They were men – and for decades, only men – who retained an allegiance to the old country but quickly identified with their new home.

The Spanish grandees, on the whole, hated the New World, the Puritans were stuck with it and attempted to remake it in the image of the Old, but the Portuguese came, stayed and assimilated. They liked life in Brazil, and, because they were not allowed to bring their own women with them, they intermarried with the often beautiful indigenous women to begin a new race.

The first members of that race – the first true Brazilians – were *mamelucos*, the progeny of Portuguese white men and native Indian women. Later, when the shameful slave trade brought Africans to the Americas, other races emerged – the *cafusos*, of mixed Indian and African blood, and the *mulattos*, born of Africans and Europeans. All these racially mixed people coexist in contemporary Brazil.

Slavery

The harrowing story of Brazilian slavery is outlined in the History chapter *(see page 20)*. The trade in human beings began in 1549, when a labor force was needed for the sugar

---

LEFT: *cariocas* have a huge capacity for enjoyment.
RIGHT: vital discussions in a city street.

plantations, and was not outlawed until 1853. Slavery itself continued until 1888, when the Lei Áurea (Golden Law), signed by Princess Regent Isabel de Orleans e Bragança finally brought it to an end.

By 1835, the year of a bloody slave revolt in the interior of Bahia, there may have been more blacks in Brazil than whites – a situation that must have caused concern to those members of the ruling class who were aware of it.

In some respects, however, Brazilian slavery was more liberal than its equivalents in other New World colonies. Owners were prohibited by law from separating enslaved families and were required to grant slaves their freedom if they could pay what was deemed a fair market price. A surprising number of slaves were able to achieve this liberation, even in the earliest colonial days. Slaves in the cities also benefited from the *innandades*, lay brotherhoods supported and encouraged by the Catholic Church, particularly the Jesuit missionaries. These organizations gave slaves and free blacks permission to hold assemblies on religious holidays, and to raise money to buy their freedom and that of other slaves.

Socioeconomic development

Brazil's history of racism and slavery and their aftermath left its non-white population unpre-

LEGACY OF SLAVERY

Most of the written records of slavery were destroyed when the system came to an end in 1888, but its legacy remains in the social structure of the country. And there are some tangible reminders, as well, such as the Cemitério dos Pretos Novos (Cemetery of the New Blacks) in the Gamboa area of Rio. Here, the remains of thousands of bodies, mostly those of young men who, it is believed, died on the voyage from Africa to Brazil, were discovered, piled on top of each other, by a couple working on the foundations of their home. This incident hit the headlines, but such finds are not uncommon in and around the city.

pared for the 20th century, let alone the 21st. Today, Afro-Brazilians lag behind in socioeconomic terms, creating a vicious circle that has resulted in persistent discrimination. A recent study by the UN showed that Afro-Brazilians comprised 63 percent of the poorest sector in Brazil as a whole.

Mixed-race Afro-Brazilians have a far lower level of personal income and further education – as measured by college degrees – and far higher rates of illiteracy and infant mortality, although the overall national rate for the latter declined steeply in the last decade of the 20th century, to stand at 29.61 per 1,000 live births in 2003.

Some academics have described Brazil as an emerging "racial democracy." This claim must be questioned against the background of continuing discrimination – albeit more subtle than before – and incipient racial tension. In a recent article, Alzira Rufino, director of the Casa de Cultura da Mulher Negra (Black Women's Cultural Institute) points out that the UN considers a country to be democratic when the racial breakdown of those in governmental positions is the same as that among the general population. By this standard, Brazil still has a very long way to go.

A nation of immigrants

Although 55 percent of Brazilians are white, there are numerous cultural groups making up that percentage. Like the United States, Brazil is a nation of immigrants, and they do not just come from Portugal, the original colonizing country. Rodrigues, Fernandes, de Souza and other Portuguese names dominate the phone book in some Brazilian cities, but in others, names like Alaby or Geisel, Tolentino or Kobayashi also appear a number of times. The sprawling commercial district around Rio's Rua do Ouvidor features hundreds of shops owned by people of Middle Eastern origin who came to Brazil in the first decades of the 20th century from the lands that are today's Syria and Lebanon, many of whom have made good lives for themselves in the city.

Statistically, Rio comes closer than any other metropolis to reflecting Brazil's overall racial balance. While the national population is 55 percent Caucasian, 39 percent *mulatto* and 6 percent Afro-Brazilian, Rio's 6.4 million inhabitants are 63 percent white, 28 percent *mulatto* and 10 percent Afro-Brazilian.

The nation's racial mixture is evident on every street corner and along every sandy beach of Brazil's second-largest city. For many people, part of Rio's charm is precisely its racial commingling. This has given rise to the notion that Rio, and the rest of Brazil, has resolved racial tension through an increasing mix of black and white. This is not entirely true, but in many respects the city does seem to be at ease with its racial and cultural iden-

tity. It has certainly produced some interesting physical characteristics that are rarely seen in other multiracial cultures. Some *cariocas* (Rio residents) have all the attributes of the African except for their skin color. Others have black skins, but green eyes and Caucasian features.

However, there are many who insist that talk of harmony and happy coexistence is a myth – one that clashes daily with harsh reality and allows the problems of racism to be hidden behind talk of social disadvantage. For many Afro-Brazilians, being poor is synonymous with being black. It is patently obvious that Rio's population becomes progressively

darker as its sprawling suburbs stretch away from the famous beach neighborhoods.

Religion and spiritualism

Much of Rio's racial variety results from internal migration. Bantu-origin slaves of colonial Rio mixed with Nagô-nation Africans migrating from Minas Gerais after that state's gold rush had petered out by the end of the 18th century. Starting in 1877, when a drought devastated much of the northeast of Brazil, blacks of Iorubá origin poured into Rio from Bahia.

The mixture is most intriguing when it comes to religion. The beliefs of African *umbanda* and *candomblé* exist among many

---

LEFT: fruit-sellers at the end of the 19th century.
RIGHT: Portuguese immigrants came seeking work.

of Rio's white residents, while European practices, such as faith healing and modern, alternative cults, have penetrated the traditional African religions.

Stereotypical elements of Brazil's African religious heritage were exploited in Marcel Camus's 1959 film, *Orfeu Negro*. Building on the ancient Orpheus and Eurydice myth, Camus's Black Orpheus speaks with the spirit of his dead Eurydice through the sly intervention of a medium – an elderly, pipe-smoking black woman, surrounded by chanting spiritualists in flowing gowns, loaded down with charms, not unlike the *alas das Baianas*, the elderly but extremely agile women who dance in the Carnival parades. The noisy, smoke-filled session is one of the climaxes of this atmospheric cult movie.

The majority of *cariocas*, including those who embrace spiritualism, consider themselves Catholics – even though many of them are agnostic. In Rio's suburbs, it is quite common for couples to get married in two separate ceremonies, first an *umbanda* ritual, then a Catholic Mass.

However, in Rio de Janeiro, as in the rest of the country, the Evangelical churches are gaining numerous adherents. The largest, and most controversial, is the Igreja Universal do Reino de Deus (Universal Church of the Kingdom

CHICO XAVIER

For many years, Chico Xavier (1910–2002), who was born in Minas Gerais, was the most popular medium in Brazil, regarded by many as a spiritual leader. He first came to prominence in the 1930s, and over the course of a long life wrote more than 400 books, using a process known as psychography, in which it was believed that his hand was guided by spirits from the life beyond. It is said that he always hoped that he would die on the day of a festival, and his death finally came on the day the Brazilian soccer team won the World Cup in Japan, June 30, 2002 – surely a festival of sorts for many Brazilians.

of God). New churches are opening all the time, some modest, some showy – the Igreja Universal in Rio is a huge modern "cathedral" built, it seems, as cathedrals always were, with no expense spared.

Evangelical radio and television programmes are widespread and influential, and many young people have embraced the faith. The 1980 census showed that 89 percent of Brazilians described themselves as Catholic, but only 70 percent do so now. Some 30 million people in Brazil now define themselves as Evangelicals, and the figure appears to be growing, much to the consternation of the Catholic Church.

Natural riches

From an outpost peopled by slaves and their masters, to seat of government of a strategic European nation, to independence, military dictatorship, and embryonic democracy – all this occured within a space of 200 years or so. Brazil has often been referred to as the country of the future, but with things tripping along at such a rapid pace, the country is not ready for all the challenges it faces.

The natural richness of the country needs no elaborate description: everything grows here. Many observers wonder why more people are not living in the rural areas, off the prodigiously fertile land. Isn't it better to be poor in a self-sustaining rural situation than to live a life of destitute underemployment in the big city? Logically, the answer should be yes, but cities have long held out a promise to those living in rural poverty, and the exodus from the countryside shows that Brazil is no different in this respect. The many families arriving daily in already overcrowded cities indicate that the move to misery continues.

Entire books are written about the Brazilian economy. It takes a special sort of analytical mind to understand the social effects of galloping inflation, soaring interest rates, serious corruption at the highest levels, and prohibitive import duties that place cheap staples from international markets out of range of many people. But the effects of these and other economic factors can be experienced by anyone who cares to look beyond the dramatic beauty of Sugar Loaf and the glory of the beaches, into the heart of the city: its people.

The northern suburbs

Beautiful though it is, the topography of the region does not make it an easy one to manage. The massive hills parallel to the seashore effectively cut off the industrial north zone from the commercial and residential south zone. These same hills are also the physical manifestation of the great cultural and social divide that separates the north zone from the more glamorous south.

For much of the working-class sector, the reality of Rio is the northern suburbs, far from

the beaches, a constantly growing maze of slums, housing projects and *favelas* (shantytowns), with pockets of middle-class housing. Even here, land values, pushed up by a chronic housing shortage, are steadily forcing the poor further north and consequently further away from the sites of their jobs, most of which are downtown or in the south zone.

At the same time, new waves of immigrants from the less developed states of the northeast and the underdeveloped interior of Rio de Janeiro state make demands for housing and public services that the government cannot meet. This has led to a population explosion in the northern flatlands, an area called the

Baixada Fluminense, where most live in abject poverty. Lacking sanitation and clean water, awash in garbage, the Baixada is a public health disaster where meningitis, typhoid and tetanus are rife, especially among the children, and infant mortality rates remain high.

The *favelas*

For some people living in the Baixada, even a hillside *favela* in Ipanema or Copacabana is something to aspire to. Many Baixada residents face a two-hour bus ride to reach their jobs in downtown Rio, while for south-zone *favelados*, work is often only a few minutes away, and they have the advantages of

LEFT: an hypnotic dance, part of an *umbanda* ritual.
RIGHT: celebrating St Sebastian, patron of the city.

spectacular views and immediate access to the beach. Life on the hillsides of Rio is precarious but, bad as things may be, they are seldom as bad as they are in the flatlands of the northern suburbs.

For most residents of the Baixada, even progress to the southern hillsides is out of reach. Ever-increasing demand and the improved housing within these *favelas* have produced an inevitable by-product – rising rents. Originally, the principal attraction of the *favelas* was that they were rent-free, but this is no longer the case. Organized tours of *favelas* are commonplace now: if you are going to visit one, make sure you go with somebody

Irmãos (Two Brothers Mountain) separating Leblon from São Conrado. While some *favelas* have been razed to the ground and their inhabitants forcibly resettled miles away, nothing can touch Rocinha, which gained official status in 1992. With a resident population of 120,000 – a figure the embarrassed authorities will be quick to diminish – it is a town within a city. Hundreds of commercial establishments function here, as do four state schools and a post office. *Favelas* like Rocinha are climbing the social ladder, and nowadays there are a number of residents with lower-middle-class occupations such as clerical and secretarial work.

reliable who knows what they are doing *(see pages 132 and 221)*.

Favelas have become a part of the folklore of Rio. Out of them come the samba schools that march in splendid costumes during the Carnival parades. Out of the *favelas* comes the samba itself, the seductive rhythm that is both song and dance *(see page 100)*. And out of the *favelas* come the construction workers who build the high-rises for the wealthy; the employees of the rich man's companies and industries; the waiters who serve the visitor in bars and restaurants.

Rio's largest *favela* is Rocinha, which sprawls across the south and sea side of Dois

At the time of writing, the Vila Alice *favela*, above Laranjeiras suburb, was one of a number under threat of *remoção* (eviction). The authorities promise that they will rehouse the residents in low-cost housing further from the city, but even if these promises were realised, it would still mean tremendous upheaval, and the evicted people would face lengthy journeys to work.

Drugs and guns

Not surprisingly, most illicit drug activity in Rio is connected with the *favelas*. The economic power of the traffickers has made them the dominant force. Gangs of drug dealers now control the majority of the large *favelas*. In return for the support of residents, they offer protection from petty criminals and distribute some of their profits from the drug trade among the local population.

These cocaine bandits have been elevated to the status of folk heroes for the slum dwellers, although this is a two-edged sword, as rival gangs often fight it out in the streets, and innocent victims get caught in the crossfire. Fernando Meirelles's 2002 film *Cidade de Deus (City of God)* gives a pretty accurate picture of the violent side of *favela* life.

With drugs, of course, go guns. The UN states that guns are the biggest cause of death a large percentage of the population lives has its effect on the city's bill of health, especially in the un-sanitary, polluted areas of the city.

There are 130 cases of tuberculosis diagnosed per 100,000 inhabitants, which is more than double the national average of 57 per 100,000. Dengue fever is proving hard to stamp out, and each summer sees the disease return with renewed vigor. HIV/AIDS is a big problem in Rio, too: 778 people in every 100,000 died of AIDS in 2003, the majority of them aged between 25 and 50, although due to the use of antiretroviral drugs this figure has declined steeply since 1995, when it was 1,507 per 100,000.

among young people in Rio, and in Brazil as a whole. In 2004, some 36,000 people were shot dead. Despite this, in an October 2005 referendum, 64 percent of those who voted rejected the proposal to ban the sale of guns, with the gun lobby arguing that weapons were needed for personal security.

City statistics

While at the top end of Rio society people live clean, healthy lives and are treated in the best hospitals if they do get ill, the squalor in which

Recent figures also indicate that between 1999 and 2002, more than 2,000 women died in Rio's public hospitals from complications related to illegal abortions. Most of these women were poor, black, and relatively uneducated. In September 2005, a bill to legalize abortion was presented to Congress, but the power of the Roman Catholic Church means there is little chance of it being approved.

The unemployment situation in the city may be illustrated by one statistic: An advertisement recently appeared in a Rio newspaper for street cleaners. Successful applicants would earn about $US200 per month, with breakfast included. There were 390,000 can-

LEFT: Rocinha *favela* sprawls over the hillsides.
ABOVE: growing up in the *favela*

didates for the 1,200 jobs available, 78 percent of which were submitted via the internet.

It is not all bad news, though. As well as a fall in the rate of deaths from AIDS, the literacy rate for Rio de Janeiro has increased to nearly 90 percent, higher than the national average. This means that many young women are better educated, understand about contraception, have fewer children in quick succession, and provide better care for their babies. Brazil's public vaccination programs are the envy of many countries, and the infant mortality rate is dropping *(see page 38),* albeit far more slowly among the underprivileged. There are 5.1 doctors per 1,000 inhabitants in Rio, compared to a shameful average of 1.9 in Brasília, the nation's capital.

On a lighter note, it is said there are more Avon ladies *(revendadoras)* in Brazil than there are members of the armed forces – although figures vary widely between 600,000 and 800,000. An indication, perhaps, of the country's obsession with physical beauty, although it could also be that it is a job that many unskilled women find easy to combine with childcare responsibilities.

Powerful elite

All cities have social divisions, and most have extremes of wealth and poverty, but perhaps

DIVORCE LAWS

Until 1977, Brazilians could not obtain a divorce, but there was a provision for legal separation, known as a *desquite*. This guaranteed that a separated woman could claim alimony, but did not mean that a marriage was legally terminated, so neither party could remarry. However, it was common practice for people who had obtained a *desquite* to marry a new partner in Bolivia, which regarded a *desquite* as a divorce, even though the marriage was not valid in Brazil. Changes to the law since 1977 have rationalized the situation and mean that it is now possible to convert a *desquite* into a divorce, after three years' separation.

Rio more than most is a city of multiple contrasts – wealth and penury, luxury and squalor, health and disease. The rich are dependent on the poor for the quality of their lives; the poor depend on the rich for their livelihoods.

What distinguishes some members of Rio's wealthy residents from their counterparts in other countries, though, is not so much their means as their power. The elite-driven nature of Brazilian society means that those on top enjoy almost unchallengeable authority and impunity. There are white-collar crimes in Brazil but, strangely, it would appear there are no white-collar criminals. Rio's business elite, the top layer of the upper crust, does not wash its dirty linen in public. Cases of fraud or corruption are in general handled quietly, usually behind closed doors. The elite is careful to protect its own.

Rio, like the rest of the country, is wound up in red tape, and Brazilians are masters of the *jeito*, a term which, roughly translated, means a compromise, or a quick fix. There is a whole class of professionals *(despachantes)* whose role is to *dar um jeito* or find a solution to a specific situation, whether it is a business impasse or, in many cases, a confrontation between an ordinary citizen and bureaucracy. It is a role that seems absolutely essential in order to get anything resolved.

just because it's red, when there is nothing coming in the other direction and nobody is attempting to cross the road?

Former president Tancredo Neves once said, "It's not the fact but the interpretation that counts," and in keeping with this sentiment, Brazilians, and perhaps *cariocas* in particular, will interpret rules as they see fit.

Cariocas also have a reputation for a sense of humor, and a serious approach to fun, and it is perhaps these characteristics that enable them to cope with the glaring social disparities that exist in their beautiful city, and prevent the whole place from flaring up in a tinderbox of revolt.   ❑

Carioca characteristics

It is difficult to sum up national characteristics, or more specifically, those of the residents of a particular city. To do so, you have to generalize (always a dangerous thing to do), but a few of the adjectives used to describe *cariocas* are "hospitable," "extrovert," and "spontaneous." *Cariocas* can also be described (along with many of their fellow Brazilians) as fairly laid-back about punctuality, and disinclined to obey rules they think don't make sense. Why, for example, stop at a traffic light

LEFT: a market trader; Rosângela Matheus, governor of Rio. **ABOVE:** soccer unites all colors and classes.

TELENOVELAS

To escape from the realities of everyday life, there is always television. Brazil has a huge commercial television system. TV Globo, the biggest company, is the fourth-largest network in the world *(see pages 35 and 62)*. The country is famous for its *telenovelas*, the prime-time serials that we know as "soaps." Sometimes aired six days a week, they command the highest advertising rates. With their universal themes of love, jealousy and intrigue, *telenovelas* are hugely popular throughout Latin America, and many of the Portuguese language ones made in Brazil are dubbed into Spanish and sold to the rest of the continent.

WHEN THE STARS SHONE IN RIO

For several decades the rich and famous went flying down to Rio to enjoy a hedonistic lifestyle beneath a blazing sun

Copacabana has been a magnet for visitors since the 1930s. It's a place where the tempo is set and trends are established; for many years Copacabana epitomized the glamor of Rio, racy modern lifestyles, and all that was cosmopolitan. The "Princess of the Sea," as the place was known, is gradually aging into a somewhat overworked queen, now overshadowed by other neighborhoods, but her memories are enough to keep her going for a long while yet.

Famous visitors included Orson Welles, who managed to cause trouble wherever he went. With *Citizen Kane* already under his belt, he never did complete the movie he went Rio to make, but had a glorious time nonetheless. Marlene Dietrich was another iconic star visitor, whose 1959 performance, in a skintight dress, at the Copacabana Palace's Golden Room, was legendary.

ABOVE: Louis Armstrong had a legendary thirst, made worse by the heat of Rio. Everywhere he went, he took his hip flask, reportedly filled with water. Before long, he was converted to the excellent local beer.

LEFT: Carmen Miranda, the Brazilian Bombshell, was a giant of the entertainment industry, but only 1.5 meters (5 ft) tall; the eccentric extra-tall hats and crippling high heels made up the difference.

BELOW: Orson Welles and Marlene Dietrich: neither of them came to Rio to enjoy a quiet time.

LEFT: Carmen Miranda took refuge in a room in the Copacabana Palace, devastated after her Brazilian fans accused her of becoming too "Americanized."

THE COPA PALACE

In terms of style and celebrities, the Copacabana Palace Hotel has always been the focal point of the city, indeed, of the whole country, even though Rio has not been the seat of government since 1960. It was hostess to hedonism and the fine art of keeping oneself amused and in the spotlight. Under its immense roof, VIPs of all kinds have slept – and eaten and drunk, gambled and performed, plotted and schemed, lived and died.

Gambling was the entertainment of choice for many, and the casinos became the nursery for budding stars and the podium for veterans. They were first closed down in 1924, but reopened nine years later by President Vargas, who enjoyed mingling with the rich and famous. They gave nightlife a special focus in Rio, which would persist until President Dutra closed them down again in 1946, mainly at the instigation of his pious but impractical wife: some 50,000 jobs were lost in the entertainment industry as a result of the croupiers' collective retirement.

RIGHT: King Carol of Romania took up residence in the Copacabana Palace in 1942, cooling off in the tropics from some heated situations back home. He and Magda Lupescu, the mistress he would marry some years later, kept eight Pekinese pooches in their suite at the Copacabana. Thenceforth, "no pets" became the hotel's policy.

RIGHT: President Getúlio Vargas, who reopened Rio's casinos in 1933, and enjoyed the high life himself when he was not concentrating on affairs of state.

LEFT: multifaceted Josephine Baker was another to enchant audiences at the Copacabana's Golden Room. This star's career involved dropping out of school at the age of 12, significant work for the French Resistance during World War II, and a serious involvement in civil rights movements. She was passionate about children and pets.

BELOW: in the late 1920s Santos Dumont, known as the Father of Aviation, spent sad days at the Copa, suffering from depression. He later committed suicide, horrified at the way aviation was being used in the conduct of war.

THE TASTES OF BRAZIL

From luscious tropical fruit to fresh seafood, melt-in-the-mouth cuts of prime beef and the national dish, *feijoada*, Rio caters for those with healthy appetites, and offers ice-cold beer and the liquid fire called *cachaça* for those with equally healthy thirsts

Bom dia! Good day! And you probably will have a very good day if you begin by doing justice to the vast freshness of a Brazilian buffet-style breakfast. Forget vats of steaming eggs and soggy sizzling sausages. Think fruit: watermelon, papaya, pineapple, bananas – even caramelized bananas if you're feeling really indulgent. Think juice: melon, passion fruit, cashew and orange. Think crusty French rolls and slabs of cornmeal bread. Think thinly sliced ham and chunks of farmer's cheese. Think coffee, real Brazilian coffee. It's a great way to start the day.

Tempting fruits

Among the vast array of fruits on offer, there may well be some with which you are unfamiliar. One such is the pink, pellet-like *acerola*, a member of the hawthorn family that has a long recorded history – it was mentioned by Homer in the 9th century BC. It is used mainly for juice and is said to contain the highest concentration of Vitamin C of any fruit in the world.

Guava fruit may be familiar to some visitors, as it now appears on the exotic-fruit counters of supermarkets in the UK and the United States, but the guava trees that drop their fruit on many a Rio sidewalk will be an unfamiliar species. Yellow on the outside, and a surprising pink inside, the fruit is extremely perishable, and so is frequently made into preserves. Sticky guava paste, *goiabada*, con-

trasts with sharp white cheese in a favorite Brazilian dessert, known as *Romeu e Julieta*.

Brazil is one of the world's main producers of orange concentrate, and the variety of fruit on display is impressive; oranges for consumption on the local market are not waxed and polished as they are for export.

Avocados are plentiful, but are not seen in a salad, or served with vinaigrette. They appear on the dessert trolley, blended with lime juice and sugar to produce a tasty puree. There are very few lemons grown in Brazil, but bright-green limes are a delicious substitute. They should not be confused with *Lima da Pérsia*, which is very bland, and reserved for babies.

LEFT: a colorful way to spice up your life.
RIGHT: fruits of all kinds flourish in the local climate.

Juice bars

The juice bars of Rio are great places in which to familiarize yourself with the local fruits. There's a vast choice – *açai, acerola, graviola,* as well as fruits that will be more familiar. Or you can opt for a *vitamina*, a thick, creamy shake that will include banana with one or two other types of fruit, and sometimes oat flakes or wheat germ, and is similar to what is now marketed abroad as a "smoothie." If you are watching calories make sure they don't ladle in the sugar, though – ask for *sem açúcar* (without sugar).

Curiously enough, fruit is also sold at traffic lights in Rio: mangoes, strawberries, limes, persimmons and sweetsop are all offered to the driver waiting for the lights to change.

Guaraná

A fruit that is rarely seen but widely consumed is *guaraná*. The reddish, seed-filled fruit is borne, in the Amazonian wild, on woody vines that seek the sun in the rainforest by climbing up other trees. In cultivation, the plant is trimmed to a shrub-like form. The seeds are highly prized and have been used by the indigenous population for centuries.

Guaraná was rediscovered in the 20th century; it can be found in capsules, powder or paste form, and is being heavily exported.

A FRUIT WITH ATTITUDE

The reptilian-looking durian fruit, called *jacas*, grow easily in the Brazilian climate, and may reach an astounding weight of 20 kg (44 lbs). They can been seen growing in various parts of the city, and the mess they can make of a car's windscreen when they come crashing down may easily be imagined. Less easy to imagine are their reputed aphrodisiac qualities, so revolting is their smell. Durians are said, also, to contain an enzyme that anaesthetizes the digestive tract, which is why they used to be consumed by slaves, in an attempt to fool their bodies into thinking they were not starving.

Like so many exotic "new" foods, it is imbued with magical powers, according to many. Its chemical composition is akin to that of ginseng, high in caffeine and other, reputedly aphrodisiac, substances. But visitors and residents are most likely to encounter the product in its canned form, in the refreshing, sparkling soft drink Guaraná, whose sales rival those of the cola producers.

Sustainable sources for salad

Controversial as it is, *palmito* (heart of palm) is a great addition to a salad in its pickled form, and a real feast when served freshly baked on a banana leaf, with a little melted butter and salt. The white, tender inner portion of the trunk is an expensive delicacy anywhere in the world. Indiscriminate harvesting of palm trees has resulted not only in severe deforestation but also in the near extinction of at least one of the better varieties of palm.

It is estimated that 95 percent of *palmito* production is illegal, while a tiny sector is trying hard to establish new, ecologically sound sources. The chief hope for this is the Pupunha palm, actually a coconut palm, which sprouts again after being cut. If the ecological aspect of this food is likely to give you indigestion we suggest you search the product label for information about its source. Don't expect any guidance in a restaurant, though: in all but the finest places, the waiter is most unlikely to be able to help you identify the source.

Savory morsels

Salgadinhos are little savories, and a great favorite at almost any time of day: as a midmorning snack with *cafézinho* (a small, black coffee) or early in the evening with an ice-cold *chopp*, Brazil's delicious draft beer (as opposed to *cerveja*, which is bottled beer). Their nearest European equivalent are tapas.

Some chefs wrap puff pastry around creamed chicken, heart of palm or shrimp to make a rissole; others serve morsels with a foreign flavor, such as the *kibe*, a Middle Eastern deep-fried meatball made with cracked bulgar wheat and mint. *Pastéis* are little deep-fried triangles of pastry containing anything from shrimp to cheese. *Empadas* are tiny pies, made with a crumbly dough and filled with cheese, shrimp, or chicken.

Brazilians have never lost the taste for *bacalhau*, the dried salt cod introduced by the Portuguese. On sale in shops and markets, it looks like sheets of stiff, gray cardboard, but when soaked and cooked it is transformed. It is most often served in rissole-like balls, which are meltingly rich. These *bolinhos de bacalhau* are the subject of an annual election for "the best of...," and to be voted the best supplier of these deep-fried goodies is to ensure a line of hungry customers at the door every weekend.

LEFT: there's a juice bar on every corner; fruit for sale on the beach. **RIGHT:** *acarajé* comes from Bahia.

African influences

Perhaps the strongest regional influence to be found in Rio is that of the northern state of Bahia, a reminder of the African slaves and their edible ritual offerings to their gods. *Acarajé* blends dried shrimp and ground beans into fiery, fried morsels. Soft-shell crabs join shrimp, lobster, and sea bass, and garlic, onions, coriander, and peppers in fragrant *dendê* palm oil, topped off with a dash of coconut milk, to produce *moqueca*, the traditional fish stew of the region.

Manioc roots are boiled and pounded into a creamy thickening ingredient for the shrimp casserole known as *bóbó de camarão*, often

served inside a whole pumpkin; and the exotic *Vatapá* recipe, which combines cornmeal, *dendê* oil, cashew nuts, peppers, dried shrimp, coconut, ginger, and coriander, has even been immortalized in a song.

None of these things, however, can be served without a large dish of white rice to accompany them. In fact, most Brazilians do not consider a meal to be complete if there is no rice on the table – regardless of the presence of potatoes or pasta.

Rice and beans

The vast majority of working-class *cariocas* sit down to a plate of rice and beans at lunchtime, accompanied by whatever meat or vegetable is available. Black beans are the norm in Rio, while other states prefer brown or red varieties. All are cooked for hours with garlic, onions, choice bits of sausage and sun-dried beef, or bacon – whatever the cook can afford. If an unexpected visitor should appear, the whisper *"bota mais água no feijão"* – put more water in the beans – will be heard.

Accompanying the rice and beans is usually *farofa*, ground manioc root toasted with garlic and onions, which is another staple of the Brazilian table. *Farofa* is an acquired taste, and is often descriptively referred to as saw-dust by foreigners. Small dishes of *farofa* are

while leaving the less noble parts for the slaves to eat. Usually the slaves did not know where their next pig was coming from, so they salted and dried portions of it for future use. These portions could include ears, tongues, feet and tails, as well as chunky portions of fat-marbled meat.

Nowadays, the dish has been much gentri-fied, with the addition of roasted loin of fresh pork and melting spare ribs, but all the meats are set out in separate bowls, so visitors need not fear the appearance of an ear on their plate unless they really want one. The amount of food served in some of Rio's *feijoada* restau-rants is mind-blowing.

placed on the table in many restaurants for customers to sprinkle on food if they wish.

Festive *feijoada*

Ironically, the staple of the poor is also the fes-tive dish of the wealthy. Saturday lunchtime in Rio means *feijoada*, black-bean stew and all the trimmings, to be followed, if possible, by a horizontal afternoon. The major hotels vie with each other for the title of Best *Fei-joada* in Rio, and outdo themselves in the ser-vice of this feast.

The origins of the dish go back to the Por-tuguese slave owners, who would slaughter a pig and keep all the best bits for themselves,

Sliced oranges may seem a strange addi-tion, but they serve as a tangy foil for the rich-ness of the dish, and thinly sliced, stir-fried kale provides a fresh and slightly bitter vege-table accompaniment. Hot pepper sauce is served separately, and carefully added at the diner's discretion; visitors should take care not to contaminate their entire plate with this liquid fire, but to test its strength on a corner first.

Docinhos

Docinhos – little sweets – are consumed at all times of the day. Often just miniature versions of traditional desserts, many of them are based on thick, egg-yolk-rich custard, a cardiologist's nightmare. This custard can be enriched with coconut to form a *quindim*, a typically Bahian sweet. The custard makes another appearance in *olhos de sogra* (mother-in-law's eyes), in which it is used to stuff prunes.

Brigadeiros (brigadiers) are essential at children's parties: fudge balls rolled in chocolate "worms" and served in fluted paper cups; while condensed milk, boiled up into supersweet *doce de leite*, is a perennial favorite.

Passion fruit, *maracujá*, is a healthier alternative, and is very popular whipped into fluffy mousses. Guavas, pineapple, star fruit and papaya are among the many fruits incorporated into *docinhos*, cakes and puddings.

option. Designer coffee *has* caught on, however, and you can now indulge in espresso, cappuccino and latte at a variety of smart cafés in the south zone.

Getting a caffeine fix

Brazilians drink coffee all day long. Standing up at a bar, they gulp down two mouthfuls of steamy black liquid, so sweet your tongue may curl. While they are waiting in the bank or for an appointment, a plastic thimble full of short-term energy is often offered. This is the traditional *cafézinho*, or little coffee, and it is found just about everywhere. In many Brazilian households, coffee is made by the drip

Coffee

Contrary to what many would expect, especially those old enough to remember the song "There's an awful lot of coffee in Brazil...," buying coffee in Brazil is quite straightforward. You won't be confused by too much choice, because only in the most specialized delicatessens are there many different blends to choose from. Basically, you buy coffee in two forms: ground or instant. Decaffeinated coffee is available, but has never really caught on. In only a very few restaurants will it be an

method, several times a day, it not being the done thing to reheat a pot.

Milk is never added to the *cafézinho*; in fact, there's no room for any in the tiny cups. Sugar is a different matter, and in many cases the cup is half full of it before the coffee is poured. For some reason, sugar is never added after the coffee. If you want milky coffee, other than at your hotel at breakfast time, your best bet is to ask for a *media*, available in snack bars or *lanchonetes*. In this case, the ratio will be about two thirds milk to one third coffee, and lots of sugar unless you stop them in time. What's more, it will be served in a tall glass, rather than a cup or mug.

Chilled tea

Cariocas are great consumers of tea. Not the dainty cups of English-style tea, and not served with milk, but chilled glasses of *maté*, or *matte* (pronounced *máh-chee*), a refreshing infusion of *ilex paranaensis*, a member of the holly family. Laced with a shot of lime juice and often over-sweet, this beverage is sold on the beach and at football matches, often dispensed from large tin barrels strapped to the back of a vociferous salesman. Nowadays, *maté* is always available in cans.

This same tea is widely consumed hot in the southern states of Brazil, and the *gaúchos*, the cattlemen of folklore and legend, are often

which averages out at about 10 liters (21 US pints) per capita.

Cachaça's promotion to polite society came in the guise of the *caipirinha*, which translates as "little hillbilly," and is Brazil's national drink. Sugar and chopped limes are pounded in the bottom of a glass which is then filled with ice and *cachaça*. It is refreshing and delicious, and it is often only after you've drunk it that you realise how powerful it was. For the faint-hearted, a *caipirinha* can also be made with vodka, in which case it becomes a *caipiroska*. *Cachaça* purists, of course, disdain the ice-and-lime routine, and savor the neat spirit reverently, in shot glasses.

seen, somewhat incongruously, nursing a silver-decorated gourd with a straw poking out of it, drinking *maté*.

Cachaça

Another form of liquid fire is traditionally served with a *feijoada*, and that is *cachaça*, the Brazilian firewater, literally *aguardente* (burning water). Fermented and distilled from sugar-cane juice, *cachaça* is yet another of the slaves' contributions to national culture. For many years it was considered the beverage of the lower classes, but in the last few decades it has grown in status. Brazilians drink a staggering 1.8 billion litres of *cachaça* annually,

Wine

The appreciation of wine in Brazil is still pretty much in its infancy, and the local product, too, has a long way to go. However, the picture is changing: consumption has risen by 35 percent in a recent three-year period, and is increasingly on the up. What started out as an occasional glass of one of the sweeter white wines is gradually changing to an appreciation of dryer, more sophisticated whites, and full-bodied reds.

For some time now it has been apparent that some producers have begun to market a better quality of wine – at least, better than the national average. New technology, more experience and, most of all, pressure from foreign markets, has made many local producers sit up and pay attention to their product, and the winners in this race are members of the wine-drinking public.

Times are changing

Brazil's answer to the Napa Valley is in the southernmost state, Rio Grande do Sul, which produces about 90 percent of the country's output. The chief wine-producing area here is in the mountains in the northeast of the state, known as the Serra Gaucha, with special mentions for the regions around the small towns of Bento Gonçalves, Caxias do Sul and

this country will never be a leader in wine production or marketing, but things will undoubtedly improve, and they are certainly changing fast. The time when the only safe wine to order on the menu was a Chilean one is a thing of the past – although Chilean and Argentinian wines are widely available, fairly inexpensive, and often very good; Brazil is the principal buyer of Argentinian fine wines.

In the meantime, if you want to taste the local offerings, you will find perfectly acceptable table wines. The most prestigious wines to look out for are the ones with the Valduga or Miolo labels – especially the more expensive Reserva.

Garibaldi. Indeed, some companies are running wine tours of the region, a sure sign that it is being taken seriously. Conditions here are near perfect for viniculture, except for an occasional excess of rain, which tends to occur just before harvest time, thus compromising the quality of the grape. This area was settled in the late 19th century by Italian immigrants from the Veneto, who were quick to establish vineyards and start production.

There is no tradition of wine drinking in Brazil, and the climate and soil are such that

LEFT: *caipirinhas* – the national drink.
ABOVE: a bar that specializes in beer.

Best beers

While in Rio, you can always do as the *cariocas* usually do, and opt for beer *(cerveja)*. There are a number of local brands worth trying: Antártica and Brahma are ubiquitous, while the popular Bohemia beer, introduced by German immigrants, has been brewed in the nearby hill town of Petrópolis since 1853. *Chopp* is the name given to a draft beer, which is wonderfully thirst-quenching, but high in alcohol. Most commonly this is a light, lager-type brew, but you can also get a dark *(escuro)* version in some specialist bars. The important thing is that it should be ice-cold. ❏

BEAUTY AND THE BEACH

Life in Rio revolves around the beach for people of all ages, both the active and the indolent. When bodies are so openly displayed, it's perhaps not surprising that the city also has the world's foremost cosmetic surgeons

What makes Rio's beaches so special? Or is it a case of the beaches making Rio special? *Cariocas* scoff at the residents of São Paulo, the *Paulistas*, saying they are a boring, work-obsessed bunch, who have no idea how to enjoy themselves. They put this down to the lack of a beach. While this judgment of the *Paulistas* is clearly unreasonable, it is a fact that public parks and gardens do not have the same effect on people as sand and sea. With no paths, no railings, no trees to divide up the space and nowhere to hide, the beach is distinctly different.

In Rio, if you want to know what the weather has in store, you ask: "*Vai dar praia este fim de semana?*" "Will it be beach weather this weekend?" A good look at the beaches of Rio de Janeiro can reveal a lot about how this city works. Look beyond the golden-tanned, sunbathing bodies on the sands of this metropolitan sundeck and you will see the customs, personalities and amusements of the *cariocas*.

The sandy world

The beach is a place where you read, gossip, flirt, jog, work out, or just do absolutely nothing. It is a concert hall, an exercise center, a clinic and an office, too. It is also a place to swim, but most *cariocas* merely amble down to the waterfront, stoop to douse themselves in the water, and possibly wander out to waist depth – but no further. Apart from the surfing

---

LEFT: volleyball on the sands.
RIGHT: dressed for the promenade.

and watersports fanatics, actual head-under immersion is far from widespread. In fact, for many years immersion was considered harmful to one's health, and only undertaken if prescribed by a doctor.

Alongside the many who seemingly sit around on the beach and do nothing, there are those in constant motion. It may be another day of boiling 38°C (100°F) heat, but the weekly (or daily, for some) volleyball games on the scorching sands continue regardless. Brazil's success in Olympic volleyball started, as so much in this country does, on the beach. It is a game that requires incredible fitness, and it is no wonder that the participants in these hotly contested matches all look like movie stars on the set. Paddleball, or frescoball, is also a popular activity, and of course there's always a game of beach soccer in progress.

Futevolley, as the name suggests, is a challenging mixture of soccer and volleyball. It only began about 20 years ago, but has since become very popular and has its own organized tournaments. Then there's the lone beach jogger, pounding the sand, concentration etched on his sweaty face, as he pushes his body through his challenging routine. Less energetic are the fishermen. No, there isn't much left to catch, but it's relaxing and beautiful just the same.

alongside simple old-fashioned bicycles ridden by pretty girls in shorts and T-shirts.

Beach-going starts early for Brazilians, and even tiny ones are taken out in their strollers in the early morning. Each beach has its babies' meeting point, where rows of baby carriages are parked while the toddlers fight it out over each other's toys. The babies will all be safely back home by 9am, when the sun becomes dangerously hot. There's no discernible class distinction here, as mothers, fathers and nannies race around trying to keep their charges in check.

For true economy of movement, watch a *carioca* housewife pack up from the beach and

The sidewalk
The paved sidewalk that borders the beach and the adjacent cycle track are both part of the beach experience. The population of Copacabana, for instance, is predominantly made up of senior citizens. Watch the elderly couples as they take their constitutionals along the sidewalk, often hand in hand, and wonder if they haven't reached their twilight years in such great shape because of their healthy walking routines. The cycle tracks can produce some amusing sights: complicated wheeled vehicles whose pilots are dressed from head to foot in sprayed-on cycle gear topped by strange pointy helmets drift past

head for home. The beach umbrella and rush mat are rolled up; a small pail is filled with seawater and off she goes. By the time she's finished with her foot-stamping routines and the pail of water is emptied on the sidewalk, not one grain of sand will remain on her body or even her feet. But not everyone is so careful, and many *cariocas* know when it's time for the beach because the elevator floors in the buildings where they live are grittily sandy underfoot.

Punctuation marks
The kiosks and the funnel-shaped lifeguard stations are the punctuation marks on the sidewalk. Planning permission, building licenses,

environmental impact: no, we are not talking about building a new city. The fuss is all about the refurbishment of the kiosks, which are currently rather rudimentary but which, if plans go ahead as they stand, will have glassed-in, air-conditioned decks, underground toilet facilities, and much more. At the time of writing, a question mark hangs over this subject, and it is too soon to tell how this necessary remake of the kiosks will proceed.

Whatever happens to the kiosks, there will always be vendors plying up and down the beach, with ice-cold drinks, biscuits, homemade sandwiches, sometimes oozing mayonnaise, which you consume at your own risk, raw egg and hot sun being a risky combination. The grilled prawns, speared on sticks, may also be for those who like to live dangerously. You can buy kangas, sunglasses, towels with pictures of Christ the Redeemer in vivid color, and all kinds of souvenirs.

You can have a massage, if you don't mind the lack of privacy: tables are set up in shady spots, and you lie there while someone takes the knots out of your system. Or you could have your ears pierced. And you can be impressed by the imaginative and painstaking sand sculptures, whose patient creators ask for a donation from those who want to photograph them. The beach is a thriving commercial world.

Body beautiful

The one obvious fact about the beach experience is that the vast majority of the people involved are wearing very, very little clothing. Does that mean that if you bulge a bit here, sag a bit there and wrinkle a little somewhere else you will feel a fool on the beach? Not at all; the *cariocas* are very forgiving, and come in all shapes and sizes themselves.

But that doesn't mean they won't go to painful, and expensive, lengths to ensure their birthday suits are as near to perfect as they can make them. You can see them working on their bodies on the beach and sidewalk. All the walkers have their own style and speed, governed by some beat within. Plugged into Walkmans, squeezed into skintight suits, attached to pedometers, weight belts, heart-

rate monitors or just their dogs, they push forward along the road to physical fitness.

On the sand itself you will find groups doing aerobics, t'ai chi, Pilates, or just a simple stretch class, a forest of legs and arms moving gently in time to the waves. Many an Adonis will hang from iron bars, his face contorted with the pain of this self-inflicted suffering and sacrifice.

Off-beach beautification

Is the beach to blame for the incredible position Brazil occupies in the world of cosmetic surgery? Indirectly, it must be. Is it a coincidence that the world's foremost plastic sur-

LEFT: keeping the body beautiful can be hard work.
RIGHT: some know when it's time to take it easy.

geon, the man of a million well-kept secrets, is Brazilian Ivo Pitanguy? Certainly not!

Daily, Rio's clinics – many by no means as outstanding and reputable as that of Dr Pitanguy – engage in a game of new lamps for old. They do battle against wrinkles, blemishes, fatty deposits, cellulite, sagging derrières, imperfect noses, and breasts that are never quite the right size. The struggle to rejuvenate *carioca* matrons or to give the young the perfect body involves all the techniques of the profession, and everyone talks quite openly about it.

And it does not only involve women: men – mainly lawyers, economists and financial executives – between the ages of 35 and 45,

much shorter recovery time. But if you haven't started these injections by your late twenties, you'd better get going. The young are using prevention now – anyone over 35 may get left with only the cure.

Waxing fashions

Hairdressers abound in Rio, too. And they don't just dress hair. All sorts of beauty treatments are carried out, as well as manicures and pedicures. Hair removal is a big issue: non-existent moustaches are removed, eyebrows reshaped, legs waxed and the way made clear for those skimpy Rio bikinis.

And here is the great dichotomy: while for

on their first or second marriages, are the new patrons of the plastic-surgery clinics.

Non-surgical treatments are acquiring more devotees every day. Currently, many dermatologists claim to be seeing a higher percentage of people seeking aesthetic treatments than patients with skin diseases. Vast quantities of Botox are injected daily into the faces of dissatisfied Brazilians. Expression lines on the forehead and around the eyes magically disappear, and lips regain their youthful fullness – at least for a few months.

The advantages of this type of treatment, as opposed to surgery, are manifold: less expensive, less invasive, and less painful, with a

the local people it is essential to have a great body, those who don't need not feel out of place. You may well be past your prime or carrying more weight than you would like, but that won't affect your welcome or acceptance on the sandy playgrounds of Rio. Working out and looking good are *carioca* obsessions, and it sometimes seems that beautification and beach-going are all that people are concerned about. This isn't quite the case; they do have other preoccupations, but as you pan the sands and peek at those around you, you'll see that a great deal is done in the name of beauty and the beach.❏

ABOVE: sunbathing is a serious business.

New Year's Eve

New Year's Eve on the beach in Rio has become almost as much of an event as the city's spectacular Carnival which takes place about six weeks later. The local authorities do not mess around when it comes to having fun, and the massive, open-air party is organized down to the last detail, just like Carnival. Cruise-ship itineraries now feature December 31 in Rio de Janeiro; flights are impossible to get hold of unless you book them way in advance, as are hotel rooms; and people flock from all over Brazil in buses that line the roads.

People have always popped down to the beach on New Year's Eve, to dip their feet in the water for good luck, or to take part in the ritual homage to Iemanjá, whom adherents of the ancient *umbanda* religion venerate as the goddess of the seas. Iemanjá is a very vain lady who is used to being worshipped, and little purpose-built boats laden with perfumes, combs, scented soaps and white flowers are floated out to her by the faithful. If the boat comes back, it could be a tough year ahead; if it disappears, it is a sign that Iemanjá is pleased with the gifts it contained, and a good year is guaranteed.

Many people also place lighted candles at the water's edge, which adds to the magic of the scene, as does the fact that almost everybody wears white.

To the large numbers of faithful followers of the goddess who have always engaged in the beachside rituals have been added thousands of spectators, local people and tourists alike. But nobody seems to mind, and the cigar-smoking women in their white robes coexist quite peacefully with the partying crowd. And what a party it is! Up to three million people gather on Copacabana Beach, dancing to the music of the big-name live bands emanating from specially-built concert stands, or making their own music with improvised percussion instruments.

The five-star hotels that line the beach-front host sumptuous parties which sell out months in advance. At a more humble level, street vendors offer every form of refreshment imaginable. Tiny, portable barbecues are set up, and kebab-like morsels are grilled to order.

On this special night, Copacabana traffic does not get snarled up, simply because there is none: no cars are allowed in the area. Security is good, and the day's newspapers provide maps of how to get about and where the action will be.

On the beach, at the magic moment of midnight, rich and poor embrace and crane

their necks to see the skies illuminated by the multicolored explosions of millions of dollars' worth of fireworks. The cascade of fireworks flowing down the 30 floors of the Meridien Hotel provides a heart-stopping moment all of its own.

Listen to the sound of three million people sighing with satisfaction. Whether you are celebrating the Festa de Iemanjá or the birth of a new year, it is undoubtedly a night to remember. Tomorrow, people will be subdued. Little boats rejected by the goddess will lie forlornly on the sands, street cleaners will be hard at work, and you will be left with memories to treasure. ❑

RIGHT: fireworks illuminate the sky at midnight.

THE MOVIE INDUSTRY

Rio is the hub of Brazil's thriving cinema industry,
and its directors and actors are making a
big splash on the international scene

Rio de Janeiro may no longer be the political capital of Brazil, yet despite São Paulo's best efforts, it remains the cultural capital of the country, and cinema is one of its great strengths.

The nascent Brazilian film industry had its ups and downs in the early days, reaching its first peak in the 1940s when the Atlântida Studio opened in Rio. For the next 25 years it turned out popular films targeting the masses, many of whom could not read the subtitles on the silent films. Only free delivery into thousands of homes of a similar style of entertainment via television was to burst its bubble.

The box in the corner

Television had started in a small way in Brazil in 1950 with TV Tupi, but only truly began to affect the Brazilian population with the launch of TV Excelsior's daily soaps in 1960. In April 1965, TV Globo was launched by Roberto Marinho, who, in the 1920s, had taken over *O Globo*, one of the city's principal newspapers, from his father. Some two decades later, Marinho launched Radio Globo, which became the country's only truly national radio network; and 20 years after that he did the same with TV Globo *(see page 35)*. The network's influence has not been restricted to the small screen, however, and many of its stars have moved to cinema and been the key to attracting paying audiences to the movie houses. Globo has also financed or part-financed many of the most successful Brazilian films of the past decade.

Glittering prizes

The popularity of television did not stifle artistic endeavours on the big screen. In 1962 Anselmo Duarte's *O Pagador de Promessas* won the coveted Palme d'Or at Cannes, and it was at the same festival in 1964 that the world started to take notice of Brazil's Cinema Novo. Both Glauber Rocha's *Deus e o Diabo na Terra do Sol* and Nelson Pereira dos Santos's *Vidas Secas* were in competition, while Caca Diegues's *Ganga Zumba, Rei dos Palmares* was the closing film in Critics' Week.

If Cannes was good for Brazilian cinema, the Berlin Film Festival was even better, with Brazilian films picking up a string of top prizes and critical acclaim throughout the 1970s, 1980s and late 1990s. "Of all the European festivals, Berlin has always been the most curious about our filmmaking," says Walter Lima Jr, who won a Silver Bear in 1969 for his *Brasil Ano 2000*.

When government subsidies were pulled in the 1990s, Brazilian filmmaking virtually came to a halt. Despite the barren years, some filmmakers never gave up, most significantly Brazil's most successful and prodigious producer, Luiz Carlos Barreto, responsible in 1976 for *Dona Flor e Seus Dois Maridos*. Directed by his son, Bruno, it remains the most successful Brazilian movie of all time, selling over 12 million tickets and being nominated for a Golden Globe.

Academy Award nominations in consecutive years for producer Barreto put the Brazilian film industry back on track and bolstered its confidence in competing critically and commercially. In 1996 and 1997 Brazil received nominations for best foreign-language film, first for Fabio Barreto's *O Quatrilho*, a gentle story of pioneering Italian immigrants in southern Brazil, and then for *O Que é Isso Companheiro?*, Bruno's movie (given the English title *Four Days in September*) based on the true story of the kidnapping of the American Ambassador to Brazil by a left-wing group in 1969.

Spotlight on Brazil

In 1998, Walter Salles Jr's *Central do Brasil* premiered at the Berlin Film Festival. The reception was rapturous. It won the Golden Bear for best film, while its leading lady, Fernanda Montenegro, won the best actress Silver Bear. Over a year later, *Central do Brasil's* bandwagon rolled into Hollywood, with a nomination for best foreign-language film, Brazil's third nomination in three years. Montenegro was nominated for best actress, a first for a Brazilian performer. The global success of the film, both critically and commercially, turned the spotlight on Brazilian cinema and Salles, and neither has disappointed.

Salles has gone on to direct the highly acclaimed *Motorcycle Diaries*, the story of the young Che Guevara's journey through South America, and the English-language thriller, *Dark Water*.

But Salles does not have to stand alone on the international stage. In 2003 Fernando Meirelles served up the stunning *Cidade de Deus (City of God)*, a movie about life in Rio's *favelas* that was considered by many critics, and the public, to be not only the most innovative and fresh movie of 2003, but quite sim-

ply the best. Going full circle, Meirelles has since produced and part-directed a series for TV Globo, *Cidade dos Homens*, which is based on his film, and in 2005 directed the English-language adaptation of John Le Carré's novel *The Constant Gardener*.

It is still not easy to find the funding to make new films, but the industry survives, especially in Rio, and will continue to entrust its existence to the city where South America's premier film festival, **Festival do Rio**, takes place each September and October. In 2005, the festival jury voted Sergio Machado's *Cidade Baixa* the best home-grown movie, and its star, Alice Braga, who also appeared in

City of God, the best actress. October 2005 also saw Breno Silveria's *2 Filhos de Francisco (Francisco's Two Sons)*, a film that tells the story of two of Brazil's favorite country and western music stars, become the biggest Brazilian movie since 1990, with more than 4.7 million tickets sold, surpassing the sale of 4.6 million for Hector Babenco's prison drama *Carandiru* in 2003.

Of course, no consideration of filmmaking in Brazil would be complete without mentioning the number of foreign films and TV series that have used beautiful Rio as part of their backdrop, all the way back to 1933. Who will ever forget *Flying Down to Rio*? ❑

LEFT: a shot from Fernando Meirelles's *City of God*.
RIGHT: the talented Alice Braga, who starred in *City of God* and *Lower City*.

CARNIVAL

There has been some form of Carnival in Rio ever since the Portuguese arrived, but they would have been amazed at the flamboyant, excessive festivities that now preoccupy the city's residents and draw in thousands of visitors

Rio's Carnival is often described as "the world's biggest open-air party," a state of being that permeates the Brazilian soul, and influences even those who protest they hate it. Carnival equals big business, too. An estimated US$30 million is directly invested, from the private and public sectors; 60,000 full-time jobs are created by Carnival, with this figure rising to 120,000 during the three months preceding the bash. No wonder it is taken seriously; it spreads its economic tentacles into every sphere of activity.

Influencing the arts

Novelist Jorge Amado recognized this when he gave Carnival the highest honor by making it the title of one of his books – *País do Carnaval (The Country of Carnival)*. It has been an important theme in Brazilian literature for as long as it has been an important event in Brazilian life. All the great poets and writers make of it a metaphor for Brazil itself. Vinicius de Moraes placed it at the center of his lyric play *Orfeu Negro, Uma Tragedia Carioca (Black Orpheus, A Carioca Tragedy)*, which audiences the world over knew as the luminescent 1959 film *Black Orpheus*.

Édouard Manet was deeply impressed by the many moods and colors of Carnival when he visited Rio in 1875. According to historian João Ribeiro, the French artist later told him that the images he recalled from Carnival influenced the development of Impressionism.

LEFT: putting the final touches to a Carnival figure.
RIGHT: posing for the camera in Cinelândia.

CARNIVAL FANATICS

For some, Carnival is the most important thing in life. Turn-of-the-century poet Olavo Bilac eloquently described the Carnival fanatic: "He is a different person altogether, from another race. Those who merely love Carnival do not deserve the title, 'carnavalesco.' The true fanatic is an individual who was born for Carnival... alone. He lives for it; he counts the passing years according to the number of Carnivals he has celebrated; when he is about to die, he has only one regret – he will miss next year's Carnival and all the other Carnivals which will mark the life of Rio de Janeiro until the end of time."

Brazilian writer Isis Valeria captures the essence of Carnival in her short story *Folião*. A suburban worker who has spent an entire year preparing for Carnival dies at the moment his name is called out as winner of a costume competition: "He took his first steps, dragging behind him the weight of his costume, almost in a trance. He was in his glory. The crowd in the hall was at his feet. He fell before reaching the other side of the room. His face changed expression with the pain but his dentures, even in death, kept grinning. He was carried out of the theater. Outside, he was surrounded by enthusiasts who unmindfully congratulated him on his victory." What a way to go.

stink bombs, water balloons, mud balls, and even arson as forms of entertainment. It was entertainment for some – but others saw it as a public nuisance. The *entrudos* became so bad that, by the mid-19th century, decent men and women spent the time before Lent in their homes, scared to venture onto the streets. *entrudos* were outlawed in 1853, but the ban was hard to enforce as the police were often among the most active participants. It wasn't until the early 1900s that a strict campaign put an end to this antisocial form of fun.

A reversal of roles was an essential element of the Roman and Renaissance Carnivals, and today, too, a temporary class inversion takes

Ancient origins

Modern Rio has the most famous Carnival celebrations in the world, but Carnival's roots go back to Roman times. The ancient Romans had more than 100 annual festivals, of which the most famous was the week-long Saturnalia, a precursor of Carnival, held at the end of December. Some kind of pre-Lenten observance has existed in Brazil for as long as the Portuguese have been here – *carnevale* coming from the Latin for "goodbye to meat." But until the early 20th century the tradition tended to emphasize pranks, not celebration. The practitioners of the absurd were called *blocos de entrudos*, and their antics featured

place. In Rio, the poor dress up as royalty and strut in front of the rich, who come to the parades dressed down. Many believe that when class lines blur in Brazil, Carnival will begin to die. No fear of that yet, though.

How Carnival developed

A Portuguese immigrant named José Nogueira Paredes (dubbed Ze Pereira by revelers) is credited with inventing the first Carnival club. One of his innovations was to get everybody in the club to play the same kind of drum, creating a powerful, unified sound that is the basis for the modern samba-school *bateria,* or percussion section.

The working-class clubs were called *blocos* or *ranchos*, and played ballads of European origin known as *choros*, many of which are still popular. The late 19th century also saw the first involvement of blacks in Carnival. This was at least partly due to an 1877 drought in the northeast of Brazil which sent many *nordestinos*, including some freed black slaves, to Rio and São Paulo. The former slaves brought their own brand of musical and dance traditions with them to the city's Carnival celebration.

The most colorful event

While Carnival is hundreds of years old, the samba-school parade was a 20th-century innovation. The very first samba school was called Deixa Falar (Let 'Em Talk), and was organized by the mainly black residents of Rio's Estacio district in 1928. Deixa Falar paraded for the first time in the Carnival of 1929. Paraders followed no fixed route and weren't well organized, but their very size made them different from the ordinary *blocos* and *ranchos*. Unlike the other parading groups, Deixa Falar designed colorful costumes and clever dance routines.

Other black neighborhoods set up rival samba organizations almost immediately. During the 1930 Carnival, there were five such groups, and so many spectators that police had to clear a special area around Praça Onze on the day of their parade.

Things became even more sophisticated when the *Mundo Esportivo* newspaper offered a prize to the best samba group in 1932. By then the black-dominated Praça Onze parade groups had acquired the name "school," probably because local schools let them practice on their grounds on the weekends before Carnival. The 1932 prize went to Mangueira, one of the schools which first paraded in 1930.

By 1935, the samba parade had blossomed into one of the major Carnival events. In that year the city government paid a small subsidy to the largest schools and took over the parade organization and the awarding of prizes. By 1935, 25 schools were participating *(see picture story, page 100)*.

LEFT: Carnival is an event where anyone can join in.
RIGHT: gay pride adds to the social diversity.

Modern trends

Today's celebration of Carnival in Rio de Janeiro has two main features: colorful, often frenzied street events, and the world-famous samba parade. Like any popular outpouring, it is evolving all the time. Organized Carnival balls, for instance, which saw so many of the stars of Hollywood "flying down to Rio" in the 1950s, have not made it into the 21st century intact. The exception is the brilliant, black-tie or gala-costume Baile do Copa at the Copacabana Palace Hotel on the Saturday of Carnival. Street Carnival, on the other hand, whose death knell was tolled prematurely some years ago, is on the up, with the city

authorities investing infrastructure, cash, and organizational skills to enrich the enjoyment of the average man and woman in the street at this very special time of year.

Another element that has become an integral part of the Rio Carnival scene is the warm welcome extended to the international gay community, which has only served to enrich the social diversity of the event. On the downside, the increasing participation in the major parades of just-got-off-the-plane, high-paying visitors who have never attended a rehearsal strikes a jarring note. Their place, clearly, is in the street Carnivals, where they can blend into the background.

Street Carnival

Street Carnival starts on the Friday afternoon of Carnival in a hectic we'll-never-be-ready ceremony on Avenida Rio Branco downtown; the mayor delivers the freedom of the city of Rio, in the form of an oversized key, to Rei Momo. This roly-poly monarch will rule the city until Ash Wednesday. Momo's classical predecessor was Momus, the chaotic personification of sarcasm and ridicule.

This particular earthly king, though, is elected in December, two months before Carnival. The job description is staggering: the minimum weight requirement for contenders is 110 kg (242 lbs, or over 17 stone), and their

height must be at least 1.65 meters (5ft 5 in). Candidates must also have excellent communication skills and embody the spirit of Carnival. On top of all this, they are also expected to be light on their feet.

During Rei Momo's reign, fun and folly will take over. Old and young join rich and poor to parade joyfully down the streets, stopping for a beer here and there, snarling up the traffic and generally having a great time.

Costumes are not essential, although crossdressing has always been part of the fun. A conservative bank manager or accountant who usually wears a pin-striped suit can be seen wearing his wife's dress, with a pair of balloons strategically in place, and tottering on a pair of her ruined-for-ever high heels.

A simple and age-old way to dress up is to wear a mask; these are often satirical renderings of the political villain of the moment. And, every year, there's a cartoon likeness of whichever local politician has been most featured in the "bad news" press.

This all takes place to the atonal accompaniment of a few dozen drums and other percussion instruments, plus the incessant hooting of car horns. The latter are pretty much ignored, as it is accepted that anyone who attempts to get from A to B during Carnival must want their head read.

The more organized bands will have their own sound car, a hulking mastodon of a vehicle fitted with deafening speakers, and a rudimentary *bateria*. The master of ceremonies is poised atop the sound car, endlessly belting out Carnival favorites in full voice.

District bands

Each district has its own *banda* or *bloco*, which will, essentially, reflect the affluence and humor of its residents. Possibly the most famous of them is the Banda de Ipanema, which musters in Praça General Osório at 4pm on the Saturday two weeks before Carnival, and then again on the Saturday and Tuesday of the big week end itself. Copacabana's rival to the famous Ipanema band is the Banda da Sá Ferreira, which takes to the streets on the Saturday and Sunday of Carnival, also at 4pm, starting on the beachfront, at the corner of Rua Sá Ferreira. Leblon's pride is the Banda Empurra que Pega, which starts its meanderings at the corner of Avenida Ataúlfo de Paiva and Rua Carlos Góis on Saturday and Sunday of Carnival, around 6pm.

The irreverently named Carmelites Band takes its name from Santa Teresa's convent, and crawls around that hilly area on the Friday before Carnival and on Shrove Tuesday. The band meets at the Ladeira de Santa Teresa, on the corner of Rua Hermenegildo de Barros, from about 5pm. The most irreverently named of all, though, is the Sovaco de Cristo, Christ's Armpit, which starts just under the statue of Christ, on the Sunday before and during Carnival, at 5pm, at Rua Jardim Botânico 594.

Terreirão do Samba

The Terreirão do Samba – Samba Land – is a temporary venue that is set up during the lead-in to Carnival in the less salubrious area of the Sambadrome. Originally used simply as a support system for the major parades, with bars, food vendors and somewhat primitive facilities, Samba Land has become a Carnival destination in its own right. A vast stage hosts the big names in samba, who are accompanied by a chorus numbering thousands. On parade nights, non-ticket-holders can see members of the schools warming up before the off, making last-minute alterations to costumes that will never actually fit them, adjusting hats and

actually a series of interconnected buildings, most of which house classes during the elementary school year.

Amazingly, everything works at the Sambadrome. Security is strict; taxis are plentiful; entry is controlled; facilities are adequate; food and drink are readily available; there are no blind spots and few deaf ones. Tickets are essential, and they are not cheap. Many of the cheaper stands, near the beginning of the parade, however, are bought by the schools at heavily subsidized prices for the families of the paraders, and the friends of the influential school directors. Sambadrome capacity is officially 58,824 people, but that does not include

straps, and gulping down one last gasp of something fortifying to keep them going for the next couple of hours: the whole atmosphere is electrified. Stakes are big in the samba competition, and tempers can run high.

The Sambadrome

The Sambadrome is proof of the importance of Carnival in the life of Rio. Designed by the father of contemporary Brazilian architecture, Oscar Niemeyer, this monster edifice was built in a record-breaking nine months. It is

LEFT: Carnival is a time for looking really silly.
ABOVE: strutting their stuff in the Sambadrome.

the peripatetic vendors of food and drink, the security guards, the police, the bar staff, or the press; not to mention the 6,000 people who might be on the parade area at any given time (*see Activities, page 220*, for more detail on tickets, and on who parades where and when).

The samba parade is an all-discipline presentation, encompassing design, literature, rhythm, color, painting, costume, music, dance, sculpture, poetry, harmony… it is rather like staging an opera on the move.

It is no surprise that the overall director, the *Carnavalesco* (*Carnavalesca* if it is a woman) is paid a handsome sum. The director is a professional, and it is not unusual for schools to poach the best from their rivals, much as soccer players are traded among the clubs.

Every detail of a parade must relate directly to its theme, which may be a historical event, a literary work or a personality. The costumes must reflect the historical time and place; the song must recount or enhance the theme. The huge floats that push down the avenue must detail it in depth through the papier-mâché figures, styrofoam sculptures and painting.

Schools are judged on their theme song, their floats, their costumes, and their enthusiasm. Winning matters – it is not just about taking part. The judges are not to be envied for this always controversial task.

PARADE STATISTICS

The competitive parade covers some 540 meters (1,770 ft) of the 1,700-meter (5,800-ft) purpose-built area. The areas before and after the competitive stretch are left for muster and dispersal. The floats – there must be between eight and 12 – must not exceed 8 meters (26 ft) in width. The height of each must not be greater than 10 meters (33 ft). All floats must be pushed or pulled by manpower alone. Each school must complete the marathon in no less than 60 and no more than 85 minutes; huge clocks line the parade ground, and hearts can be heard stopping when a school overruns its allotted time and loses precious points.

Essential elements

Finally, the samba parade is a nostalgic commemoration of classic samba traditions of the past. There are certain constant elements which must be present whatever the theme. These include the *abre-alas*, literally the "opening wing," which consists of a group of *sambistas* dancing just in front of or behind a large float, which depicts something like an open book or a scroll and is, in effect, the title page of the samba school's theme.

Behind the *abre-alas* is the *comissão de frente*, literally "front runners," and for many spectators the best part of the parade. The *comissão* has evolved into a special show all of its own, with carefully choreographed dances, involving anything from the courting rituals of emerald hummingbirds to entire winning volleyball teams, lobbing volleyballs at each other.

The principal *porta bandeira* (flag bearer) and the *mestre sala* (dance master) appear near the front of the school. They are dressed in lavish, 18th-century formal wear, irrespective of the samba school's theme. The *porta bandeira* is a woman who holds the school's flag. While sharing the flag with the applauding spectators, the *porta bandeira* performs an elaborate dance with her consort. The pair develop a complicated set of steps without breaking rhythm, and they have to do it while proceeding very slowly down the avenue.

Serious samba

The bulk of the samba school comes next, the most instantly recognizable of which is the *bateria* – a small army of percussion enthusiasts, whose job is to maintain a constant thundering rhythm, so the other members of the school can keep up with the tempo of the samba song, and to provide an exciting, pulsating undercurrent to the overall enterprise. All members of the *bateria* wear the same uniform, which must reflect the school's theme.

The rest of the musical responsibility falls to the *puxador de samba*, who rides on the sound car. He is a revered figure who belts out the school's song, with serious amplification. If he stops, everything stops. Everybody in the parade is expected to sing the song all the way to the end of the presentation. Members of the school often distribute copies of the lyrics in the grandstands just before the parade begins.

Animals and Indians

Marching both in front and behind the *bateria* are the major *alas* of the samba school. These groups, comprising scores of people, present different aspects of the school's theme. If the theme is based on an Amazon myth, one of its main *alas* might present *sambistas* dressed as Indians; another could have its members dressed in costumes suggesting the animals of the Amazon; a third could represent figures of Amazon Indian mythology; a fourth might evoke the flora of the region.

The *Ala das Baianas* must parade, even though their presence can often be only tenuously linked to the theme. This group consists of sometimes hundreds of older women, dressed in the flowing attire of the northeastern state of Bahia, home to Brazil's African traditions. Their presence commemorates the earliest history of samba. To be chosen for the *Ala das Baianas* is a high honor.

Destaques and passistas

In between the major *alas* are a number of lavishly costumed individuals depicting the main motifs of the school's theme. These *sambistas* are called *destaques*, literally "prominent figures." They usually include local celebrities, with a preference for voluptuous actresses and strikingly handsome young men, with glitter almost their only attire.

The *passistas* are incredibly agile dancers, who stop in the middle of the street to perform complicated routines. They often use a tambourine as a prop and perform suggestive acrobatic feats as part of the show. The female *passistas* often wear little more than G-strings.

The floats are a show apart, huge structures bearing small houses, gardens, phantasmagorical figures, or fountains of soap bubbles and scent. Celebrities, in heavily sequined courtly costumes, crown the floats; they are hoisted there by forklift truck and they dance and sing for the applauding crowds.

Financing the Carnival

Most of the members of the samba schools are working-class people, who spend the whole year preparing for the event. Support for their

efforts comes from a small government subsidy, from dues paid by members, and from donations made by businesses and individuals in the neighborhoods where the schools have their headquarters. In addition, in recent years the samba schools have become popular entertainment in the off-season. Most of the big-name schools appear at nightclubs or concerts during the year, where they earn a percentage of the gate takings or a flat fee.

In practice, however, most of the schools' money comes from donations, and most of the donations come from the bosses of Rio's time-honored *jogo do bicho (see page 124)*, the illegal numbers game, and also, sad to relate,

from the drugs business. The numbers chiefs support the parade because it is great public relations. Most of Rio's poorer inhabitants have three passions: soccer, samba and the *jogo do bicho*.

Some critics say the parade has become too extravagant, with major schools spending as much as US$300,000 a year on preparations. Largely responsible for the move toward Las Vegas-style opulence was Joãozinho Trinta, former artistic director of one of Rio's largest samba schools, Beija-Flor. Trinta defended his insistence on big-budget productions with the classic remark: "Only the rich enjoy poverty. The poor want luxury." ❑

LEFT: Carmen Miranda contestant at a hotel ball.
RIGHT: a member of the *Ala das Baianas*.

THE MUSIC SCENE

Samba and bossa nova are the two forms of music most closely associated with Brazil, but the country is known for an eclectic and exciting range of music, with devotees of all ages

There are few nationalities that can rival the Brazilians for their love of music and song or for their innate sense of rhythm. Leave a group of Brazilians to their own devices, and it won't be long before somebody is tapping out a rhythm on a tabletop or using a box of matches as a percussion instrument.

Brazilians' sense and feel of rhythm can be seen in the way they walk – even in the way they talk: just compare the way Brazilians handle and use the Portuguese language with the way the Portuguese do, and you will notice a marked difference. Music and its diverse rhythms percolate right through Brazil, to the extent that while other leading sports teams might play with a swagger when they are on top, the Brazilian national soccer team simply plays with a rhythm that is all its own.

Eclectic tastes

Brazilians are extremely open-minded when it comes to musical taste. They will happily embrace the latest English-language hits and acts coming out of the US and the UK, although they will embrace more warmly the multitude of musical styles and rhythms to be found in Brazil itself – styles that include the internationally known samba and bossa nova and the all-encompassing MPB *(Música Popular Brasileira)*. There are also musical styles with exotic sounding names like *axê*, *choro*, *forró*, *frevo*, *pagode* and even Brazil-

LEFT: Marisa Monte is a Brazilian megastar.
RIGHT: Zeca Baleira has a huge following.

ian rock'n'roll, jazz, reggae, afro reggae, heavy metal, electronica and the home-grown country and western, known as *sertaneja*.

While each musical form will have its regional roots, the glue that holds them together has always tended to be Rio de Janeiro. In the same way that Brazilian actors gravitated to Rio, seeing it as the cultural capital of the country, so did many musicians.

During the 1960s, a period of political repression, Rio was home to the main television and radio networks *(see page 62)*, and the best recording studios, and samba and bossa nova were driving the musical agenda, thanks to innovative musicians such as Tom Jobim, João Gilberto, Baden Powell and Sergio Mendes, among others.

The people's choice

To understand the contemporary Brazilian music scene it is important to know that, unlike in the US, the UK, and many other countries, the music Brazil is listening to at any one time is not driven by the charts or formulated playlists, but by personal choice. The result is that some of the biggest names in Brazilian music today started off back in the 1960s as contemporaries of the Beatles, Rolling Stones, and Bob Dylan. Never having

lost popularity, they are as big today as they were when they started some 40 years ago, and their new output and material is considered equally relevant. They share the stage and the space with new stars, some of whom explode onto the scene and shine brightly for a short time, others who seem likely to carry the baton forward for many years to come.

Musical godfathers

The godfathers of contemporary Brazilian music are the triumvirate of Chico Buarque, Caetano Veloso, and Gilberto Gil. Chico is a native *carioca*, while Caetano and Gil both hail from Bahia. If they have female equivalents, they are Maria Bethânia, who is Caetano's sister, and Gal Costa. All started out in the 1960s and have been household names in Brazil ever since, even when some of them were forced into exile *(see page 34)* to avoid the oppression and censorship of military dictatorships. Ironically, Gil, despite a heavy commitment to recording and touring, has still found time to go from political exile to his role as Brazil's Minister of Culture.

As well as being singers and performers in their own right, Chico, Caetano, and Gil are also prolific songwriters, and it is almost a rarity when a Brazilian album doesn't have a composition that is credited to one of the three, or to Tom Jobim, who died in 1994. They are also unusual in that their fan base is spread evenly across all age groups, and their work can be found in the CD collections of children, teenagers, parents and grandparents.

In truth, in Brazil it is often the song that is

WHERE TO FIND IT

Visitors to Rio will not have to look far to discover which of the big names are playing, as they all tend to use one of two large show houses. The most traditional is Canecão, which opened in 1967 and has been going strong ever since. It is located next to the Rio Sul shopping center in Botafogo. Who is playing there, and when, can be found on the venue's website (www.canecao.com.br).

Newer and larger is the Claro Hall in Via Parque Shopping in Barra, which can seat over 3,000 people at tables or 12,000 standing. Details of who is about to play the Claro Hall can be found on the Brazilian site for Ticket-Master (www.ticketmaster.com.br).

There are plenty of record stores in Rio, making it easy to pick up CDs of the best of Brazilian music, including hits by some of the performers mentioned here, most of whose names are unfamiliar to foreign visitors but are well worth checking out. Most artists have compilations of their greatest hits, and once you are in the store it will soon be quite clear which is the hot-selling CD or DVD of the moment. It is worth remembering that most music DVDs are "zone-free" – which means they are suitable for any DVD player. CDs and DVDs of Brazilian stars' music are also exported all over the world, and a selection can be found in most of the major record stores.

the star rather than the singer, and at times it appears that the singers and the public share out the great bossa nova, samba and MPB standards democratically. Brazilian songwriting can also be very personal, and can reflect the locations about which the songs are written. Jobim's *The Girl from Ipanema* would be the best-known example, but he was a master of painting life in Rio, using a location such as Corcovado or, in *Aguas de Março (The Rains of March)*, signaling the end of summer. For songs about people rather than places, check out Adriana Calcanhotto's *Cariocas*, which lists, perfectly, the foibles of Rio's residents.

Following in famous footsteps

It would be a mistake to think that the ongoing popularity and impact of Buarque, Veloso, and Gil is down to a lack of imagination or of other options. Numerous Brazilian artists have flourished since the 1960s and had equally long and distinguished careers. They include the likes of Jorge Benjor, João Bosco, Roberto Carlos, Rita Lee, Marina, Milton Nascimento, and Elba Ramalho. Then there are the big names from the samba scene that include Beth Carvalho, João Nogueira, Martinho da Vila, and Zeca Pagodinho.

All the above were born and brought up in diverse regions of Brazil, but made their way up by playing the clubs and bars of Rio de Janeiro. The same is true today, so the Rio public is always on the lookout for the rising stars playing clubs and bars such as **Mistura Fina** on the Lagoa, **Vinicius** in Ipanema, **Bar do Tom** in Leblon, and **Alegro Bistro Musical** and **Bip Bip** in Copacabana.

If the music scene in Brazil in the 1960s and 1970s was dominated by solo artists and singer-songwriters, the 1980s onwards saw the growth in popularity of groups. These include Biquini Cavadão, Kid Abelha, Legião Urbana, and Paralamas do Sucesso, while AfroReggae, Charlie Brown Jr and Jota Quest are among the new kids on the block.

New names and stars are always emerging. Among those to stake a place recently are Zeca Baleiro, Carlinhos Brown, Ana Carolina, Cassia Eller, Seu Jorge, Kelly Key, Vanessa

da Mata, Margareth Menezes, Fernando Porto, Nando Reis, Maria Rita, and Ivete Sangalo.

Two bright stars

Two new Brazilian singers to make a huge impact in recent years are Bebel Gilberto and Marisa Monte. Bebel, daughter of the bossa nova star, João Gilberto, exploded on the international scene with her album *Tanto Tempo* in 2002. In truth, New York-based Bebel is probably a bigger star internationally than she is in her native country, but in taking the contemporary sound of Brazil into millions of homes around the world she has opened the door for others.

One of the brightest stars in Brazil is Marisa Monte. She stepped into the spotlight in the early 1990s on the back of a much-talked-about show that combined old and traditional compositions with modern Brazilian and international music. Her first album went platinum and she has never looked back, with four more acclaimed albums and a number of shows and tours to her credit. She also found time to join forces with Arnaldo Antunes and Carlinhos Brown to form Tribalistas, which resulted in another best-selling album and DVD. Marisa could probably be a global star if she put her mind to it, but prefers to concentrate on Brazil, with just the occasional international tour. ❏

LEFT: Caetano Veloso, still going strong.
RIGHT: Gal Costa is a household name.

PLACES

A detailed guide to the entire city, with the
principal sites clearly cross-referenced
by number to the maps

Rio de Janeiro is a sensuous city whose character is expressed both by its extrovert people and by its geography. The city is divided into two zones, the north and the south – *zona norte* and *zona sul* – but for most visitors it is the south that is of most interest. This is the zone that is home to Rio's scenic wonders – Sugar Loaf (Pão de Açúcar), Corcovado, the Floresta da Tijuca, and the Lagoa Rodrigo de Freitas, as well as the famous beaches of Copacabana and Ipanema, and the slightly more distant ones of São Conrado, the Barra da Tijuca, and Grumari.

Life for the residents of Rio and for visitors revolves round the beach, the city playground. Fortunately, there are enough beaches to go around, each with its own personality, its distinctive quality, and its status.

But Rio is more than the sum of its beaches, mountains, and stunning views. As befits a city with a 450-year history, there is also a historical and cultural side to it, concentrated in its downtown area, where there are numerous imposing squares, interesting churches, and a number of excellent museums and galleries. Then there are the hillsides of Santa Teresa, reached via quaint, clanking trolley cars; the imperial enclave of Quinta da Boa Vista; and the vast expanse of Guanabara Bay and its islands, all of which merit a long, reflective look.

At night, Rio comes alive for a second time, and stays vibrantly awake until late. Residents and visitors flock to the city's bars and restaurants, many of which are blessed with spectacular views just outside their windows, then move on to lively music venues.

The chapters that follow – each of which includes a section on some of the most interesting places to eat – will introduce you to some of the best that Rio de Janeiro has to offer, help you find your way around, and avoid pitfalls, but will always bear in mind that independent travelers like to make their own discoveries, too.

An Excursions section *(see pages 169–203)* describes easy-to-reach and interesting destinations outside the city.   ❏

PRECEDING PAGES: an aerial view shows Rio in all its glory; ride the cable car to the top of Sugar Loaf and see the city spread out before you.
LEFT: visitors at the foot of the Cristo Redentor statue, on the summit of Corcovado.

Central Rio de Janeiro

0   400 m
0   400 yds

Rua Visconde Inhauma
Rua Presidente Vargas
Praça Pio X
Nossa Senhora da Candelária
Casa Franca Brasil
Centro Cultural Banco do Brasil
Santa Cruz dos Militares
Nossa Senhora da Lapa dos Mercadores
SÃO CRISTOV.
Av. Prefeito Olímpio de Me
Rua Visconde de Niteroi
Uruguaiana
Rua de Buenos Aires
Nossa Senhora do Carmo
Praça 15 de Novembro
Estação das Barcas
Av. Ana Neri
Rua Visconde de Niteroi
CENTRO
Nossa Senhora da Conceição a Boa Morte
São Benedito
Rua do Ouvidor
Nossa Senhora do Monte do Carmo
Paço Imperial
Praça Ancora
Av. Presidente Kubitschek
São Francisco
São Francisco de Paula
Teatro Caetano
Rua 7 de Setembro
Assembléia
Avenida Rio Branco
Rua Uruguaiana
Museu Naval e Oceanográfico
Av. Alfredo Agache
VILA ISABEL
Mara
Praça Tiradentes
Rua da Carioca
Convento Santo Antonio
Avenida Nilo Peçanha
Praça Henrique Lage
Praça do Expedicionário
R. Castro
Nossa Senhora do Bonsucesso
Museu Histórico Nacional
MARACAN
R. Vinte e Oito de Setembro
R. Maxwell
São Francisco da Penitência
Largo da Carioca
Carioca
Chile
Av. 13
Teatro Municipal
Museu Nacional de Belas Artes
Av. Almirante Barroso
Pres. Antônio Carlos
R. Mal. Aguinaldo
Santa Casa da Misericórdia
Praça Antenor Fagundes
Av. General Justo
CASTELO
ANDARAÍ
Av. Maracana
Praça Tiradentes
República do
Av. República do Paraguai
Estação do Bonde
Rua Senador Dantas
Av. Graça Aranha
R. Araújo Porto Alegre
Palácio G. Capanema
Av. Churchill
AV. F. Roosevelt
Santa Luzia
Rua de Santa Luzia
Catedral de São Sebastiao
Biblioteca Nacional
Praça Floriano
Cinelândia
Av. Nilo
Rua de Santa Luzia
Santa Luzia
Praça Virgilio de Melo Franco
Marechal Câmara
Arcos da Lapa
R. Evaristo da Veiga
Teatro Mesbla
Rua Branco
Av. Presidente Wilson
Praça Itália
Trevo dos Estudantes
Praça Senador Salgado Filho
Av. Almirante Silvio de Noronha
R. Bonde Joaquim
Ld. de Santa Teresa
Rua da Lapa
Rua do Passeio
PASSEIO PUBLICO
R. Teixeira de Freitas
Lg. da Lapa
R. Mestre Valentim
Praça Déodoro
Rua João Neves de Fontoura
Avenida Infante Dom Henrique
Rua Jardel Jercolis
Museu de Arte Moderna
Parque Nacional da Tijuca
Estrada
Praça Paris
Praça Pistoia
Monumento dos Mortos da II Guerra Mundial
PARQUE FLAMENGO
Enseada da Glória

Floresta da Tijuca
ALTO DA BOA VISTA
JAR
FURNAS
Estrada de
Mesa do Imperador
Vista Chinesa
Vista Chinesa
Estrada das Furnas
Estrada da Pedra
Parque Nacional da Tijuca
PARQUE DA CIDADE
R. Marques de São
Pedra Bonita
da Gávea
Estrada da Barra
Parque Nacional da Tijuca
Morro Dois Irmãos
Túnel Dois Irmãos
VIDIGAL
ITANHANGÁ
SÃO CONRADO
Pedra da Gávea
Estrada da Tijuca Cascatinha
Avenida

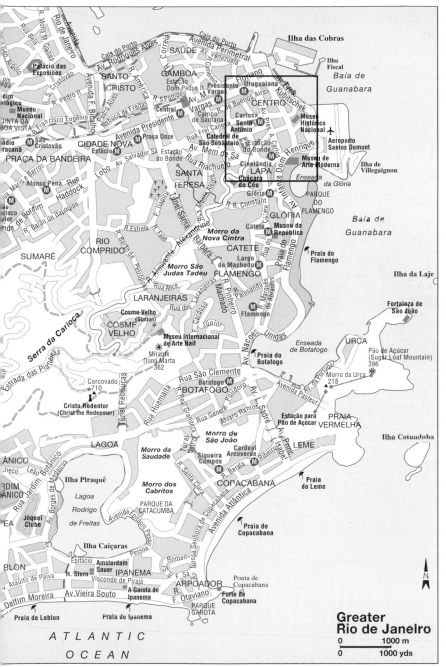

Greater Rio de Janeiro

| 0 | 1000 m |
| 0 | 1000 yds |

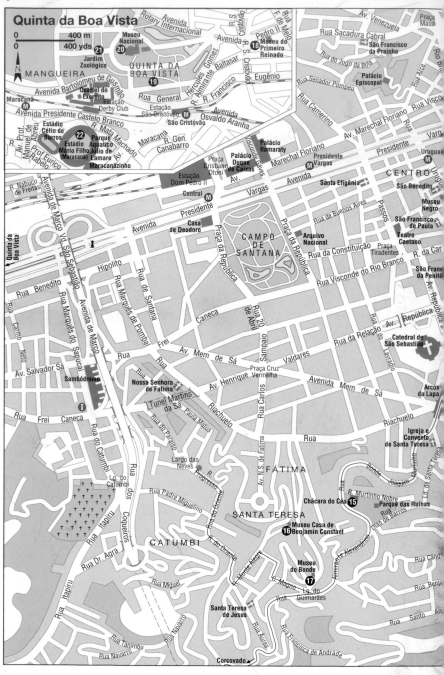

Quinta da Boa Vista

0   400 m
0   400 yds

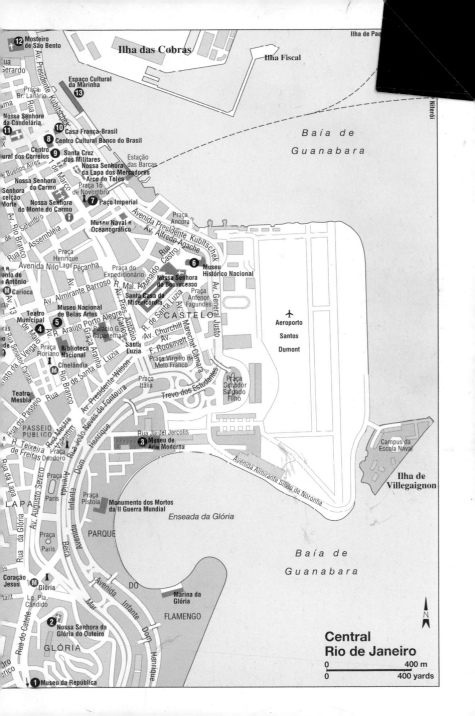

12 Mosteiro de São Bento

Rua Gerardo

Av. Presidente Kubitschek

Praça Br. Landário

13 Espaço Cultural da Marinha

Ilha das Cobras

Ilha Fiscal

Ilha de Pa...

Niterói

Nossa Senhora da Candelária **11**

10 Casa França-Brasil

8 Centro Cultural Banco do Brasil

Centro ...ural dos Correios

e Buenos Aires

9 Santa Cruz dos Militares

Estação das Barcas

Nossa Senhora da Lapa dos Mercadores

Arco do Teles

Baía de Guanabara

Nossa Senhora do Carmo

Senhora celção Morte

Av. Rio Branco

Nossa Senhora do Monte do Carmo

Praça 15 de Novembro

7 Paço Imperial

Praça Ancora

Avenida Presidente Kubitschek

Av. Alfredo Agache

Assembléia

Museu Naval e Oceanográfico

Praça Henrique Lage

Rua Castro

Praça do Expedicionário

R. Mal. Aguinaldo

Av. Almirante Barroso

6 Museu Histórico Nacional

Avenida Nilo Pécanha

Nossa Senhora do Bonsucesso

M Carioca

Teatro Municipal **4**

Museu Nacional de Belas Artes **5**

R. Araújo Porto Alegre

Graça Aranha

Av. Pres. Antônio Carlos

Palácio G...

Santa Casa da Misericórdia

Praça Antenor Fagundes

CASTELO

Av. General Justo

Biblioteca Nacional

Rua de Santa Luzia

Santa Luzia

R. de Santa Luzia

Av. Churchill

Aeroporto Santos Dumont

Cinelândia

Rua do Passeio

Praça Floriano

Av. Presidente Wilson

Av. Marechal Câmara

Av. F. Roosevelt

Praça Virgílio de Melo Franco

Teatro Mesbla

Rua 13 de ...

Rua do Passeio

Av. João Neves de Fontoura

Praça Italia

Trevo dos Estudantes

Praça Senador Salgado Filho

PASSEIO PÚBLICO

Praça Mestre Valentim

Av. Henrique ...

Rua Jardel Jercolis

3 Museu de Arte Moderna

R. Teixeira de Freitas

Praça Deodoro

Campus da Escola Naval

Av. Augusto Severo

Av. Beira

Dom

Rua da Lapa

Praça Paris

Praça Pistoia

Monumento dos Mortos da II Guerra Mundial

Avenida Almirante Sílvio de Noronha

Ilha de Villegaignon

LAPA

Rua da Glória

Praça Paris

PARQUE

Enseada da Glória

Coração Jesus

M Glória **1**

Lg. Pla. Cândido

DO

Av. Infante Dom Henrique

Av. Mar

Marina da Glória

Baía de Guanabara

Rua do Catete

2 Nossa Senhora da Glória do Outeiro

FLAMENGO

GLÓRIA

1 Museu da República

N

Central Rio de Janeiro

| 0 | 400 m |
| 0 | 400 yards |

CENTRAL RIO

Rio is not just beaches. The downtown area has a
wealth of museums, churches, and remnants of its
imperial past, as well as good restaurants
and trips around the bay

A tour of the historic city center
of Rio de Janeiro provides the
visitor with a glimpse of its
past, its present and an appreciation
of the people who make this area a
permanent bustle of comings and
goings. Here, latest-generation com-
puters are plugged into crumbling
100-year-old walls, and modern,
"intelligent" high-rises offer all that
is contemporary in office security
and comfort.

The sights recommended in this
chapter are the pillars around which
daily life revolves. Some of the
locations mentioned are of a religious nature, and seriously under-
dressed visitors may be challenged,
or even lent a skirt or jacket in order
to gain admission.

Other places, especially the cultural centers and museums, do not
necessarily have important collections on permanent display, but serve
as interesting backdrops for a huge
variety of temporary exhibitions.
Carry your camera – if you must –
discreetly. Most of the places recommended here open around noon and
are closed on Monday; many of them
also close down during Carnival.

Presidential memories

The **Museu da República** ❶ (Rua
do Catete 153, tel: 2258-6350;
Tues–Fri noon–5pm, Sat–Sun and
public holidays 2–6pm; admission
free on Wed) is housed in the Palácio do Catete. Guarded by menac-
ing-looking eagles, the palace is the
former residence of 18 Brazilian
presidents. It came into federal government hands in payment of a bad
debt in 1896, when its owners were
thwarted in their ambition to turn
the building into a hotel.

The museum highlights presidential memorabilia of every period
from the 1889 proclamation of the
republic to the end of the military

Map
on pages
84–85

LEFT: a flavor of old Rio
in Arco do Telles.
BELOW: downtown
rush-hour.

You will often find street entertainers performing outside the Museu da República.

BELOW: the sacristy of Nossa Senhora da Glória do Outeiro.

regime in 1985; more recently it has been equipped as an impressive high-tech research center.

A red-carpet welcome leads to the ground-floor meeting room, dominated by the Cabinet table used by Deodoro da Fonseca (1827–92), Brazil's first president. Each place is marked with the dispatch book of one of Fonseca's ministers. Wood, which put Brazil on the world map in the first place, is well evoked in the stunning floors. Above all this formality, Bacchus and Adriane are there to keep a watchful eye on presidential doings.

The second floor features elegant, but stiltedly ceremonial, reception rooms. St Sebastian, patron saint of Rio de Janeiro, guards the chapel in the incongruous company of Diogenes the Cynic. An 1812 pedestal vase in the Blue Room belonged to Napoleon, and the Moorish Room has a wonderfully authentic feel to it. Furniture in the Banquet Room is carved with motifs suitably suggestive of fish, fruit, and game.

The private quarters of the country's presidents were situated on the third floor. It was in the Quarto do Presidente Getúlio Vargas that the dictator shot himself in the heart on August 24, 1954. The room is preserved exactly as it was that day, right down to the soiled pajama top the tortured man was wearing when he "left this life to enter history."

The extensive gardens are certainly worth visiting. Covering 24,000 sq. meters (28,000 sq. yds), they were formally laid out by French landscapers. They have all the elements of an old-fashioned garden: plenty of water, bridges, grottoes, winding paths, and statues, one of which represents the birth of Venus. The tropical content is provided by the palm avenue and the numerous fruit trees, which attract a colorful variety of birds.

The perfect church

Close by, on a hill overlooking Guanabara Bay, is the postcard-perfect **Igreja de Nossa Senhora da Glória do Outeiro ❷** (Praça Nossa Senhora da Glória 135, tel: 2557-4600; Mon–Fri 8am–5pm, Sat–Sun 8am–noon; free). Dating from 1714, this attractive church is the first important example of baroque architecture in Brazil, and its design is based on two interlocking octagons.

It was a great favorite with the royal family, and still dubs itself "imperial," long after the end of the empire. The tile work is especially noteworthy, though there is some controversy as to whether the inspiration for the tiles was the ancient Book of Tobit or the Song of Solomon.

Adjacent to the church is the **Museu da Irmandade de Nossa Senhora da Glória do Outeiro** (same hours as the church but closed Mon), where the generosity of the church's royal and noble parishioners can be observed through a rich, if not particularly attractive, collection of religious items.

Parque do Flamengo

To get from the pretty Glória church to the Museum of Modern Art the visitor needs to cross the Aterro (Landfill) do Flamengo, which was created in the early part of the 20th century and is otherwise known as the **Parque do Flamengo**. Needless to say, the pedestrian walkways over the high-speed road are the only way to get to the greenery, although at weekends the area is closed to traffic and becomes one of the world's truly gigantic recreation areas.

The vegetation of the park bears all the trademarks of its creator, the committed *carioca* landscaper Roberto Burle Marx (1909–94), with its contrasting colors and textures, and striking selection of plants. This vast area measures 1,200,000 sq. meters (1,436,000 sq. yds), of which 58 hectares (143 acres) are lawns, and contains some 13,000 trees. This means that at any given time, there's bound to be a clump of something in flower.

The Amazonian Cannonball Tree *(Curoupita guianensis)*, also known as the Monkey's Apricot, produces spectacular football-shaped fruits and pink flowers directly on its bark. Majestic palms guard the war memorial, honoring those who died in World War II, and the Tomb of the Unknown Soldier, which was built in the late 1950s.

Museum of Modern Art

The **Museu de Arte Moderna** ❸ (Avenida Infante Dom Henrique 85, tel: 2240-4944; Tues–Sun noon–6pm; last admission half an hour before closing) is a striking edifice. Designed in 1954 by Affonso Eduardo Reidy, its style was considered outrageous for its time; the architect's intention was to leave wide, open spaces in the building so that its glorious setting could be viewed through it, from almost every angle. The gardens that surround the MAM, as it is affectionately known, were, like the Parque do Flamengo, originally designed by Roberto Burle Marx.

From the early 1950s to 1978, the MAM amassed a respectable collection of contemporary art, and was

Map on pages 84–85

A piece of sculpture outside the Museu de Arte Moderna.

BELOW: a fortune-teller at work.

BELOW: the Teatro Municipal in tree-lined Praça Floriano.

the country's pride. Its massive proportions seem to welcome the huge sculptures and installations that have become a hallmark of Brazilian modern art. In 1978, however, disaster struck in the form of a fire, which consumed almost the whole collection. Solidarity and support poured in from all parts of the world, and the collection is now back up to scratch, with works by Fernand Léger, Alberto Giacometti, Jean Arp, Henry Moore, Barry Flanaghan, Max Bill, Carlo Carrà and Lucio Fontana, among many other artists.

In addition to the international collection, the MAM is the custodian of works by notable Latin American artists, such as Joaquín Torres García, Cruz Díez and Jorge de la Vega. Brazilian art at its best is represented here in works by Bruno Giorgi, Maria Martins, Di Cavalcanti, Lygia Clark, Helio Oiticica, Franz Weissmann, Amílcar de Castro and Wyllis de Castro.

The MAM is one of Rio's outstanding exhibition sites, and consequently plays host to important traveling exhibitions. It is also the stage for a variety of events and "happenings," from jazz festivals to fashion shows.

Star turns and tantrums

Cinelândia, reached by an overhead walkway away from the MAM, is a large, open square, surrounded by imposing public buildings, which gained its name and fame from the numerous cinemas it used to house. Its name on the map is **Praça Floriano**. All around the square are hawkers selling bits and pieces, from pirated CDs to peanuts in long paper cones, which are kept warm by glowing coals in specially adapted paint cans. The local legislature holds court in the area, and demonstrators, from half a dozen to hundreds, can often be seen waving placards. In the early evening the bars fill up as office workers "wait until the bus empties out a little" over an after-work beer.

The most monumental structure in the square is the august **Teatro Municipal ❹** (Praça Floriano, tel: 2299-1643; Mon–Fri 10am–5pm).

A truly magnificent building, oozing atmosphere, it is a scaled-down replica of the Paris Opera and was inaugurated in 1909. What tales it has to tell.

Nijinsky danced here in 1913, Pavlova four years later. Maria Callas slapped director-general Barreto Pinto in the face one night in 1952 when he had the temerity to tell the great diva that her Norma (in Bellini's opera of the same name) "stank." Nureyev stopped the orchestra mid-dance, striding – his eyes wide with ire – to the front of the stage, stating that he couldn't dance "to that noise." Pavarotti brought a usually boisterous audience to its knees in silence. The late Princess of Wales endured a power cut during a ballet performance here. Both on and off stage, it's all pure theater.

Check what's on while you are in Rio, as performances here are of a consistently high standard, and ticket prices modestly priced by international standards. *(See more about classical music in the Activities section, page 216.)*

Brazilian artists

Across Avenida Rio Branco from the Municipal Theater is Rio's fine-arts museum, the **Museu Nacional de Belas Artes ❺** (Avenida Rio Branco 199, tel: 2240-0068; Tues–Fri 10am–6pm, Sat–Sun 2–6pm; free on Sunday). It was built in the French neo-classical style and completed in 1908. The original collection consisted of art brought to Brazil by Dom João VI when the Portuguese royal family fled the Napoleonic threat 100 years earlier. This collection was added to by the French Artistic Mission, led by Joachin Lebreton, and has been growing ever since. It includes works by Cândido Portinari, one of Brazil's greatest 20th-century painters *(see box below).*

Brazilian printmakers are very well represented through the work of Fayga Ostrower and Carlos Oswald; painters include Tarsila do Amaral, Eliseu Visconti and Alberto Guinard. The intriguing work of Iole de Freitas is emblematic of the daring practiced by contemporary Brazilian sculptors. These names

Map on pages 84–85

A detail on the façade of the magnificent Teatro Municipal.

BELOW: cooling waters cascade from a fountain in Praça Floriano.

Cândido Portinari

Cândido Portinari (1903–62) was born in Brodósqui, in São Paulo state, the son of Italian immigrants. He received little formal education, but his artistic talent soon became obvious, and at the age of 15 he enrolled in the Escola Nacional de Belas Artes in Rio. International recognition came when he painted three panels for the Brazilian pavilion at the New York World Fair in 1939. A brilliant portraitist, Portinari became increasingly concerned with social themes and the hardships of rural people, a subject that was reflected both in his work and his growing political activism. He became a member of the Brazilian Communist Party in 1944.

Moorish touches demonstrate that Rio has an eclectic architectural history.

BELOW: buses stop outside the National Library building.

may not be familiar to foreign visitors, but it is certainly worth making their acquaintance. The African collections are endearingly straightforward, and pay homage to the ties between two continents. The museum is undergoing major restoration at present, and may well be shrouded in hoardings during your stay; do not let this deter you, as it is well worth a visit.

Museu Histórico Nacional

A short walk southwards is one of Rio's most important landmarks, the **Museu Histórico Nacional** ❻ (Praça Marechal Ancora, tel: 2550-9224; Tues–Fri 10am–5.30pm, Sat–Sun and public holidays 2–6pm). The museum – actually a series of interconnected buildings – is a rambling structure reflecting different architectural styles and historical epochs. Wings and improvements have been added and subtracted at various times since 1603, when a small fortress was built on the site. In 1922 much of it was remodeled to accommodate the fair held to celebrate the centenary

of independence. An injection of 21st-century cash has added escalators and modern conveniences to the historic building.

It pays to get your bearings and approach the exhibits in an organized fashion, as there is plenty of content, and it is well explained in the informative panels. Various aspects of Brazil's history are presented in modules; one is entitled "Colony and Dependence," another "Memories of the Empire." Impressive, large-scale oil paintings set the tone and allow the visitor to place the exhibits in context.

The Farmácia Teixeira Novaes is the recreation of a real apothecary's premises, and has a wonderfully authentic feel to it. The adjacent Casa do Trem houses the coin collection, the largest in Latin America, numbering some 127,000 items. The carriages are a show apart, and always a great hit with the kids. There's a lovely internal patio, which houses the huge collection of cannons, and is a wonderful place to stop and put your feet up for a few moments.

Ferryboat station

Across from the museum is the Estação das Barcas, the ferry terminal linking Rio to Niterói, Paquetá and other destinations within the bay; there is always a fast flow of frantic pedestrian traffic as people rush to catch their boat. A green-shuttered tower pokes its turreted head above the trees; this is the Albamar Restaurant *(see page 99 for details)*. This is all that remains of the Municipal Market, built in 1906. The view and ambience are more inspired than the food, which is only adequate. A lively antique and bric-a-brac fair – Parker pens, silver salvers and teacups – takes place here every Saturday from 9am to 6pm, when barter and bargaining set the tone.

The hub of power

A short walk in a northwesterly direction brings you to **Praça XV de Novembro**, named in honor of the date (November 15, 1889) on which the Republic of Brazil was officially proclaimed. This square is widely known as **Praça Quinze**

(quinze meaning 15 in Portuguese). Carefully restored, it is one of the most interesting points in the center of the city.

One of Rio's most historic structures, the **Paço Imperial** ❼ (Imperial Palace; Praça Quinze de Novembro 48, tel: 2533-4407; Tues–Sun noon–6pm) dominates the plaza's south side. Its straight rows of windows give it marked architectural unity, while its iron and woodwork make it pleasingly home-like. Work on the building was completed in 1743, and for 63 years it served as headquarters for Brazil's royally appointed viceroys.

King João VI made it his palace in 1808 when he arrived in Brazil, accompanied by the entire Portuguese court, fleeing Napoleon. In January 1822, Brazil's youthful regent, Pedro I, used the palace window as a backdrop for his announcement that he would remain on Brazilian soil – *"Diga ao povo que fico"* – thus defying Portuguese orders to return home, and consequently preparing the way for Brazilian independence.

Map on pages 84–85

A monument to baroque artist Mestre Valentim in Praça Quinze.

BELOW: the Petit Palais restaurant in the Paço Imperial.

The former imperial palace now serves as a multipurpose cultural center. It maintains three permanent exhibitions, one relating the history of the building itself, the second, a homage to Brazilian architecture, and a third, inaugurated in 2002, commemorating the life and work of Rio-born Sergio Camargo (1930–90), a trailblazing sculptor.

The Paço also hosts high-quality temporary exhibitions, and musical performances of every style. You can also find one of Rio's best CD shops here, a perfect place to buy Brazilian music.

The cultural corridor

The best way to get to know a bit of old-style Rio de Janeiro is to enter **Arco do Teles**, next to Praça Quinze, opposite the Paço Imperial. Here there are narrow, traffic-free streets and colorful old buildings, quaint restaurants and storefronts leading to high-ceilinged interiors. On Friday nights, *cariocas* working in the center gather here to eat and drink before going home, thus avoiding the often gridlocked rush

hour. These streets are known as the city's "cultural corridor" because of the concentration of galleries and cultural centers.

The jewel in the crown

The jewel in the cultural crown is the **Centro Cultural Banco do Brasil 8** (Rua Primeiro de Março 66, tel: 3808-2020; Tues–Sun 10am–9pm; free), Rio's pride. The former headquarters of the national bank was turned into a multipurpose cultural center in 1989, and its success spawned several similar institutions around Rio. The sheer grandiosity of the building, the wonderful natural light provided by the skylight roof, and the graceful, circular mezzanines make it a perfect backdrop for any number and variety of activities.

The marbled halls host a theater, video-screening rooms, a cinema, a bookshop, a concert hall, snack bars, and tearooms, as well as the best exhibition sites in the city. Your own, private English-speaking guide will show you around and impart lots of interesting informa-

The Arco de Teles area was built in the mid-18th century. The lovely, two-story buildings are known as sobrados.

BELOW: attractive old buildings clustered near the Arco do Teles.

tion, at no cost – just ask at the reception desk. Treat yourself, and take the elevator – a highly polished gilded cage if ever there was one – to any floor.

An average of 6,000 people visit the place daily, and peak attendance reaches 19,000 per day when a particularly popular exhibition is being staged. It is a great meeting place, or somewhere cool just to sit and take a pause. Although admission is free, there may be a charge for a particular performance or screening. The Centro Cultural Banco do Brasil is certainly worth a place on your itinerary. Even if you do not particularly connect with what you see or hear within, you can admire the grandeur of its architecture and the creativity of its mentors.

More than a post office

The **Centro Cultural dos Correios** ❾ (Post Office Cultural Center; Rua Visconde de Itaboraí 20, tel: 2503-8770; Tues–Sun noon–7pm; free) is the cultural arm of the post office, and cannot rival the Centro Cultural Banco do Brasil in terms of size or funding, but this outwardly unassuming building packs a punch in terms of content. It houses up to five temporary exhibitions, always of the highest standard, beautifully showcased by the perennially creative local designers.

Hardwood floorboards are polished to a mirror-like shine, occasionally lit by shafts of sunlight from the outside world. Rare and precious glimpses of the rooftops of old Rio can be spied from the windows. The elevator itself is a giant step back in time. There is a bar, a pocket theater, and a peaceful open patio where frequent "happenings" take place. And, of course, there's a post office.

Rio's forum

Further down the same street is **Casa França-Brasil** ❿ (Rua Visconde de Itaboraí 79, tel: 2253-5366; Tues–Sun noon–8pm; free). Originally designed as a trading center for local produce, it served this purpose for a mere two years, and by 1821 was already being used as a meeting place for politicians,

An old-fashioned postbox outside the Centro Cultural dos Correios.

LEFT: the Centro Cultural dos Correios.
BELOW: inside the Centro Cultural Banco do Brasil.

A detail on the fountain outside the church of Nossa Senhora da Candelária.

BELOW: a peaceful corner in the São Bento monastery complex.

just like the Roman forum it so clearly evokes. Nowadays, it houses exhibitions of every nature. The visitor experiences the surprising architectural mix of neo-classical and Renaissance styles. The ceiling is impressive, and the flagstone floor ankle-breakingly irregular, so caution is essential.

Anachronistic glory

Surrounded by swirling traffic, right in the middle of Avenida Presidente Vargas, is the impressive **Igreja de Nossa Senhora da Candelária** ⓫ (Praça Pio X, tel: 2233-2324; Mon–Fri 8am–4pm, Sat 8am–noon, Sun 9am–1pm; free). Although work had already begun on this church in 1775, it was only finally dedicated by King João VI in 1811. Construction took so long that the building suffered numerous architectural influences, resulting in it now being classified as an "anachronistic colonial neo-classical structure," which is an apt, if somewhat clumsy, description. The dome, which weighs 600 tons, was finished in 1877, and the magnificent

bronze doors were cast in France, and exhibited at the Paris World Fair in 1889 before being hung in Rio in 1901.

Monastery with a view

Five blocks north is one of Rio's oldest churches, the **Igreja e Mosteiro de São Bento** ⓬ (St Benedict's church and monastery; Rua Dom Gerardo 68, tel: 2291-7122; daily 7am–noon, 2–6pm), commanding a magnificent view of Guanabara Bay. The church is famous for its beautiful sung Masses, in the rich Gregorian tradition, something that is rarely heard these days. Masses are held on Sunday at 8am, 10am, and 6.10pm, and from Monday to Friday at 7.15am and 5pm (the latter in the side chapel), but if you want to hear the sung Mass you must go at 10am on Sunday or at the early hour of 7.15am during the week.

It may sound a little surprising, but in order to reach the monastery on foot you must enter the office block at No. 40, and take the elevator to the fifth floor.

The elevator will deliver you into a beautiful setting, home to one of Rio's most beloved places of worship. As you approach the building, surrounded by trees and the sound of song birds, the section to the right of the magnificent gates is the secluded workplace of the studious Benedictine monks who live in cloisters here. Obviously, it is off-limits for visitors.

Ornate interior

Work on the Benedictine monastery began in 1586 and continued for two centuries. The façade shares the flat, solid, Mannerist style that was prominent in 17th-century Brazilian religious architecture. But the simplicity of this façade is deceptive, for São Bento is noted for the opulence of its interior, highlighted by the extensive application of gold leaf and an absolute explosion of intricate baroque woodcarving. Each side chapel seems to be vying with its neighbor to outdo it in embellishment.

The gold leaf has turned out to be something of a savior for the church, although of an unexpected and non-religious kind: much of the building has succumbed to termites, and suffered massive damage. But termites don't eat gold, so the many gilded portions of the church have been preserved.

Proceed down the right-hand side of the nave, and you will come across the chapel devoted to the unfortunate St Lawrence, who was roasted over glowing coals in AD 248. The statue of the saint shows him carrying the grille upon which he met his fiery end.

The high altar is dedicated to Our Lady of Montserrat. To her right she is guarded by St Benedict and to her left by the saint's beloved sister, St Scholastica. It seems fitting that these holy siblings should stand forever in each other's company; while they lived, they were allowed to meet but once a year.

Extensive renovation work is expected to take some time to complete, but even if it is still in progress when you visit Rio, that should not deter you from coming to this delightful spot.

The bay before you

For a most unusual view of Rio, leave the church and veer off to the right, beyond the facilities and still within the compound of the church. You must enter an uninviting-looking tunnel, and stick to the narrow sidewalk on your right. Soon you will emerge into daylight, and before you lies the great Bay of Guanabara. Somehow, the fast-moving traffic on the overpass seems less hostile from this viewpoint. The hill on which the monastery stands is one of the few that survive in downtown Rio. The others that existed during the colonial period have long since fallen victim to *carioca* progress, and the local penchant for removing hills to fill in the bay *(see page 27)*.

Map on pages 84–85

The feast day of Nossa Senhora de Candelária is August 15, which is also celebrated as the Day of the Assumption.

BELOW: baroque chapel in the São Bento church.

Map on pages 84–85

It is worth getting to know Rio's metro system if you are doing a lot of sightseeing in the city.

BELOW: exhibit in the Espaço Cultural da Marinha.

The maritime past

Close by is an area designated the **Espaço Cultural da Marinha** (Navy Cultural Center; Avenida Alfredo Agache, tel: 2104-6025; Tues–Sun noon–5pm). Dynamic, fun, and well laid out, this is a great place to while away an afternoon, especially if you are traveling with children – even those who don't usually like museums will find something to interest them here.

Displays chart the history of Brazil's colorful maritime past, but the highlight for most visitors of all ages are the detailed model ships. Dom João VI's rowboat, in which he traveled to visit favorite spots in the bay, can be seen, as well as an extensive display of shipping and seafaring memorabilia.

Shipwrecks have also contributed to the display, and the visitor can examine objects brought up from the deep during the period between 1648 and 1916. There is also a realistic reconstruction of conditions on board a galleon, and a diorama illustrating the techniques used to explore underwater sites.

Getting to know the navy

The Brazilian navy has entered into the spirit of putting historical Rio back on the visitor's map with the program called "Get to Know our Navy." This takes place every second weekend in the month. Visitors board the *Laurindo Pitta*, a tug built in Britain in 1910, and cruise the Bay of Guanabara in the company of a qualified guide. The cruise takes about one and a half hours, and visits Ilha das Cobras and Ilha de Villegaignon, the latter named after the admiral of a French fleet that arrived here in 1555.

The highlight of the cruise, however, is the visit to Ilha Fiscal, venue for the last Imperial Ball, patronized by 3,000 guests, which took place a mere week before the downfall of the monarchy in November 1889, when Pedro was sent into exile *(see page 110)*. Booking is essential for this popular excursion, so be sure to phone ahead, on the number given above, for information and reservations. (For more details on visiting the bay and its islands independently, *see pages 107–12.*) ❑

RESTAURANTS & BARS

Restaurants

Central Rio has virtually no resident population, but there are plenty of people about and they all need to eat. It seems that every other doorway leads to an eatery of one kind or another. Many places open for lunch only; evening options are better in other parts of town.

Albamar
Praça Marechal Ancora 186. Tel: 2240-8428. 11.30am–6pm daily. **$$**
The setting is more inspiring than the food, and the view is best of all. A long-standing (built in 1903) favorite with visitors, very well located for the museum visits. Fish in all forms.

Bar Luiz
Rua da Carioca 39. Tel: 2262-6900. L & D Mon–Sat; L Sun. **$**
A stalwart on the downtown circuit, which opened its doors in 1927. Still famous for its icy-cold draft beer, and a gathering place for people in the news. A German slant: bratwurst, kassler, potato salad.

Bistrô Jardins
Rua do Catete 153. Tel: 2558-2673. B & L daily. Closes at 6pm. **$**
Lovely location in the tree-filled gardens of the Museu da República.

Simple pasta dishes, quiches, grills, good desserts, and a daily breakfast.

Brasserie Rosário
Rua do Rosário 34. Tel: 2518-3033. 8am–8pm Mon–Fri; 10am–5pm Sat; closed Sun. **$–$$$**
Fine dining in an extraordinary setting. Gourmet and sandwiches, salads on the snacks menu. Full lunches for the business community. Wine bar with a good selection of wine by the glass.

Cais do Oriente
Rua Visconde de Itaboraí 8. Tel: 2203-0178. L & D Tues–Sat; L Sun–Mon. **$$–$$$**
A melting pot of tastes, combining oriental food, pasta, Mediterranean recipes, and seafood, in a historic building. Extra cover charge if there is live music.

Colombo
Rua Gonçalves Dias 32. Tel: 2232-2300. 8am–8pm Mon–Fri; 10am–5pm Sat. **$–$$**
One of Rio's most beloved treasures, often used in film sets. Mirrors, marble and memories. À la carte or buffet, with special emphasis on teatime: famous for cookies and cakes.

Eça
Avenida Rio Branco 128. Basement of H. Stern. Tel: 2524-2300. L Mon–Fri. **$$$**

Foie gras and truffles are the daily fare at this exquisite businessmen's favorite. Creative contemporary cuisine with a Belgian accent.

Giuseppe
Rua Sete de Setembro 65. Tel: 2509-7215. L Mon–Fri; happy hour from 4.30pm. **$$**
Tasty sandwiches at the front of the house, Italian specialties at the rear. Prompt and efficient service.

Kotobuki
Rua do Rosário 102. Tel: 3852-0880. L Mon–Fri. **$$**
Few pretensions at this always-popular spot, which serves Chinese, Japanese, and seafood, from the menu or the buffet. Also has branches in Botafogo and Barra.

Bars

Amarelinho (Praça Floriano 55B). Literally, "the little yellow bar," but it seats 700. Feels like Venice's St Mark's in the tropics. Sit and sip and watch Rio buzz. **Lidador** (Rua da Assembléia 65). In the long-established Lidador wine-and-food store. Fine wines by the glass, simple sandwiches, unbeatable people-watching.

PRICE CATEGORIES

Prices for a two-course meal for two. Wine costs around $20 a bottle:
$ = under $35
$$ = $35–60
$$$ = $60–100
$$$$ = more than $100

RIGHT: the famous Colombo Café.

DANCE: THE RHYTHMS OF RIO

From improvised beginnings, such as a beer can filled with pebbles, rhythm is born, and where there's rhythm, dance follows

From an early age, *cariocas* dance. Every samba school has its children's department, where the tiny tots gyrate and wiggle just like their teenaged sisters. Parading in a samba school, however, is a far cry from conventional dance, and often turns into a race to beat the clock and conclude the parade in the allotted time.

Brazil is a crucible of cultures, and Rio concentrates them all. There is evidence of all manner of foreign influence in its rhythms and dance, too. At the grass-roots level, the samba is perennial, with fads that come and go adding a different twist. The side-to-side salsa from Cuba, the more linear merengue from the Dominican Republic, even hopping Scottish country dancing have all made their contributions to local rhythms and forms of bodily expression. The *choro* is another style of music that has never lost its popularity, possibly because it contains elements of tango, rumba, polka, and even waltz.

The bossa nova, which, thanks to *The Girl from Ipanema*, epitomizes Brazilian beat, is not so much a style as a musical movement. It was born in the 1960s of the talents of some of the world's finest musicians, who wanted to make samba music easier to listen to.

ABOVE: Rio's many clubs are filled with enthusiastic dancers – expert and otherwise – until the early hours of the morning. Once *cariocas* get on their feet, they can keep going indefinitely.

BELOW: swinging to the rhythm of the salsa in a music venue in the Lapa district of Rio de Janeiro, where an old colonial house has taken on an exciting new role.

LEFT: Wax figures portray a performance of Carnival samba. Not as energetic as the real thing, but just as elegant.

CAPOEIRA

Capoeira is a uniquely Brazilian phenomenon, although it now has adherents all over the world. The word *capoeira* describes the flat terrain with scrub-like vegetation in which fugitive slaves hid after escaping the brutality of captivity. Knowing that recapture was a certainty, they evolved a system of self-defense that used the only resources they had: their hands and their feet. From these aggressive beginnings, *capoeira* has evolved into part-dance, part-ritual, part-sport, and a celebration of freedom. The music that accompanies *capoeira* may seem atonal, and its rhythm is certainly a world away from the all-join-in feeling of other Brazilian musical styles. It is played, as one would expect, on the most rudimentary of instruments. The *berimbau* resembles a bow with a noisy rattle attached to one end; the *atabaque* and *pandeiro* are types of drum. *Capoeira* is permeated with an aura of seriousness and mysticism totally absent from other elements of the Brazilian music scene.

BELOW: the lambada is a dance craze that swept through Rio – and much of the rest of the world. Not everybody does it quite as well as these two, but it is an infectious rhythm that gets everyone on the dance floor, determined to have a go.

ABOVE: *Capoeira* is performed or practiced wherever space allows, and is taken very seriously, even by youngsters.

BELOW: the music of rudimentary drums accompanies *capoeira*. The rhythm is insistent and hypnotic; listening to it, it is not difficult to imagine the roots from which the dance developed, as a symbol of freedom and defiance.

SANTA TERESA

Rio's Bohemian quarter, which is best reached by a trolley ride over the arches of the old aqueduct, is a neighborhood of pastel-colored houses and art galleries, with stunning views over the city

Santa Teresa is a place of old-fashioned gables and trolley cars, dense vegetation, pastel-shaded masonry, and zigzagging staircases: a magic mountain, indeed. Every major city has one area – its Greenwich Village, its Bloomsbury, its Montmartre – that unique place with its own personality that for some reason, past or present, will always remain special: such a place is Santa Teresa.

History has it that slaves hid among Santa Teresa's mountain trails when escaping from their owners at the height of the 18th-century slave trade. More permanent residents took refuge there when yellow fever epidemics forced the city's population to flee to the hills to escape from the altitude-shy, disease-bearing mosquitoes.

Since then, writers, artists, and musicians have installed themselves along its winding streets. Bankers and businessmen have followed, constructing palatial homes, often built at fantastic angles to the slopes, surrounded by gardens the size of small countries.

A peek behind the scenes

Many local artists open their workshops to the public on special weekends throughout the year, when people flock up the hill and wander from home to home. There is a strong neighborhood feeling about Santa Teresa, which has led to the establishment of Rio's only organized bed-and-breakfast association. More than 50 homeowners have been specially trained to receive guests in their homes. These homes range from a gorgeous, pink colonial house, dating from 1908 and set in a tree-filled garden to an apartment with modern furnishings.

While the district can be reached by bus or car from many points in

Map on pages 84–85

LEFT AND BELOW: colorful houses in Santa Teresa.

A ride on the Santa Teresa trolley is an experience in itself, as well as a good way of seeing the district.

downtown Rio, much the best way to see Santa Teresa is by trolley car. Indeed, getting there is half the fun. You should be careful of your belongings and travel light when exploring the area.

The trolley system

The trolleys – or *bondes* in Portuguese, so named because foreign bonds financed the system – have been in operation since 1896. A ride on the *bonde* provides some really special views of Rio, and a fresh take on the city's contours. But it's a bumpy ride, and you need to hang on tight as you watch the antics of schoolchildren who cling to the trolley's exterior and leap on and off as it clanks slowly along.

The ride starts at the **Estação do Bonde ⓮** (Rua Professor Lélio Gama, tel: 2249-5709) in the downtown region, behind the massive Petrobrás building, and winds over the arches of the former aqueduct, the **Arcos da Lapa**. The station's well-maintained garden is a rural oasis amid the bustle of downtown Rio. A special ecological tour is run by the trolley company on Saturday, leaving the station at 10am to return two hours later. Charges are truly minimal. Get a local person – perhaps your hotel porter – to call ahead on tel: 2240-5790 to check that the special tour is running.

Food for the soul

One of the most surprising highlights of a district noted for surprises is the **Chácara do Céu ⓯** (Little House in the Sky; Rua Murtinho Nobre 93, tel: 2224-8981; Wed–Mon noon–5pm; admission free on Wed). This romantically named modern art museum was once the residence of a collector and generous patron of the arts, Raymundo Ottoni de Castro Maya.

The archive includes work by some of the greatest European artists of the 19th and 20th centuries: Braque, Dalí, Degas, Matisse, Modigliani, Monet, and Picasso. While the collection cannot rival international museums, there is a special charm in seeing works by these world-renowned painters hanging in what was, in effect, a private home.

However, pride of place goes to the finest examples of Brazilian art, including works by Antônio Bandeira, Iberê Camargo, Volpi, Di Cavalcanti and Cândido Portinari, all of whom have caught the discerning imagination of international collectors and are fetching handsome sums at auctions. The temporary exhibitions held here are of an unwaveringly high standard.

Castro Maya was as passionate about his city as he was about his collection, so it is natural that the museum includes some stunning images – by Frenchman Jean-Baptiste Debret among others – of old Rio and its early inhabitants.

The house provides a perfect setting for the paintings, being something of a work of art itself. The

corridors and anterooms are full of precious and beautiful objects: Persian rugs, Indian and Chinese ivory, and a white, smooth torso carved by a Greek sculptor more than 2,400 years ago. Even the staircase qualifies as a work of art, made of solid *peroba* or amberwood, now an endangered species.

A stroll through the silent gardens, gazing down at the spectacular view of bustling, beautiful Rio spread out below, will illustrate to the visitor just why this unique spot is called the Little House in the Sky, even if the "Little" does not seem quite accurate.

Virtually all Santa Teresa's public buildings are proudly well preserved and smartly painted. Most residents have contributed to the overall esthetic effect of the area by careful adornment of their own homes. Flower gardens are everywhere – many seeming to pour over the chipped retaining walls.

Perusing the past

Benjamin Constant (1836–91) was a leading member of Brazil's republican movement, and became the country's first Minister of War and a professor at the military academy. He is perhaps better known as the founder of the Institute for Blind Children, on Praia Vermelha.

Constant's former estate has been transformed into the **Museu Casa de Benjamin Constant** ⓰ (Rua Monte Alegre 255, tel: 2509-1248; Thur–Sun 1–5pm). Here visitors can wander through the recent history of the country by examining the furniture, books, documents, and other personal memorabilia belonging to a public figure. The museum is surrounded by pleasant, tree-filled gardens which are open daily from 8am until 6pm.

Not far away is the tiny **Museu do Bonde** ⓱ (Trolley Car Museum; Rua Carlos Brant 14, tel: 2242-2354; daily 9am–4.30pm), which gathers under one roof myriad transport-related memorabilia, harking back to the times when the trolley cars were pulled by mules. Exhibits include bells, replicas, and old-style railway workers' uniforms. Absolute heaven for train buffs. ❏

Map on pages 84–85

TIP

There is no shortage bars in Santa Teresa, although they change with the winds. There's a lively music-bar scene in the evenings, which is well worth checking out.

RESTAURANTS

Dining in Santa Teresa is fun but pretty basic and pretty cheap, the exception being the Aprazível, which is rather more expensive, but extremely pleasant.

Adega do Pimenta
Rua Almirante Alexandrino 296. Tel: 2224-7554.
11.30am–10pm Mon–Fri ; 11am–8pm Sat; 11am–6pm Sun. **$**
Features German-style sausage, sauerkraut and potato salad, but there are also duck and rabbit recipes on the menu.

Aprazível
Rua Aprazível 62. Tel: 3852-4935. Noon–midnight Thur–Sat; 1–6pm Sun. **$$$**
The name translates as "giving pleasure," which is apt enough. Spectacular views of Rio, or the leafy ambience of garden tables. Brazilian ingredients treated with originality. Be warned: there are steep steps.

Bar do Arnaudo
Rua Almirante Alexandrino 316, shop B. Tel: 2252-7246. Noon–8pm Tues–Fri; noon–8pm Sat–Sun. **$**
Northeastern Brazilian food. Simplicity itself, and full of charm. Jerked beef with squash, and some less ethnic dishes.

Bar do Mineiro
Rua Paschoal Carlos Magno 99. Tel: 2221-9227.
11am–2am Tues–Thur; 11am–4am Fri–Sat; 11am–8pm Sun. **$**
Minas Gerais country food. Chicken with okra is a specialty, and they do a great black-bean stew at weekends.

Sansushi
Rua Almirante Alexandrino 383. Tel: 2252-0581.
7pm–midnight Tues–Fri; 1pm–midnight Sat; 1pm–8pm Sun. **$**
Unpretentious Japanese place; friendly service.

Sobrenatural
Rua Almirante Alexandrino 432. Tel: 2224-1003.
11am–11pm Tues–Sun. **$$**
Dishes include Bahian-style tangy fish stews.

● ● ● ● ● ● ● ● ● ● ●

Prices for a two-course meal for two. Wine costs around $20 a bottle. **$$$$** *= more than $100,* **$$$** *= $60–100,* **$$** *= $35–60,* **$** *= under $35.*

THE BAY

This is where the Portuguese and the French fought for mastery of the coast. You can take a ferry trip to the island of Paquetá, or visit Niterói on the other side, a place with treasures of its own

L ike a big buttonhole cut out of the Atlantic coast, the 380-sq. km (147-sq. mile) **Baía de Guanabara** is a living map of Rio's maritime past. Its narrow entrance is guarded by two historic forts, the 17th-century Fortaleza de Santa Cruz, which is situated on the eastern bank, today's Niterói; and the 19th-century Fortaleza de São João on the western, Rio de Janeiro side. Their walls were constructed from solid granite blocks, cemented together with whale oil.

Where it all began

These two surviving forts lie on much older foundations, dating back to 1565, when the Portuguese realized that they would have to fortify the bay if they were not to lose it to the French. For some 50 years after its discovery in 1502, Guanabara Bay attracted numerous freewheeling Portuguese and French adventurers.

Ships returned to Europe loaded with rare birds, parrots, monkeys, Indian slaves, and Brazil wood – the heavy, red hardwood from which the *brasilin* dye was extracted, and which gave Brazil its name. The Portuguese made their base on the Rio side of the bay, the French on the eastern shore, and the two sides clashed frequently in sea skirmishes.

In 1555, the French launched a definitive effort to conquer Rivière Guenère, as they called the bay (the Portuguese had originally called it Santa Luzia). A fleet sent by Henri II took possession of a region on the Rio side, building Fort Coligny on the Ilha de Villegaignon. But "Antarctic France," as they called their new territory, was short-lived. Within five years the French were driven off by the Portuguese, the survivors taking refuge with the Tamoio Indian tribe in Niterói.

When surveying the bay today, it

Map on page 108

LEFT: the sweeping entrance to the bay.
BELOW: boarding the Paquetá island ferry.

is sad to think that nothing remains of what the French and the Portuguese fought over – no Indians, no Brazil wood trees, and no parrots.

A thing of tainted beauty

Looking to the tops of the granite hills, one can easily believe that the areas surrounding Rio must be much the same as they were when the first Europeans arrived.

But the lower one drops one's glance, from the high-rises along the Rio and Niterói shoreline, the industries and oil refineries, to the silted-up mud-flats – where lush mangrove swamps once sheltered exotic fauna – and the murky water itself, the more one becomes aware of the toll that predatory development has taken on one of the world's most beautiful natural wonders.

Spiny lobsters have disappeared. The nurse sharks cannot survive without the rays, octopus, squid, clams, and crustaceans that make up their diet. Few blue crabs can survive the lack of oxygen. And the Tucuxi dolphin, the symbol of the city of Rio de Janeiro, can no longer cruise the bay.

Cleaning up the bay is a challenge that no government to date has met fully. While various impressive sanitation projects have been put together, many of them relying heavily on hard-won international funding, the problems that plague Guanabara Bay seem to move faster than any solution for them can be implemented.

Impressive statistics

The numbers are impressive indeed: the surface of the bay measures 400 sq. km (152 sq. miles), its perimeter is 131 km (81 miles), and it contains some 3 billion cubic meters (800 billion US gallons) of saline water.

BELOW: the ferry station in Praça Quinze.

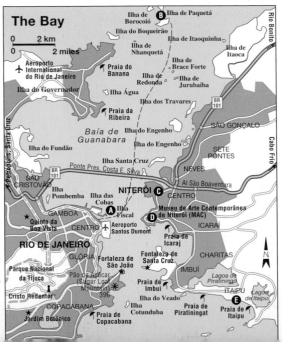

Map on page 108

Fifty-five rivers flow into the bay, whose depth is an average of 7.5 meters (24½ ft), reaching 50 meters (164 ft) in its central channel. Some 8 million people live directly in contact with the bay, which also houses 14,000 small industries, 14 oil terminals, two commercial ports, several shipyards, two oil refineries, and more than 1,000 gas stations. Daily, more than 450 tons of untreated domestic waste – enough to fill Maracanã Stadium – are poured into the bay. Mangroves, which can reduce the pollutants and keep nature in balance, used to cover 260 sq. km (100 sq. miles); now they cover no more than 82 sq. km (30 sq. miles) of the area. No wonder it's a mess.

Center of recreation

Until the 1930s, when *cariocas* started moving out to the ocean beaches, the bay was the main center of recreation for the city, whose residents held picnics on its shores and fished and swam in its waters. Well-heeled *cariocas* built holiday homes on Paquetá, the largest of the bay's 84 islands. A ferryboat trip to Paquetá's beaches, lapped by the gentle waters of the bay, so different from the crashing waves of the Atlantic, was a welcome treat.

Ferry facts

A trip to Paquetá still makes a very pleasant day out *(see next page)*. The island can be reached by regular ferry, carrying 1,000 passengers for the leisurely 70-minute cruise; the faster alternative is the 20-minute trip on the hydrofoil, which carries 75 passengers. The regular ferry fare is approximately the cost of a cup of coffee; the hydrofoil costs a little more. The boat station (Estação das Barcas, Praça XV de Novembro, tel: 2533-7524 or 2532-6274) in downtown Rio is the point of departure for both vessels.

The islands

Soon after departure from Praça Quinze, one passes **Ilha de Ville-gaignon**, which was joined to the mainland by a 1929 landfill during the building of Brazil's naval academy. In times gone by it was the seat

You will still see small fishing boats in the bay waters, as well as ferries and larger vessels.

BELOW: the green-spired palace on the Ilha Fiscal.

TIP

Luz del Fuego's colorful life and controversial death was the subject of a 1982 Brazilian feature film of the same name.

BELOW: bikes for hire on Paquetá, where private cars are not allowed.

of government of the ill-fated Antarctic France. **Ilha das Cobras** (Snake Island), today a naval port, was in its time an unloading area for slave ships and then a monastery.

Ilha Fiscal is recognizable by its strange, green-spired palace, which was formerly a barracks for customs officers. It was here that the imperial government held its last ball in 1889, shortly before the downfall of the monarchy. Ilha Fiscal is now joined by landfill to Ilha das Cobras. Guided tours to Ilha Fiscal are organized by the navy as part of a program run by the Espaço Cultural da Marinha (*see page 98*; for further information, tel: 2104-6025). A magic moment on the boat ride to Paquetá takes place when you drift under the enormous bridge connecting Rio and Niterói.

A vast panorama of water and islands now opens up, although the scene is hardly the tropical paradise portrayed by French engraver Jean-Baptiste Debret in the 19th century. The islands that have not been turned into promontories by landfills, such as the 44-sq. km (17-sq.

mile) Ilha do Governador, which houses Rio's international airport, have been given over to oil tanks and military depots.

Further into the bay, however, some islands retain a thick crop of wild tropical greenery. One of these is **Ilha do Sol** (Sun Island), where the 1950s cabaret star and striptease artist, Luz del Fuego (who apparently including live snakes in her routine), set up Brazil's first nudist colony. Her parties attracted guests from Europe, but she met a mysterious end. Whether she was murdered by her politician lover or by a jealous fisherman, or whether she merely drowned, has never been known for sure.

Step back in time

The island of **Paquetá** has survived the passage of time well. No private cars are allowed on the island, which imposes a relaxed rhythm of life. This timelessness is captured by the island's one-story houses, surrounded by well-tended gardens. The residents are proud of their zero crime rate, and zealous in maintaining it. Transport is by bike (rental outlets are everywhere) or by a horse-drawn buggy, which does a trip around the island at a 19th-century pace for a very modest fee. Eating options on the island are very limited, and the visitor would do well to stick to packaged snacks and build up an appetite for the return to the mainland.

Every Sunday, the ferryboats run a special two-hour tour of the bay, departing from the Rio Estação das Barcas at 10am. The itinerary covers Botafogo Bay, the two forts at the mouth of the bay, Jurujuba Beach, the Museu de Arte Contemporânea, and many other sights. It's a great ride for children, for whom professional entertainers are provided. At the top end of the market, cruise operators will customize any tour of

the bay, and provide food and drinks aboard luxurious vessels. *(See the Activities section, page 223, for names of some operators.)*

Niterói

In the past, *cariocas* have generally thumbed their noses at **Niterói** , claiming that it was a second-class version of their own city. Its only claim to fame, they sniffed, was that it offered an excellent view of Rio. This patronizing attitude has changed in recent years, however, as the quality of life in Niterói has remained high and relatively affordable, while Rio becomes ever more crowded and expensive. For exploring Niterói, there are ferries and hydrofoils leaving Praça Quinze every few minutes. Avoid rush hour, as many residents of Niterói cross the bay to work in Rio.

Niemeyer's great design

One of the most attention-grabbing attractions in Niterói is the **Museu de Arte Contemporânea de Niterói** (Museum of Contemporary Art; Mirante da Boa Viagem,

Niterói, tel: 2620-2400; Tues–Sun 10am–6pm; free on Wed). This is truly a superlative site, in every sense. Designed by Brazil's star architect, Oscar Niemeyer *(see pages 114–15)*, the structure is over 16 meters (50 ft) high, supported by a sole cylindrical base measuring less than 9 meters (30 ft) across. The roof has a diameter of 50 meters (165 ft), and the access consists of 100 meters (320 ft) of winding walkways. It may not look safe, but it is designed to support 400 kg (880 pounds) per square meter/yd, and to withstand 200-km (125-mile) per hour winds. The building is pure Niemeyer, at his outrageous best. Together, the ambience and view are all that man and nature can combine to offer.

The contents of the building are no less noteworthy. Collector João Sattamini has gathered together a significant and representative cross-section of postwar Brazilian art, and his collection features the works of – among others – Lygia Pape, Anna Bella Geiger, Charles Watson and Franz Krajberg. If anything, the

Map on page 108

This pretty church is one of the most photographed features of Paquetá island.

BELOW: generous helpings can be had at this Mineiro restaurant in Niterói.

Map
on page
108

Cariocas *have built some very attractive beach houses as weekend retreats.*

BELOW: the impressive bridge that links Niterói with Rio.

MAC (as the museum is known) was born of necessity, as the output of modern Brazilian artists is demanding in terms of space: huge installations and constructions, large-scale canvases and sculptures. The museum also hosts temporary exhibitions of high-quality work.

Seeking the beaches

The further away you get from Niterói city center, the prettier and more unspoiled are the beaches: **Samanguaiá**, with its yacht club, **Jurujuba**, with its seafood restaurants, and, last of the bayside beaches, the small twin coves of **Adão e Eva** (Adam and Eve).

Continuing along the coast road beyond São Francisco, you will soon reach the oceanside beach of **Itaipu ⓔ**, a long, low curve of sand separating the Atlantic from a pair of attractive lagoons. From here there is a glorious panorama of Rio across Guanabara Bay. The view embraces the entire city, from the flat top of Pedra da Gávea to the 1,030-meter (3,370-ft) height of the Pico da Tijuca.

Santa Cruz fort

On a promontory poking out into the bay is one of Niterói's treasures, the **Fortaleza de Santa Cruz** (tel: 2711-0462; Tues–Sun 9am–4pm; free), in the Jurujuba area. Along with the twin fort of São João on the Rio side of the bay in Urca, it was key to the protection of Rio during the colonial period. It is a magnificent compendium of three centuries of military architecture. The oldest parts, such as the Santa Barbara chapel, date from the late 16th century, and the Cova das Onças (torture chamber) was constructed in the 17th century.

Legend has it that the image of Santa Barbara had been taken to Niterói in error and was to be moved to another site, a move that could only take place across water. But every time the saint's image was embarked on the waters, the sea became rough and hostile, making transportation impossible. It was decided that the saint liked it where she was, so a chapel was built in her honor. You could say she was one of Niterói's first fans. ❏

Rio–Niterói Bridge

As an alternative to going to Niterói by boat, it's exhilarating to take a bus ride across the extraordinary Ponte Rio–Niterói. Buses run from the Rodoviária (bus station), and the fare is minimal. When winds are high, the bridge is closed to traffic, for obvious safety reasons. Drivers should note that a small toll is payable at the Niterói end. Inaugurated on March 4, 1974, the six-lane bridge is a stunning sight. It is more than 13 km (9 miles) long, of which almost 9 km (5.5 miles) is over water. The cost of building the bridge, financed by British banks, was estimated at around $US22 million *(see page 33)*.

RESTAURANTS & BARS

Restaurants

This chapter covers an area of hundreds of kilometers. Here is a selection of special places to go for a meal, and others where the view is really what you're there for.

Alcaparra
Praia do Flamengo 150, Parque do Flamengo. Tel: 2557-7236. L & D daily. **$$–$$$**
Director's dining room for many of the businesses in the area. Well-presented food from an imaginative menu; duck is a house specialty. Stylish, efficient.

Barracuda
Avenida Infante Dom Henrique, Parque do Flamengo. Tel: 2265-4641. L & D Mon–Sat; L only Sun. **$$$**
Located inside the Glória Marina, the emphasis is on fish. A Portuguese slant brings variations on the salt-cod theme, as well as the rich Portuguese sweets.

Casa Suiça
Rua Cândido Mendes 157, Glória. Tel: 2252-5182. L & D daily except Sat L. **$$$**
Inside the Swiss consulate and run with clockwork efficiency. Fine ingredients treated with respect, and presented with panache. Owner Mr Wendlnger prepares a mean Steak Diane, flambéed at your table.

Churrascaria Estrela do Sul
Praia de Botafogo 490. Tel: 2539-0188. L & D daily. **$$**
Don't go unless you're hungry! Eat all you can from the buffet or let the waiter carve slices of beef straight onto your plate. Salad bar, lots of side dishes.

Emporium Pax
Praia de Botafogo 400, shop 704. Tel: 2559-9713. L & D daily. **$**
Inside the Botafogo Praia shopping mall, with great views over the bay. Fine cooking and wide-ranging menu. Excellent desserts. Branches in Rio Sul, Shopping da Gávea, Barrashopping malls.

La Mole
Praia de Botafogo 228, shop 105. Tel: 2553-2467. L & D daily. **$–$$**
A Rio institution, with 10 branches, all delivering basic Italian-style food in pleasant surroundings. The nibbles they bring you on arrival obviate the need for a starter.

Porção Rio's
Avenida Infante Dom Henrique, Parque do Flamengo. Tel: 2554-8535. L & D daily. **$$$**
There aren't enough superlatives to describe the premier branch of "the big pig." Stunning design, abundance of salads and side dishes, and more meat than

you'd normally eat in a month. Plenty of vegetarian options, too. Worth saving up for. Branches in Copacabana, Ipanema and Barra.

Da Carmine (Niterói)
Rua Mariz e Barros 305, Icaraí, Niterói. Tel: 3602-4988. L & D Tues–Sun; D only Mon. **$–$$**
Handmade pasta blends interesting ingredients to produce some memorable meals. In the evening, the pizza oven is lit. Owner-operated; warm welcome.

Torninha (Niterói)
Rua Nóbrega 199, Santa Rosa, Niterói. Tel: 2714-1750. L & D Tues–Sun. **$$**
Mediterranean take on quality local ingredients, matched to a better-than-average wine list. A

favorite with Niterói residents in the know.

Bars

Belmonte (Praia do Flamengo 300). Pure Rio. The original Belmonte has been serving honest beers and filling snacks for many years. Famous for its pasties, filled with shrimp, palm hearts, and crabmeat. No credit cards. Branches in Leblon, Ipanema and Jardim Botânico.

PRICE CATEGORIES

Prices for a two-course meal for two. Wine costs around $20 a bottle:
$ = under $35
$$ = $35–60
$$$ = $60–100
$$$$ = more than $100

RIGHT: Porção Rio's is a carnivore's delight.

OSCAR NIEMEYER

Niemeyer is one of the world's most respected architects, and a man who refused to compromise his political ideals

The giant of Brazilian architecture is undoubtedly Oscar Niemeyer, born in Rio in 1907, who started his working life under the controversial Lúcio Costa. Costa was the precursor of Modernism in Brazil, and both he and Niemeyer were much influenced by the then-revolutionary ideas of Le Corbusier. From an early age, Niemeyer made a name for himself with the unconventional nature of both his designs and his politics. A die-hard communist, his strongly held views on man's role in society permeate his work. The clearest evidence of this is found in Brasília, whose master plan was laid out by Costa, and whose buildings were designed by Niemeyer. This, truly, was an opinionated architect's dream come true: to design buildings for the future seat of power of a massive country in a city built from scratch on barren countryside in the middle of nowhere.

But there are many buildings in Rio that demonstrate Niemeyer's unmistakable style, from the Museum of Contemporary Art to the public schools built from reinforced-concrete modules: cost-effective, easy to build and softened with an element of transparency. A school with a difference is the Sambadrome *(see right)*, designed by Niemeyer for his friend, the governor of Rio state, the late Leonel Brizola.

ABOVE: Niemeyer's most breathtaking work in the Rio area is the Museu de Arte Contemporânea in Niterói *(see page 111)*, designed when he was 89 years of age.

LEFT: Casa das Canoas, the house Niemeyer designed for himself in 1953.

BELOW: the massive arch at the end of the Sambadrome has its fans and its detractors, but it is quite unmistakable.

ABOVE: Niemeyer's ferry station complex complements the sinuous curves of the Museu de Arte Contemporânea.

CAPTURING THE ESSENCE

Long before he worked on Brasília, Niemeyer already had some important buildings to his credit, and a biography peppered with controversy. In 1943, ecclesiastic authorities refused to consecrate his church of St Francis of Assisi, part of Belo Horizonte's Pampulha Project, as he had failed to provide it with a confessional. In 1947 he was again in trouble, as the US authorities used his well-known communist views as the reason for denying him an entry visa.

By 1988, however, this black mark against his name was fully erased when he was awarded (jointly with US citizen Gordon Bunshaft) the Pritzker Prize, the world's most prestigious award for architecture. The citation reads: "There is a moment in a nation's history when one individual captures the essence of that culture and gives it form. It is sometimes in music, painting, sculpture, or literature. In Brazil, Oscar Niemeyer has captured that essence with his architecture. His building designs are the distillation of the colors, light and sensual imagery of his native land."

In his memoir, *The Curves of Time*, Niemeyer wrote: "I created [my work] with courage and idealism, but also with an awareness of the fact that what is important is life, friends and attempting to make this unjust world a better place in which to live."

ABOVE: Niemeyer in his studio. **BELOW:** on the outskirts of Rio, in a neighborhood rarely visited by tourists, is the Duque de Caxias Cultural Center, which he designed in 2002. A stunning example of Niemeyer's style, it demonstrates that, in his nineties, his work was as fresh and uncompromising as ever.

ABOVE: the interior of the Museu de Arte Contemporânea, with its flowing curves, is an impressive setting for the works of art displayed there.

RIGHT: one of the architect's signature-style public schools, built from reinforced-concrete modules, this one dating from 1984.

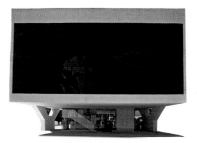

QUINTA DA BOA VISTA

Just a short metro ride away from the center is a park that contains the city zoo, a couple of imperial-style museums, and the Maracanã Stadium, the great shrine to Brazilian soccer. If you go on the weekend, you can find a lively local market

Quinta da Boa Vista Park, in the northern suburb of São Cristóvão, has long been one of the city's playgrounds. It's a pleasant, well-used, neighborhood park, the site of two museums and a zoo, and adjacent to the Maracanã Stadium. Keep well away on weekends, as crowds throng, and you will not be able to appreciate the grace with which the gardens were laid out, the twisted tree trunks, nor the interesting rock formations that dot the area.

BELOW: Quinta da Boa Vista is a family park.

Sunday market

The only reason to come here on the weekend rather than during the quieter weekdays would be to visit the Feira de São Cristóvão, a big, noisy local market. However, this is a good experience in itself. You may not want to buy the goods that are on offer, but it's a great opportunity to sample street food – there's a huge variety of it on offer, much of it emanating from Bahia, in the north of Brazil, as do many of the people who come to the *feira*.

You can also hear small groups playing traditional music, and sometimes see displays of *capoeira*, the agile mix of dance, acrobatics and martial art, performed to a rhythmic musical beat, that emanates from Salvador, capital of Bahia province.

Trysting place

The **Museu do Primeiro Reinado** ⓲ (Museum of the First Reign; Avenida Pedro Segundo 293, tel: 2299-2148, Tues–Fri 11am–5pm), lies close to but outside the actual boundaries of the park itself, and is the former home of the imperial mistress, the Marquesa dos Santos.

The home of Domitila de Castro Canto e Melo, the paramour of Dom Pedro I, is something of a poor relation in terms of museums, but it is not without charm. The gaudy checkerboard marble floors of the foyer give way to a series of public rooms, furnished in the Brazilian Empire style. Look out for the spittoon, and the collection of tortoise-shell hair combs.

The Marquesa had 13 children, four of whom were fathered by Dom Pedro. The lady herself is pictured not as an attractive young woman or a mother, but as a distinguished old granny. On either side are portraits of her semi-imperial progeny, two girls, called, sparingly enough, Maria Isabel and Isabel Maria.

The Café Domitila in the silent, leafy garden at the rear of the house, is a lovely place to stop for a bite.

City playground

The neighboring **Quinta da Boa Vista** ⓳ serves as a giant playground for the sprawling, beachless industrial zone, and suffers somewhat because of overpopulation. In its time it was the imperial backyard for Dom João VI, Dom Pedro I, and Dom Pedro II. It has been the setting for some of the most dramatic moments in Brazilian history. The formal gardens – complete with grottoes, lakes, avenues, a temple of Apollo and statuary – were laid out by the noted landscaper Auguste Glaziou. They provide some pleasant walks, especially on a dry day, as it can become boggy during the rains.

Map on pages 84–85

A musician at the Feira de São Cristóvão, the lively Sunday market.

BELOW:
inside the Museu do Primeiro Reinado.

A vast collection

The former Imperial Palace, within the park, has housed the **Museu Nacional** ⑳ (Quinta da Boa Vista, tel: 2568-8262; Tues–Sun 10am–4pm; admission charge; free for seniors on Wed) since 1892. It is an educational and research institute, and houses a vast natural history and anthropological collection.

The museum is seriously underfunded, and the exhibits are almost comically old-fashioned. One fully expects Charles Darwin to pop round a corner and elucidate on them personally. Protozoa, sponges, worms of every description and habitat, corals, insects, stuffed mammals, mothy hawks, dubious dinosaurs, all stare out at the visitor with a total lack of interest. You could almost say that it is a museum of a museum.

Rio Zoo

Although traditional bars-and-cages zoos have very much fallen from favor, the visitor could do much worse than follow the example of local people and visit the **Jardim Zoológico** ㉑ (Rio Zoo; Tues–Sun 10am–4pm; admission charge). Despite serious funding problems, the zoo has demonstrated creativity in attracting sponsorship for its activities, and rewards its 850,000 annual visitors with some memorable experiences.

At weekends the zoo gets very crowded, so at all costs avoid visiting the area on these days, and on public holidays. An upbeat atmosphere pervades its 138,000 sq. meters (165,000 sq. yds), which are lovingly tended by 180 employees. Fallen palm leaves are used as brooms to sweep the walkways, and public phones are cunningly disguised in the gaping jaws of mock caymans and kangaroo pouches. Refreshments and other facilities on site are fine.

The 2,100 animals consume on average 41 tons of food a month, and the menu may consist of watermelon, green beans, eggplant (aubergine), and sweet potatoes – very healthy and vegetarian.

In such a Catholic country, the patron saint of animals could hardly

BELOW: the birds are the stars at Rio Zoo.

be left out, and a statue of St Francis, a gift from the Franciscan community on the 800th anniversary of the saint's birth in 1182, occupies a place of honor.

The birds

Ignore the lethargic tiger and the lonely elephant, who will certainly ignore you. The real joy for the foreign visitor are the birds. The brilliant colors of the screamingly gaudy jandaia, the flame-capped parakeet, blend to produce a creature of cheeky elegance (the bird's name was adopted by the city of Jandaia do Sol in Paraná province). The inscrutable and ungainly toucans are absolutely mesmerizing. Watch them devour a piece of papaya or segment of orange for immediate results: they are said to have a digestive tract 30 seconds long. The hyacinthine and scarlet macaws are a show apart. The King vulture might look like a revolting beast, and he does suffer from a very bad reputation, but he has his virtues, being a veritable vacuum cleaner for waste matter.

Creepy things

The creepy-crawly department is well stocked, and the snakes every bit as evil-looking as they should be. The small Night House is pure spookiness. The conservation of local species is taken very seriously here, and the population of Golden lion tamarinds being returned to the wild is a tribute to the success of this program.

Brazilian temple

Although the city abounds in churches, many would say that the biggest place of worship is the Maracanã Stadium, whose official name is the **Estádio Mário Filho** ㉒ (Avenida Maracanã, tel: 2568-9962; Mon–Fri 9am–5pm, Sat–Sun 8am–11pm). A **Sports Museum** (closed on match days) is filled with photos, cups, posters, and soccer strips on display *(for more on the stadium and the passion for soccer see pages 164–5)*. A visit on a non-match day will leave you feeling you are really missing something. Go to a match if you are a fan: there's no experience quite like it. ❑

Map on pages 84–85

The Maracanã Stadium: many soccer fans see it as a place of pilgrimage.

BELOW: a Cebidae monkey at the zoo.

RESTAURANTS

This is an area poorly served by restaurants with any reputation, as it is not one where many people come to eat. The one exception, and it is a big exception, is the Adegão Português. On Sunday, the massive Northeastern Fair, pitched at the local immigrant population, occupies the Campo de São Cristóvão and offers plenty of opportunities to buy snacks, many with a Bahian flavor.

Adegão Português

Campo de São Cristóvão 212, São Cristóvão. Tel: 2580-8689. 11am–11pm Mon–Sat; 11am–8pm Sun. **$$**

Traditional Portuguese fare, heavy on the salt cod. Hearty food in gargantuan portions. Sharing a dish is the norm.

Quinta

Quinta da Boa Vista. Tel: 2589-6551. L & D Mon–Fri; L only Sun–holidays. **$**
This former imperial chapel retains an air of dignity, and provides traditional fare from a broad menu. Outdoor seating is available. Very handy for the zoo. Snacks or full-scale meals available.

● ● ● ● ● ● ● ● ● ● ● ● ● ●
Prices for a two-course meal for two. Wine costs around $20 a bottle.
$$$$ = more than $100, **$$$** = $60–100, **$$** = $35–60, **$** = under $35.

COPACABANA

Busy beach life, smart hotels, a wide selection of restaurants, and throngs of animated people make up the Copacabana scene. Who would have anticipated this when the first tunnel was blasted through the mountains in the 1890s?

t doesn't take a degree in urban planning – a simple glance at the map will do – to figure out that to get from the historic city center of Rio to Copacabana 100 years ago, you had to be able to fly or to dig. And dig they did, right through solid granite mountains, blasting open the tunnels that would give access to what is now one of the world's most densely populated areas.

It was the brave Canadian utility pioneers of the Rio Tramway, Light and Power Company who first realized the potential of this area. By building the Tunel Alaor Prata (still called the Tunel Velho, the Old Tunnel) in 1892, they linked Botafogo with the then-deserted, distant sand dunes of Copacabana, in the Rua Figueiredo Magalhães and Rua Siqueira Campos area. A second tunnel, Tunel Engenheiro Marques Porto (still, more than a century later, called the Tunel Novo, the New Tunnel), was added in 1904, and connected Copacabana and Leme, via Avenida Princesa Isabel, to the end of Botafogo Beach, where the city's showpiece, Avenida Beira Mar, had just been completed. These two tunnels were the birth canals for a new suburb, a new culture, and a new way of life – through the darkness of the tunnels to the light and life of Copacabana.

Leme ❶, at the eastern end of Copacabana Beach, retains a village feel to it – possibly because it isn't on the way to anywhere else. It is an extremely desirable residential area, although it is full of older people who tend to stay put, so very little property ever comes on the market. The beach, Praia do Leme, is relatively uncluttered, and the waves are gentle. There are some excellent restaurant options on the seafront and some hidden gastronomic treasures within.

Map on page 122

LEFT: Copacabana is as alluring by night as by day.
BELOW: enjoying coconut milk at a beachside kiosk.

TIP

For the Copacabana
Palace Hotel's gala
fancy-dress ball at
Carnival time, tickets
sell for between
US$350 and $700.

The Copa

In the 1920s, President Epitácio Pessoa embarked on a campaign to drag Brazil into the modern era by sponsoring visits to the city by foreign monarchs and international dignitaries. Clearly, a hotel on the beachfront at Copacabana was called for, and thus the legendary **Copacabana Palace Hotel** ❷ came into existence. Over the next decades, the Copa, as it is affectionately known, would set the pace and establish the trends for entire generations.

It would be lunacy to visit Rio and not set foot inside the magical Copacabana Palace Hotel, headquarters of style, monument to fine living, backdrop for dramas and hatching place of many a political plot. The Cipriani restaurant ticks all the boxes in terms of style, creativity, wine list, and elegance. The hotel's Pérgula is a delightful place, perfect for a cup of tea or a weekend blow-out brunch. Marlene Dietrich, Rudolph Nureyev, Maurice Chevalier, Robert de Niro, Francis Ford Coppola, and Rod Stewart have all been enchanted by the Copa. Even the enigmatic Janis Joplin is reputed to have found true love there, in

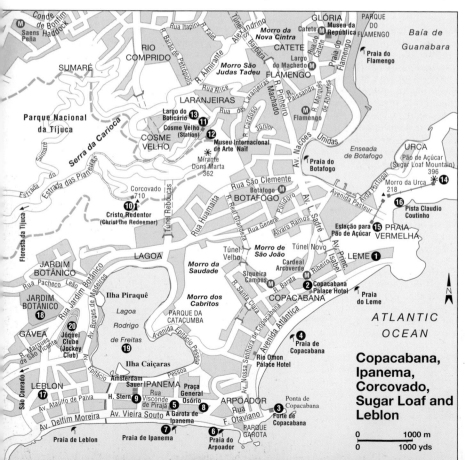

Copacabana,
Ipanema,
Corcovado,
Sugar Loaf and
Leblon

1970, although it did not last, and did not save her – she died later that year, aged 27.

Youth and age

The average age of Copacabana's inhabitants is surprisingly high – over one-third of the resident population are senior citizens. But there is still plenty of youth in Copacabana; try counting the babies, many of them being escorted by their grandparents, brought to the beach in the early morning. Or try to get one of Cervantes's famous pork-and-pineapple sandwiches at three o'clock on a Saturday morning, in the heart of the red-light district at Rua Prado Júnior 335. Not many senior citizens are to be found there.

At the eastern end of the beach are two sites of interest. One is a large covered tent which plays host to the card-playing fanatics of Copacabana. Peek inside for a curious sight: the prevailing silence as groups of four huddle over their well-worn cards is occasionally broken by a shout of glee as someone takes possession of the pile.

The fort and the fishermen

At the southern (Ipanema) end of the beach, on a little promontory called Ponta de Copacabana, and within easy walking distance, is the **Forte de Copacabana** ❸ (tel: 2521-1032; Tues–Sun 10am–5pm; admission charge). The little museum has a fine array of armaments, and an extremely well-put-together exhibition on the history of Brazil. The fort also houses a branch of Colombo, the traditional coffee shop, and the views from the café's tables are truly out of this world.

In the early mornings, visitors who are up in time are always welcomed by the local fishing community, as they haul their catches in for sale at the tiny fishmonger's next to the fort.

Exploring the streets

Residents have long abandoned any hope of parking a car, so people set out on foot to get their chores done. One-stop shopping is not a reality in Copacabana, and old-fashioned stores, many owner-operated, still thrive. The visitor could do worse

"Cooling points" along the promenade eject a refreshing spray of mist at the touch of a button.

BELOW: the great curve of Copacabana Beach and its high-density housing.

There are plenty of police kiosks along the beachfront, in case you run into trouble.

BELOW: getting ready for the massive Rolling Stones concert on the beach in February 2006.

than spend an afternoon walking around the bustling streets, whose people and places provide an insight into the lives of the residents of this quasi-city. Needless to say, valuables, including cameras, should be left at the hotel. Visitors should also beware of the occasional posse of singing and leaping urchins, who take up the whole of the sidewalk: their intention may be to surround the unsuspecting and relieve them of the contents of their pockets.

On busy Rua Barata Ribeiro, at No. 502, **Modern Sound** (Mon–Fri 9am–9pm, Sat 9am–8pm) sets a high standard: it's the best music store in Rio, and also houses the appealing Allegro Bistrô, where there is usually something of interest going on. It's a great place to spend a couple of hours.

Gambling

Gambling, a huge business and the magnet that drew people to Copacabana's glorious casinos, was outlawed in 1946. This piece of legislation fundamentally changed the character of *carioca* nightlife,

and there are many, especially in the tourist industry, who still patiently await the revoking of this law. The relatively recent permission to operate bingo was welcomed as a step in the right direction, but the bingo halls have, to date, attracted mainly overdressed matrons, out for an afternoon of fun. It doesn't quite have the glamor of the roulette table.

This is not to say that gambling is non-existent in Rio; far from it. The illegal numbers game, the *jogo do bicho*, moves millions every day. *Bicho* bankers can be seen on many street corners, sitting in their rudimentary "offices" – a wobbly chair, a clipboard, and a wastebasket taped to a nearby tree – taking pin-money bets from passers-by.

Fully operational, they are ready to decamp at a moment's notice in the unlikely event that the policeman on the corner is approaching in order to close them down. It is much more likely that the policeman has just remembered a dream – a monkey means you have to bet on number 17, perhaps – and has decided to have a flutter.

The beachfront

The enormous beach, the **Praia de Copacabana ❹**, is the entertainment center of the region, but it was not always as big as it is now. The recognition, in the early 1960s, that gridlock was the next stage for the traffic along the beachfront led to an ambitious project to widen the coast road to its current ample size, and enlarge the beach by pumping new sand in from Botafogo Bay. Many *cariocas* scratched their heads with incredulity as work progressed.

There was a general feeling that one shouldn't tamper with what God hath wrought, because it could be inviting disaster. But time has proved these skeptics wrong: the roads have stayed in place, and the waves have been kept back.

The beach is divided into numbered *postos* for identification purposes, although, with the exception of Posto Seis (6) at the Ipanema end, nobody but taxi drivers ever seems to know which is where. The sands are home to dozens of informal soccer and volleyball teams; cramped schools use the beach as an extension of their playgrounds, and organized games of various kinds are in progress throughout the day. The junior soccer players are an endearing sight, and one wonders how those small feet can bear the searing summer heat of the boiling sand, but they must have grown up hardened to it.

Weaving their way in and out of ball players and sunbathers are beach vendors, selling cold drinks, bikinis, beach towels, rubber thongs, and all kinds of other goods.

The brightly painted kiosks along the front are great gathering places, and each has its own character: motorcycle fanatics, mothers with babies, retired military men, cyclists, gays, teenagers, all have their favorites. Like finds like, and everyone shares the space in a democratic manner. They stay open until late at night, and rarely seem to lack customers.

In the morning you can watch trucks unloading vast quantities of coconuts in front of the kiosks, for *agua de coca* – coconut milk – is a great favorite. The waiters simply

Map on page 122

A life-sized statue on the promenade of poet Carlos Drumond de Andrade (1902–87), who looked on Rio as his spiritual home.

BELOW: vendors of cold drinks constantly patrol the beaches.

Service Industry

Copacabana figures in the lives of several hundred thousand people. Statistics indicate that 3.4 people inhabit every square meter/yd of the area: a tight fit. Between 10 and 15 percent of Copacabana residents live precariously in the *favelas*, living arrangements motivated by necessity, not choice. For the vast majority of them, *favela* living means that they can get to work each day. Every 10 visitors to Rio produce one full-time job in the service industry, but no employer would tolerate the tardiness implicit in relying on the chaotic public transport to travel in from the poorer northern suburbs. In Rio, if you can't walk it, you are likely to be very late.

Map
on page
122

slice off the top of the fruit and stick a straw in; the customer has a cool refreshing drink, and he has no washing up to do.

Strong currents

Copacabana beach is open to the South Atlantic, and as such is affected by strong currents throughout most of the year. This can be extremely dangerous for inexperienced swimmers, who would do well to observe what local people are doing. Watch the surfers, especially – they know the ways of the sea well. An efficient lifeguard system provides patrol boats and helicopter rescues as well as conventional lifeguards, but it is best to take no chances.

A visiting swimmer should remember that the current off Copacabana takes you down the beach and not away from the shore. This can cause some interesting problems for near-sighted swimmers when they emerge from the sea, far from their towels and friends, and have to find their way back. Needless to say, swimmers should never

leave anything more valuable than a towel on the beach while they swim, because their property might not be there when they get back.

Trinkets and discos

Back at street level, the pace never slackens. Days are busy, and the balmy nights heave. In the vicinity of the massive Othon Palace Hotel (a favorite with package operators), craftspeople set up their stalls along the central reservation of the beach road as darkness falls, and lay out their trinkets, jewelry, beach towels, kangas, and hammocks. You probably won't find much of quality here, but there's an animated atmosphere, and there's no charge for looking.

Just across the way from the market stretch is **Help**, Copacabana's most notorious disco. Things are not always what they seem, and visitors may soon discover that not all the disco's attractive habitués are there to enjoy the dancing; many turn out to be prostitutes, of either sex – or both. Caution should be the watchword for visitors frequenting Help, especially if they go alone. ❑

TIP

For details of the spectacular celebrations for New Year's Eve and the Festa de Iemanjá on Copacabana Beach, *see page 61.*

BELOW: walkers and rollerbladers take over Avenida Atlântica on Sunday.

Leisurely Sunday

Every Sunday, the broad stretch of Avenida Atlântica paralleling Copacabana Beach becomes a completely different place. The road is closed to traffic and transformed into a city playground, where a village atmosphere pervades for one leisurely day. In place of vehicles with blaring horns, and pedestrians controlled by traffic lights, there are small children on colorful three-wheeler bikes, watched by parents seated at the roadside; young couples on rollerblades engaged in earnest conversation as they sail along at a leisurely pace; boys playing football, and refreshment stalls set up to cater to everybody's needs.

RESTAURANTS & BARS

Restaurants

Judging by the number of eateries in Copacabana, you would think that no one ever cooked at home. With there being so many, there is huge competition. The beach-front restaurants all offer different styles of food, with the advantage that you can wander slowly past and see what's on people's plates.

Allegro Bistrô
Rua Barata Ribeiro 502. Tel: 2548-5005. 9am–9pm Mon–Fri; 9am–8pm Sat. $
Right inside Modern Sound, Rio's best music store, is the Allegro Bistrô, serving tasty snacks and combination sandwiches all day long. Jam sessions are frequent in this temple to Brazilian music.

Arab
Avenida Atlântica 1936, shop A. Tel: 2235-6698. 5pm–1am Mon; 9am–1.30pm Tues–Sun. $
Feta cheese, lamb, bergamot, mint, and dates, and much more, combined to produce authentic desert fare. Snacks or full meals. Has a branch on the Lagoa, at the Parque dos Patins.

Azumi
Rua Ministro Viveiros de Castro 127. Tel: 2541-4294. D only daily. $$
Exotic tempuras and fresh treatment of oriental fish staples. Daily specials always worth looking into. A trip East via an interesting menu.

Cipriani
Avenida Atlântica 1702. Tel: 2545-8747. L & D daily. $$$–$$$$
Consistently voted Rio's best, the Copacabana Palace Hotel's premier restaurant offers all you'd expect: luxuriously appointed surroundings in which to experience unique gastronomic thrills.

Colombo Café
Forte de Copacabana, Avenida Atlântica. Tel: 3201-4049. 10am–8pm Tues–Sun. $
You won't begrudge having to pay about US$1.50 to get into Copacabana Fort where the café is located. A shrimp snack or a crêpe in this setting will taste delicious: the whole of Copacabana beachfront before you, within the secure surroundings of a historic fort.

Da Brambini
Avenida Atlântica 514, shop B. Tel: 2275-4346. L & D daily. $$$
Small and welcoming place. A reservation will help secure you a table at this fine Mediterranean-style eatery, where you can savor tasty, well-prepared food. They are particularly proud of their osso bucco.

Don Camillo
Avenida Atlântica 3056. Tel: 2255-5126. L & D daily. $$
Happy atmosphere in which to enjoy Italian-style seafood and gourmet pizzas. Try for a table under the umbrella on the sidewalk, as it can be noisy indoors.

Marisqueira
Rua Barata Ribeiro 232. Tel: 2547-3920. L & D daily. $$
Select your fish of the day from the refrigerator at the door: groupers, sole, squid, shrimp, and much more. Non-fish dishes also available, including some Portuguese specialties. Portions are large, and sharing a dish is expected.

Marius Crustáceos
Avenida Atlântica 290, Leme. Tel: 2543-1767. L & D daily. $$$$
Another Rio special, all you can eat in the seafood department, in a nautically themed atmosphere. Lobster, shrimp, oysters; plain grills or with sauces. Not cheap, but it's an experience of a lifetime. No sharing dishes here. Next door is Marius Meat: the same set-up, for carnivores.

Siri Mole e Cia
Rua Francisco Otaviano 50. Tel: 2267-0894. D only Mon; L & D Tues–Sun. $$$

Many people consider this to be the most authentic Bahian-style kitchen in Rio. Steamy, spicy fish stews share space with grills and more conventional dishes on this enticing menu.

Bars

Cabral 1500 (Rua Bolivar 8). Open daily, all hours, and sitting right on the beachfront, the Cabral is a firm favorite with local families, fresh and thirsty from the beach. There's a huge menu offering all you can imagine. You can opt for snacks, portions or a full-scale meal.

Cervantes (Avenida Prado Junior 335, shop B). This venue is also open all day, every day. Traditionally, the windmills at Cervantes come into play at dawn, when party folk flock here for a roast pork-and-pineapple sandwich pick-me-up. Don't knock it until you've tried it. This is a Rio institution which is well worth investigating.

PRICE CATEGORIES
Prices for a two-course meal for two. Wine costs around $20 a bottle:
$ = under $35
$$ = $35–60
$$$ = $60–100
$$$$ = more than $100

IPANEMA

Ipanema put Rio on the map as a chic destination in the 1960s. Today, it retains the romantic atmosphere of the city more than any other beach district. It also has some of the city's best restaurants

I panema is Rio's most cosmopolitan neighborhood. It is the gathering place of the city's artists and intellectuals, the locale of chic discotheques, nightclubs, elegant and intimate restaurants, luxurious beachfront apartments, exclusive art galleries, fashionable boutiques, street vendors selling everything you can think of, and top cinemas and theaters.

Seen from above, the area forms a homogeneous unity of apartment buildings, tree-lined streets and wide expanses of water. This is the money belt of Rio, home to a mixture of traditional old money and Rio's nouveaux riches.

In search of space

Ipanema (a Tamoio Indian name meaning dangerous waters) began as an adventurous property development scheme in 1894, marked by dirt tracks running through the sand dunes, with a handful of bungalows along the sides of the roads. Considered by most to be a distant outpost on the fringe of civilization, the neighborhood was mostly ignored until the 1950s, when the crush of Copacabana became too much for its well-to-do residents.

Following the same path that had taken them from the Guanabara Bay neighborhoods to Copacabana, these well-heeled settlers carried on moving south, over to the next beach. This is a process that continues to this day, as can be seen in São Conrado and the Barra da Tijuca (*see pages 155–61*), oozing southwards in search of more space. As Ipanema became increasingly prosperous and fashionable, dirt roads gave way to paved streets and avenues, bungalows were replaced by the homes of the wealthy, and shopping arcades sprang up where sand dunes once sprawled.

Map on page 122

LEFT: eye-catching architecture in Ipanema.
BELOW: the beach is a good place to get together.

Rio's public tele-phones are known as "big ears," because that is what they resemble.

Property values

From the 1950s to the present day, Ipanema has undergone an extraordinary real-estate boom and population explosion. Its early homes were replaced first by four-story apartment buildings, some of which still survive, and since the 1960s, by a surging tide of high-rises, gradually turning the Ipanema skyline into an updated version of Copacabana, but with one major difference: Ipanema property values are the highest in Brazil, with beachfront apartments fetching huge sums by any international yardstick.

Wave of liberalism

That this should happen in Ipanema is not surprising. During the 1960s, the neighborhood was swept by a highly romanticized wave of liberalism that achieved international fame. Rio's bohemians and intellectuals gathered at Ipanema's sidewalk cafés and bars to philosophize over the movements of the decade – the hippies, the Beatles, rock and roll, drugs, long hair, and free love. Like their counterparts in the United States and Europe, Ipanema's long-haired youth were revolting against the values of their time.

Being centered in Ipanema, however, and not San Francisco or London, the movement quickly acquired a tropical, romantic strain. At its highpoint, the citizens of the Republic of Ipanema were capable of such rousingly romantic (or surreal) acts as rising from the tables of a sidewalk café to applaud the setting of the sun.

A modern legend

One of the guiding lights of the Republic of Ipanema – and the man responsible for what is now the world sound of the bossa nova – was famed composer, the late and much-lamented Tom Jobim, who made *The Girl from Ipanema* a citizen of the world. Looking back, Jobim recalled this magical period with nostalgia.

"Ipanema used to be a paradise, one of the best places in the world. Against Paris, Rome and New York, I preferred Ipanema. Not because of man-made things but because of

nature and beauty. The ocean on one side, the lagoon on the other. It had an abundance of fish, clean water and forest, and you could see the mountains. To give you an idea of what Ipanema was, when I first brought my song to the United States of America... no one knew where Ipanema was. One year later came the tourists and the hotels. Because of *The Girl from Ipanema*, I was once stopped on the street by a furious guy who said that I was responsible for rents skyrocketing in the neighborhood!"

The Girl from Ipanema

Now a pop classic, *The Girl from Ipanema* was the first big hit to emerge from the bossa nova movement of Brazilian singers and composers. The song put Brazilian popular music on the map and brought instant fame to composer Tom Jobim and lyricist/poet Vinícius de Moraes in the mid-1960s, when the wistful lyrics and the mellow, romantic melody exploded onto the music scene. It was immortalized by the tenor sax of Stan Getz and the sultry voice of Brazilian singer Astrud Gilberto.

For many years before his early death in 1994 – from complications following a relatively simple operation – composer Jobim enjoyed success as a world-renowned musician. His songs have been recorded by everyone from Frank Sinatra to Sarah Vaughan, and, with his own youthful family group, he appeared regularly at international venues such as Carnegie Hall.

Moraes, who studied law in Rio and English literature at Magdalen College, Oxford, died in 1980. He wrote reams of romantic poems and the lyrics for numerous songs, including the score for the film *Black Orpheus* (1959).

Today, Rua Montenegro, where the two men first saw the girl on whom they based their song, has been renamed after Vinicius de Moraes, and the Veloso bar on the corner from where they watched her pass is appropriately called **A Garota de Ipanema** ❺ (The Girl from Ipanema). There is a park in the vicinity called Garota de Ipanema, and the international airport has been renamed Antonio Carlos Jobim. Fame, for sure.

The end of an era

The 1964 military coup and a subsequent crackdown on liberals four years later brought all this philosophizing and free love to a sudden end. Particularly affected was the nation's most liberal neighborhood and its left-leaning bohemians; many were driven into exile. With this, as the writer and academic Heloisa Buarque de Hollanda remembers, "The neighborhood lost its innocence... a crisis came and the party ended."

Despite its brevity, and its narrowly defined location, this freewheeling period in the 1950s and early 1960s came to define the

There was a less bohemian side to Vinícius de Moraes, who was also a diplomat. He joined the service in 1943, and three years later was posted to Los Angeles, where he served as vice-consul until 1950.

BELOW: colorful beach towels laid out for sale on the sand.

Favelas

I f patronizing voyeurism sums up your feelings about touring a *favela* or shantytown, think again. One out of five people in Rio lives in a *favela*, and getting to know the *favela* way of life will give you a deeper understanding of this complex city.

Rio's first *favela* was occupied by the military, a delicious irony when one considers the atrocious lengths the more recent military went to in order to stamp out these embarrassing blots on an otherwise perfect landscape. Soldiers returning from the Canudos War in the northeast of the country in 1897 *(see page 25)* were allowed to camp, temporarily, on a hill in central Rio while accommodation was arranged for them. But the accommodation never materialized, so they stayed where they were.

By 1904 there were 100 huts; this number had swollen to 15,000 by 1933. The origin of the term *favela* is something of a mixture: it is the name of a hill where a famous battle took place and it is also a thorny shrub, a member of the bean family (*fava* = bean in Portuguese). During the 1890s, a big effort was made to clean up Rio. This involved demolishing hundreds of tenement houses, and

throwing some 100,000 people out of their homes. By way of compensation, they were permitted to take with them the planks of wood out of which their former homes were made. Lacking any other materials or resources, they used these planks to build their new homes.

There are more than 500 individual *favelas* in Rio, accommodating 20 percent of the population. A shack with a bedroom, bathroom, and kitchen can be rented for as little as US$50 per month in a suburban *favela*, while the same accommodation would cost three times that much in a more central or southern district. Consider that the average wage of a *favela*-dwelling head of household is in the region of US$100, and you start to get some sums that don't add up, and entire families crammed into a dwelling designed for one.

Favelas all have their own culture and history. Rocinha, the mammoth city within a city that dominates the São Conrado area, translates as "small vegetable garden," and in the 1940s lettuces grew where gang warfare now rages and 120,000 reside. The vast majority of the inhabitants of Rocinha were originally from Brazil's drought-ridden and impoverished northeast, and arrived in droves to join the construction industry during the building boom of the 1950s and 1960s.

Vidigal, which clings to the mountainside of the coastal Avenida Niemeyer, linking Leblon and São Conrado, was put on the world map by a papal visit in the 1980s: the ever-charismatic John Paul II visited an especially sanitized shantytown during a heavily orchestrated visit. The 1990s saw Spike Lee direct Michael Jackson in a clip filmed in the Dona Marta *favela* overlooking Botafogo; more heavy orchestration was involved, plus a run-in with the authorities, who did not want Rio's poverty exposed on the world screen. And Fernando Meirelles's 2002 film *Cidade de Deus (City of God)* provided an insight into *favela* life for many cinema-goers.

Touring a *favela* is absolutely routine for visitors to Rio. Just make sure you go with a proper tour company – only a fool would go on their own. Check the Activities section *(page 221)* for details of one reliable operator. ❏

LEFT: Favela das Canoas.

modern *carioca* spirit – irreverent, independent and decidedly liberal.

The period also propelled Ipanema into the vanguard of *carioca* style, pushing Copacabana back into second-class status. In a fad-conscious city, the trends of Rio usually begin and end in Ipanema. Today, the neighborhood is the center of chic and sophistication. If it's not "in" in Ipanema then it's simply not "in" at all.

The beaches

Separated only by a canal, the neighborhoods of Ipanema and Leblon have different names but an increasingly shared identity. At the Copacabana end, **Praia do Arpoador** ❻ is famed for its surfing and its splendid view. Passionate *cariocas* claim that the best ending to a long night out is to watch the beautiful sunrise from Arpoador, looking out at the crashing waves as early-rising fishermen cast their lines into the sea.

At the opposite end of the beach, standing sentinel is the imposing **Morro Dois Irmãos** (Two Brothers Mountain), which sets off to perfection one of Rio's most spectacular natural settings.

Between the two extremes stretch the **Praia de Ipanema** ❼ and the Leblon beachfront *(see page 147)*. In the morning, before it gets too hot, joggers and cyclists throng the sidewalk while members of exercise classes go through their gyrations on the beach. During the day, the golden youth of Rio frequent the beach and its waters. Contrary to what many people believe, topless bathing has never caught on in Rio; Brazilian women are not prepared to share their bodies with all and sundry, and Brazilian men are not keen for them to do so either, even in this most liberal of settings. They can be similarly disapproving of foreign visitors stripping off.

At sunset, the sidewalk is crowded with couples of all ages, walking hand in hand through the golden light of the day's end, a timeless ebb and flow that continues well into the darkness of the evening. Whizzing past them, seemingly oblivious, are the joggers and

Map on page 122

TIP

In 2005 Rio's legislative assembly approved a ban on postcards displaying images of women in the tiny, revealing bikinis for which the city is well known.

BELOW: the Lagoa de Freitas lies behind Ipanema beachfront.

Children don't care how fashionable or otherwise a beach is – they just enjoy playing in the sand.

speed walkers, working off the stresses of the day.

Art takes to the sands as well, and beach architects spend painstaking hours producing sand sculptures, anything from sensuous female figures to cartoon characters or simply castles in the sand (drop a few coins in the collecting bowl if you want to take a picture).

Less boisterous than the beach-front of Copacabana, Ipanema preserves the romance of Rio de Janeiro more than any of the city's 23 other beaches.

Class of its own

For more practical pursuits, such as shopping and eating, Ipanema is also in a class of its own. Until the big shopping centers and malls began to flourish, the neighborhood boutiques and shops were practically the only options for Rio's discriminating consumers. Despite the competition, the high quality of their goods still attracts a significant portion of the city's spending clientele.

Ipanema is also serious restaurant country, and in any given block

BELOW: Ipanema sidewalk.

there will be something to suit every palate and pocket. A welcome recent addition to the Ipanema scene has been a significant increase in the number of hotels in an area that was once practically hotel-free. This means that the neighborhood can now hold its head high in terms of accommodation *(see page 214).*

Hippies and jewelers

A relatively modern Ipanema tradition is the **Hippie Fair**, on Sunday at **Praça General Osório ⑧**, from 9am to 6pm. Started in 1975, the fair is now less hippie-trippy and more sophisticated, but it is still a pleasant, open-air bazaar of Brazilian handicrafts where local people and tourists mix easily. Excellent leather goods, attractive batik items, painted porcelain, and plasticized piranha fish all share space with eye-catching oil paintings and unusual souvenirs.

Ipanema has also become Rio de Janeiro's jewelry center *(see page 221).* However cursory your interest in gemstones, you will not regret paying a visit to the headquarters of one of the world's top jewelers, **H. Stern ⑨** (Rua Garcia D'Avila at the corner of Rua Visconde de Pirajá). While there are numerous other players in the jewelry game, among them Amsterdam Sauer, Natan, and a host of independent designers, the top name is, without a doubt, H. Stern.

The mixture of Brazil's mineral riches with the creativity of its designers and the tradition of its craftsmen has made the jewelry industry big business in Brazil. This is nowhere more evident than in the magical world of H. Stern, who has been in the business for 60 years. His Ipanema headquarters are impressive indeed, and visitors are always welcome. A simple, informative guided tour takes the visitor through all the stages of the creation

of a jewel. Tourmalines, aquamarines, emeralds, opals, all are cut and mounted in golden nests before your very eyes. There is no pressure to buy, but should the urge to do so take over, the choice is limitless, and ranges from million-dollar creations to inexpensive, fun mementoes of your day in Ipanema.

Near by is the gated square called Praça Nossa Senhora da Paz (Our Lady of Peace), a quiet spot surrounded by swirling traffic, where people-watching is the sport of the day. It's a great place to put your feet up, cool down, and soak up some local atmosphere.

Ambitious plans

In sharp contrast to Copacabana, there are very few commercial outlets or hotels along the Ipanema and Leblon beaches. At the Copacabana end of Ipanema, however, is one busy exception, the **Barril 1800**, a big tropical beer hall serving snacks and meals, with a vast veranda overlooking the beach. Beachside kiosks are plentiful, and there are toilet facilities in the lifeguards' stations.

Ambitious plans for the beachfront include the installation of 309 new kiosks along the 34-km (21-mile) stretch between Leme and Prainha, and the construction of underground facilities and glassed-in, air-conditioned bars. These plans, however, may take some time to implement.

Culinary treats

It is beyond the beach that the art of good eating is most evident. There are food outlets for a quick hamburger, a croissant, crêpe or pizza, and just about every corner has an ice-cream parlor and a fruit-juice bar, selling every imaginable variety of delicious juice from fruit crushed while you watch. These establishments are open-fronted, and what's available inside is easily discernible from the outside.

The neighborhood's real fame, though, is as the home of intimate, sophisticated restaurants, for special occasions or a big night out on the town. *(See pages 136–7 for some of Ipanema's best and most characteristic restaurants and bars.)* ❏

Map on page 122

Lifeguards represent a reassuring presence on the beach.

BELOW: sand sculptures are works of art – albeit somewhat temporary ones.

Restaurants

Much like Copacabana, you are spoilt for choice in terms of restaurants in Ipanema. This means that you can afford to select exactly what you want; if one restaurant isn't what you're in the mood for, there will be one close by that is. In the more upmarket establishments, sharing a dish is not done.

Armazém do Café
Rua Visconde de Pirajá 547, shop 101. Tel: 2259-0209. All hours, daily. **$**
This chain of quality coffee shops prides itself, of course, on its coffees, with the optional additions of Irish whiskey, liqueurs, and local firewater, *cachaça*. Tasty

snacks from quiches to sesame-studded palm-heart turnovers can make a delicious meal or snack.

Azul Marinho
Avenida Francisco Bhering, Hotel Arpoador Inn. Tel: 2513-5014. L & D daily. **$$**
Views of Ipanema Beach framed by fishermen's nets provide the setting for this typically regional Brazilian restaurant. Emphasis on Afro-Brazilian seafood combos, spicy and flavorsome. Occasional happy hours with live music.

Bazaar Café
Rua Barão da Torre 538. Tel: 3202-2884. L & D Mon–Sat; L Sun. **$$–$$$**
Contemporary cuisine in designer setting, serving

full meals, snacks, all well prepared and well presented. Desserts are worth saving space for.

Benkei
Avenida Henrique Dumont 71. Tel: 2540-4829. D Mon; L & D Tues–Thur. **$–$$**
An eclectic menu leaning towards Japan. Sushis, sashimis, tempuras. Plenty of steak and seafood in this always popular informal eatery.

Carpaccio e Cia
Rua Prudente de Morais 1838. Tel: 2511-4049. Noon to late, daily. **$$**
Traditionally consisting of wafer-thin slices of uncooked beef seasoned with grated parmesan and capers, Carpaccio takes on a new personality. Salmon, jerked beef, octopus: you name it, they'll slice it thin and season it. Also many attractive cooked dishes on the menu.

Casa da Feijoada
Rua Prudente de Morais 10. Tel: 2247-2776. Noon to late, daily. **$$**
Daily doses of Brazil's national dish, usually only served on Saturday elsewhere. Black-bean stew with all the trimmings. Also other traditional Brazilian fare, and some international-type dishes as well.

Da Silva
Rua Barão da Torre 340. Tel: 2521-1289. L & D daily. **$$–$$$**

Lunchtime sees a busy, value-for-money gourmet buffet, while the evenings are more sophisticated, à la carte affairs. Excellent standards of cuisine, with a faint Portuguese accent. No reservations accepted for lunch.

Garota de Ipanema
Rua Vinícius de Moraes 49. Tel: 2523-3787. All hours, daily. **$**
Tall and tan and young and lovely: she's still there! Snacks, simple fare, lots of meat. Even if only for a beer – and the beer's great – music-lovers will not miss the chance to experience the Girl from Ipanema.

Gula Gula
Rua Aníbal de Mendonça 132. Tel: 2259-3084. All hours, daily. **$$**
Don't be put off by the fact that this is a chain of restaurants: it is a benchmark in contemporary Brazilian restaurant design, management, and food. From soup through to sweets, temptations for all. All branches recommended.

Madam Butterfly
Rua Barão da Torre 472. Tel: 2267-4347. L & D daily. **$$–$$$**
Creative contemporary Japanese cooking with flair and attention to detail. One of Rio's trailblazers in oriental food.

Mil Frutas Café
Rua Garcia D'Avila 134 A.

Tel: 2521-1384. From 10.30am, daily. **$**

You are really here for the ice creams, repeatedly voted the best "homemade" ice creams in Rio, even if they do make 13,000 liters of them every month, in 160 flavors. At the café, you can order a sandwich before heading into the cold stuff.

New Garden

Rua Visconde de Pirajá 631 Tel: 2259-3455. Noon to late Mon–Sat; noon–6pm Sun. **$$**

Where Ipanema becomes Leblon, this traditional eatery caters to hungry folk. Pork ribs, and all manner of steak and duck all have their place on the menu. Nice wine list.

Osteria Dell' Angolo

Rua Prudente de Morais 1783. Tel: 2259-3148. L & D daily. **$$$**

Sophisticated Italian food in elegant surroundings, in an area rich in restaurant options. Risottos are a specialty, and all pasta is good. Above-average wine list.

Pizzeria Capriciosa

Rua Vinícius de Moraes 134. Tel: 2523-3394. All hours, daily. **$$**

Where the beautiful people eat beautiful, thin-crust pizza. The antipasto is a parade of temptations. Other branches around town, all recommended.

Via Farme

Rua Farme de Amoedo 47. Tel: 2247-9860. All hours, daily. **$$**

An unpretentious Italian-style restaurant with a veranda, sitting right in the middle of Ipanema. There's good pasta and seafood on the menu, friendly service, and great opportunities for people-watching.

Via Sete

Rua Garcia D'Avila 125. Tel: 2512-8100. L & D daily. **$–$$**

Variety is the keynote at Via Sete: burgers, wraps, and decadent desserts. Very well located for Ipanema shopping by day and wandering by night.

Zaza Bistrô

Rua Joana Angelica 40. Tel: 2247-9101. D only daily. **$$$**

A tasteful, exuberant tropical environment, rich in decorative detail, is the setting for some memorable meals. An ever changing menu bravely blends flavors to produce food that is original and fun. Upstairs, the seating is on large floor cushions; downstairs, more conventionally, there are chairs.

Bars

Barril 1800 (Avenida Vieira Souto 104). This is a geographical landmark, as it is the only bar on Ipanema Beach,

and it rests somewhat on the laurels of its location. It's a great meeting and drinking place, but the food here is only averge, and eating should be kept simple.

Shennanigin's Irish Pub (Rua Visconde de Pirajá 112A). Open from 6pm until very late, this is a popular haunt for visitors and residents, who pick up advice and exchange stories. It's got all you would expect from a pub: darts, billiards, lashings of beer and good cheer. Another branch in Barra offers much the same, plus a minimal cover charge.

Sindicato do Chopp (Rua Farme de Amoedo 85). Open all hours, this is a beer-drinkers' paradise. The name translates as "The Draft Beer Union." Not a great deal of work

gets done in this union, however, between sips and snacks. There are other branches in Copacabana and Leme.

The Lord Jim (Rua Paul Redfern 63). Evenings only, until late, except weekends, when it opens at 1pm. The Lord Jim was Rio's first pub, and it's now some 30 years old and still going strong! There are darts and drinks, and an amazing selection of dishes on a menu that goes well beyond blotting paper. It's a great favorite with singles.

PRICE CATEGORIES

Prices for a two-course meal for two. Wine costs around $20 a bottle:
$ = under $35
$$ = $35–60
$$$ = $60–100
$$$$ = more than $100.

MARKET STALLS AND STREET VENDORS

Street vendors and markets are a major feature of life in Rio, from itinerant sellers of cold drinks and T-shirts to well-established produce markets

It is said that street vendors are the soul of a city. If this is true, Rio has a colorful, vibrant, creative, and competitive soul. In Rio, you can buy things everywhere: on the beach, from sellers outside a bus window, and, surprisingly for most, at traffic lights. Weekdays see the incredible transformation of entire roads being occupied, from about 4am, by traditional food stallholders, who do brisk business in the early hours. By 11am bargain-seeking customers get some good deals; by lunchtime the very poor turn up to pan for runaway oranges and bruised papayas. By 2pm it's all over, with not a banana skin or a whiff of fish in the air remaining. An urban miracle, which takes place every day.

Then there's the Hippie Fair in Ipanema, which specializes in arts and crafts; the Antiques Fair in Centro; and the Feira do Nordestino in São Cristóvão, catering to immigrants from the northeast, where you can find lots of Bahian food, and there's good street entertainment.

ABOVE: herbs, spices, peppers, fruits, and garlic are laid out in a tempting display on a market stall.

BELOW: barbecued prawns on sticks are hawked around the beaches by hopeful vendors.

BELOW: Naïve art for sale at the long-established Hippie Market held in Ipanema each Sunday. There aren't many hippies to be seen these days, but lots of arts and crafts and leather goods.

MARKET DAYS

The neighborhood market days and locations are as follows – all are in the south zone of Rio, and within easy reach for the visitor:
Monday: Rua Henrique Dumont, Ipanema
Tuesday: Praça General Osório, Ipanema
Wednesday: Rua Maria Eugenia, Botafogo
Thursday: Praça Nossa Senhora Auxiliadora, by Flamengo's soccer ground in Leblon
Friday: Praça Nossa Senhora da Paz in Ipanema and Praça Santos Dumont in Gávea
Saturday: Rua Frei Leandro (Jardim Botânico side of Lagoa Rodrigo de Freitas)
Other markets:
Saturday: Feira de Antiguidades (Antiques Market), Praça do Mercado (near the Niterói ferry terminal) (all day, from 9am)
Sunday: Feira de Arte (Hippie Fair), Praça General Osório, Ipanema (all day, from 9am)
Sunday: Feira do Nordestino, São Cristóvão, Quinta da Boa Vista (6am–2pm)
Daily: every evening stalls are set up along a stretch of Avenida Atlântica (Copacabana) selling sandals, sarongs, sunglasses, and souvenirs.

Above: a jewelry stallholder takes a lunch break during a quiet moment at the Saturday Feira de Antiguidades. This market is a Rio institution. There's lots of bric-a-brac as well as real antiques, and you may get some bargains here if you're not too shy to haggle.

Right: masses of flamboyant flowers stand proudly in their buckets. They are so cheap they hardly constitute a luxury, even for those with very little money to spare.

Above: during pineapple season, these traditional emblems of hospitality are everywhere, and their scent is overpowering. You can smell a pineapple truck from far away.

Right: colorful scarves, bags, and sarongs for sale, by an equally colorful vendor, at the Hippie Fair, a weekly Ipanema market that holds an enduring appeal for visitors.

CORCOVADO AND SUGAR LOAF

Two of Rio's best-known sites are Corcovado and
Sugar Loaf Mountain. They also provide some of
the city's most astonishing views, which
have amazed visitors since Darwin's time

Rio de Janeiro has been stunning visitors with its spectacular views ever since the Portuguese first got here in 1502, and while much has changed since then, the landscape still provides once-in-a-lifetime vistas. The best of these are from Corcovado and Sugar Loaf Mountain.

Corcovado

Corcovado, meaning "hunchback," is the mountain pedestal of Rio's famed **Cristo Redentor** (Christ the Redeemer) statue. The best way to reach the summit – 710 meters (2,330 ft) high – is on the 4-km (2½-mile) Corcovado Railroad, and for anyone without their own transport, the only way. From the quaint **Cosme Velho station** ⑪, the little cog train makes the 20-minute journey every half-hour between 9am and 6pm, with trains leaving every 30 minutes. Tunnels of lush foliage and splendid views make the very steep but comfortable ride more scenic than a trip by car.

The railway was originally carved out of Rio's mountainsides by engineer Pereira Passos in 1884. The first trains to chug up the mountain track were foreign-built steam engines. It was a dangerous, smelly, and time-consuming trip. Then, in 1912, the Rio de Janeiro Tramway, Light and Power Company electrified the route, and it became much more popular.

Views to make you dizzy

At the summit, on a clear day, visitors are greeted by a dizzying view spread out before them. All Rio is there: Sugar Loaf, the southern beaches, tree-lined residential districts, the Jockey Club's toytown-like racetrack, the shimmering Lagoa Rodrigo de Freitas, and the Rio–Niterói bridge.

Map
on page
122

LEFT: the statue of Christ the Redeemer lords it over the city.
BELOW: Corcovado station, for the train to the top.

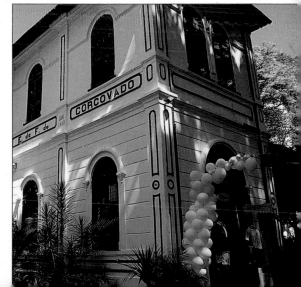

There are sometimes temporary exhibitions at the Museum of Naïve Art, when works can be purchased for sums that are surprisingly reasonable for original artworks.

BELOW:
Largo do Boticário – a glimpse of old Rio.

Once off the train, the visitor should be prepared to do some serious climbing of steps. Although lifts and escalators have now been installed, and are a boon to the less mobile, you may have to wait in line for some time to use the lifts, so if you're fit it's often better to walk. The impressive Christ the Redeemer statue presiding over the scene is 30 meters (99 ft) tall. The work of a team of artisans headed by French sculptor Paul Landowsky, it was completed in 1931. The base of the statue is usually surrrounded by visitors having their pictures taken – and it's not unusual to find a television or film crew up here as well.

Museum of Naïve Art

When you've had your fill of views, taken panoramic pictures, and maybe had a cool drink at one of the cafés, take the little train back down. Back at ground level, on the same side of the road as the Cosme Velho station, you will find the delightful little **Museu Internacional de Arte Naïf** ⓬ (Tues–Fri 10am–6pm, Sat–Sun noon–6pm; admission charge, which is halved if you have been on, or are going on, the Corcovado train). The museum is caretaker to what is estimated to be the world's largest collection of Naïve art, with 8,000 works from around Brazil and many other countries.

As you walk in, you are immediately hit by the impact of a vast canvas, measuring 4 m by 7 m (13 ft by 23 ft), by Lia Mittarakis, entitled *Rio de Janeiro, I Like You, I Like Your Happy People*, a quotation from one of the city's favorite old-time waltzes. Another quotation catches the eye, this one by Einstein: "Imagination is more important than knowledge," a statement which perfectly sums up the whole concept of Naïve art.

One unmissable work is Aparecida Azedo's *Five Centuries of Brazil*. Viewed from a mezzanine level, it measures 1.40 m by 24 m (4.5 ft by 78.5 ft). Key events in Brazilian development are shown with bold simplicity, and explanations of the historical scenes depicted are given on the mezzanine's railings.

On leaving the museum, continue for half a block up Rua Cosme Velho, then take a sharp turn to the right off the main road, which reveals a forgotten pocket of old Rio: the **Largo do Boticário** ⓭ or Apothecary's Square, a perfect little microcosm of the past, built in the 1920s in neocolonial style with materials taken from demolitions in the center of Rio.

Sugar Loaf

Among Rio's classic views, there is nothing quite like the panorama from the top of **Pão de Açúcar** ⓮ (Sugar Loaf Mountain), reached via a two-stage cable-car journey. It's all laid out before you – the vast curve of Copacabana Beach, the perfect curl of Botafogo, the Rio–Niterói bridge, and, on clear

days, when the mist isn't swirling, the jagged peaks of the Serra dos Orgãos, over an hour's drive away.

As with many of Rio's classic sights, getting there is half the fun. Visitors should be prepared for a heart-stopping glide in swaying, glassed-in cable cars. Sugar Loaf Mountain is undoubtedly Rio's best-known landmark. Today a symbol of the city, it was at its feet that the original city of São Sebastião do Rio de Janeiro was founded in 1567.

The Indians had a name for this singularly shaped granite monolith that stood guarding the entrance to Rio's Guanabara Bay. They called it Pau-nd-Acuqua, meaning high, pointed, isolated peak. To the Portuguese, this name sounded like *pão de açúcar* (sugar loaf), and the shape of the peak also reminded them of the clay molds used to cast refined sugar into a conical lump called a sugar loaf.

Still popular with rock climbers, the 400-meter (1,300-ft) summit's first known conqueror was an Englishwoman, Henrietta Carstairs, who, in 1817, placed a British flag at the top. A patriotic soldier soon replaced it with a Portuguese one.

The cable car

In the first decade of the 20th century, Brazilian engineer Augusto Ferreira Ramos envisioned an aerial link that would make the view from the mountain top accessible to all. Despite general skepticism, in 1909 he obtained authorization from the mayor for his project, and the first stage of the cable-car line to 218-meter (715-ft) Morro da Urca, the low mountain in front of Sugar Loaf, was inaugurated in 1912.

On a magical day in October, the cable car made the connection between Praia Vermelha and the Morro da Urca and back no less than 24 times, such was local people's curiosity in seeing the city's new thrill. In a miraculous engineering achievement, less than three months later, in January 1913, the final stage from Morro da Urca to Sugar Loaf was completed. The original 24-passenger cable cars were imported from Germany, and they remained in use for 60 years before being

Map on page 122

One of the many appealing pictures in the Museum of Naïve Art, a place well worth visiting en route to Corcovado.

BELOW: the cable cars make the trip to the top of Sugar Loaf every 30 minutes.

"Brazilian scenery is nothing more nor less than a view in the Arabian Nights, with the advantage of reality."

— CHARLES DARWIN

BELOW:
Praia Vermelha, with Sugar Loaf in the background.

replaced in 1972 by larger cars able to handle the increased demand for their services.

Now visitors are whisked up from **Praia Vermelha station** ⓰ in Italian-made bubble-shaped cars that hold up to 75 passengers and offer a 360-degree view. Each stage takes just three minutes, with cars starting out from the top and the bottom simultaneously, zipping past each other in the middle of the ride. (Departures are every half-hour from 8am to 10pm; the adult fare is approximately US$10 at 2006 rates, children aged 6–12 pay half-fare, and under-sixes travel free.)

Views from the top

From both the Morro da Urca and Sugar Loaf itself, you have spectacular views on all sides, and there are paths leading to viewpoints. To the west lie the beaches of Leme, Copacabana, Ipanema, and Leblon, with the mountains beyond. At your feet are Botafogo and Flamengo leading to downtown Rio, with Corcovado and the statue behind. Most visitors feel the view from Corcovado is more spectacular than that from Sugar Loaf, but the main reason for this is that Corcovado offers the best view of Sugar Loaf itself.

To the north, the high bridge across the bay connects Rio de Janeiro and Niterói, and you can see Niterói's beaches stretching away to the east. It's a good idea to bring a map with you to help you get your bearings. And do not just look into the middle distance, look around you, too: the garden at the Morro da Urca stage offers peaceful walkways and a privileged peek into the richness of Brazilian wildlife.

Needless to say, souvenir shops abound, and there is plenty to eat and drink. A prime location for a show house or restaurant, the site on Morro da Urca has had a chequered history, hosting some of the city's best samba shows in this hard-to-beat location, then falling fallow again and hosting nothing.

Pista Claudio Coutinho

If the need to feel terra firma beneath your feet overtakes you when you descend to **Praia Vermelha** (Red Beach), go for a stroll through the **Pista Claudio Coutinho** ⓰ (daily 6am–6pm; free). The walk is named in honor of the Brazilian soccer team's trainer, who died in a diving accident in the area. This is one of Rio's lesser-known treasures, and is administered by the army. It is preserved from the intrusions of modern life by the prohibition of bicycles, cars, motorcycles, and skates; the natural wildlife is kept safe by the no-pets policy. The entire walk is only 1¼ km (¾ mile) long, but if you are a nature-lover you may wish that it went on for ever.

A paved pathway hugs the mountain. To your right, the sea beats down on the barnacle-covered rocks; to your left, the abundant fertility of the rainforest is punctuated

by the bareness of granite – bare but not barren, as bromeliads bloom comfortably on the sheer rocks. Early on in the walk, you will come across a grotto, to your left, dedicated to Our Lady of the Conception, patron saint of the Brazilian army. Notice how the ferns sprout enthusiastically from the rocky altar. Look back to your right for a great view of Praia Vermelha.

Flora and fauna

Hummingbirds dart in and out of the light, in dive-bombing movements, hard to catch on film. Gentle, hissing squeaks from the trees indicate another form of life: marmosets, always playfully curious, popping their white-tufted ears out of their tree homes to check out the traffic. Weighing a mere 240 g (8.5 oz), these little creatures hate the cold, so they are happy here, and, provided they can avoid joining the food chain via birds of prey, they can live up to 20 years.

At all times of the year, the vegetation on the walk is breathtaking: black-eyed susans, pierced mon-steras, giant, elephant-ear philodendrons, blue gingers, and masses of pinky-purple epidendrum orchids all thrive in this perfect environment. Brazilwood trees have been planted on the sea side of the walk, and these slow-growing hardwood giants will one day create an impressive avenue.

Fruit trees do well here, too, including mango, papaya, and avocado. The birds know this, and are present in great numbers and variety. The yellow waistcoats of the Great kiskadees are everywhere, and even if you cannot see them, you can hear their rackety calls. Pairs of powder-blue Sayaca tanagers dance gracefully through the trees. The real prize, though, is the blood-red Brazilian tanager, one of the most beautiful birds in the world. If you see one, you'll never forget it.

If you go up Sugar Loaf Mountain late in the afternoon and stay for a little while, you can see the city in the daylight, watch the sun go down, spot the first lights coming on, and then see the city at night, a truly enchanting vision. ❑

Brazilwood trees have been planted along the Pisto Claudio Coutinho walk.

BELOW: if you are lucky, you may see a marmoset.

RESTAURANTS

The area around the Corcovado railway station is not noteworthy for restaurant choices – it is not really a place where one goes to eat, although there are snacks available if you're hungry. Two modest options are located at the base of Sugar Loaf.

Garota da Urca
Avenida João Luis Alves 56, Urca. Tel: 2541-5040. 11.30am to late, daily. **$–$$**
Try for a table near the front of the veranda; the buses whiz past, but the view is lovely. You get simple, well-prepared food, served with a smile, and it's an extremely pleasant walk from Sugar Loaf.

Praia Vermelha
Praça General Tibúrcio. Tel: 2275-7245. 11.30am to late, daily. **$–$$**
At the extreme right of the Red Beach at the bottom of Sugar Loaf, this is a good place to soak up some more wonderful views and quench your thirst. No credit cards accepted at the time of writing.

● ● ● ● ● ● ● ● ● ● ● ● ● ●
Prices for a two-course meal for two. Wine costs around $20 a bottle.
$$$$ = more than $100 , **$$$** = $60–100, **$$** = $35–60, **$** = under $35

Map on page 122

LEBLON AND THE LAGOA

Leblon still has a neighborhood feel, along with some splendid beaches. It is also the location of the lush Jardim Botânico and the Lagoa Rodrigo de Freitas, a popular spot for sport and leisure

ike Ipanema, **Leblon** is a largely residential neighborhood, traversed by busy streets that are alive with schools, banks, offices, supermarkets, and good food and excellent entertainment options. Residents need not stray far on foot to get their chores done. Leblon is somewhat short of hotels, but this lack is made up for by the numerous apart-hotels, which offer good serviced apartments at reasonable rates; these are especially appropriate for families.

There is a village feel to Leblon, especially in the area furthest away from Ipanema. Rua Dias Ferreira perhaps best illustrates the essence of the place. Fancy little cafés sit beside old-fashioned grocery stores and upmarket food emporia. Designer-clothing stores share the street with basic, stand-up bars, frequented by local workmen. There is a concentration and variety of eating places which ensures that a stroll down Dias Ferreira will supply whatever you might wish to find on a menu.

Beach babies

In the early morning, beach walkers form a special fraternity, and the noisiest part of the beach walkway is two blocks north of the Caneco 70, the only bar actually on Leblon beachfront. Here, the babies of Leblon get together to start their days. Accompanied by their white-clad nannies or their mothers (or, increasingly these days, their fathers), they are wheeled to their special kiosk in their silver baby carriages, and then the fun begins.

On a sunny day after a spell of rain, as many as 40 baby carriages may be lined up here, a sight to warm the hearts of even the most cynical. In truly democratic fashion, nannies will exchange telephone

Map on page 122

LEFT: watching the sunset at Leblon.
BELOW: swan pedalos on the Lagoa are always popular.

numbers with mothers when one's charge seems particularly enamored of the other's – or of his toys. By 9am the babies are all gone; while the early-morning sun is known to be good for them, any other kind is to be avoided by the very young and the infirm. Curiously, the early-evening air is considered noxious for infants and elders as well.

The cult of cachaça

Something else that Leblon has very much in common with Ipanema is that it abounds in food outlets: tiny storefront Arab snack bars serve up tasty, filled pastries, juice bars abound, and uncountable flavors of ice cream can be tasted. The Academia da Cachaça, at Rua Conde de Bernadotte 26G, is a patriotic showcase for one of Brazil's great sources of pride: *cachaça*, the potent firewater distilled from sugar cane, around which a true cult has been formed. This stretch of road, particularly rich in food and drink options, borders Cobal, a farmers' market that turns into a huge, open-air bar as night falls.

Botanical garden

On the Corcovado side of the Lagoa Rodrigo de Freitas, hugging the mountain, is Rio's **Jardim Botânico** ⑱ (Rua Jardim Botânico 1008, tel: 3874-1808; daily 8am–5pm; admission charge), which covers 140 hectares (350 acres). This prime piece of real estate started out as a sugar plantation and mill in 1596, and remained active as such until 1808, when Dom João VI installed a gunpowder factory on the site. He was so taken with the lushness of the surroundings that he established a garden there, in which to nurture precious imported seedlings, among the first of which was the Palma Mater palm, brought to Brazil from Mauritius. Indispensable spices and exotic herbs were grown in the garden, too. In complete contrast to today's widespread ban on the importation of plants, at that time tax incentives were made available to anyone who wanted to bring new plants into the country.

A grand collection

The collection grew, and now numbers more than 7,200 species of plants, many of which are set out in formal rows, although many others have simply sprouted as testimony to the incredible fertility of the area. Imposing iron statuary dots the arboretum, although the twisted trunks of the ancient ficus trees are monuments in themselves. Fascinating collections of carnivorous plants, bromeliads and orchids are enshrined in their own greenhouses; lakes showcase the giant, flat leaves of the Amazonian water lilies.

One garden is devoted to medicinal plants, and yet another to those which will give pleasure to the sight-impaired visitor, with highly scented, strangely shaped foliage and flowers. Bird life is especially rich, and 138 species from 34 different families have been sighted;

TIP

There's a pleasant little café in the Jardim Botânico, where you can get a light lunch or just coffeee and cake, seated at tables beneath the trees.

BELOW:
the Japanese garden in the Jardim Botânico.

the noisy, ungainly toucans are a delight to watch as they hop from tree to tree.

A local paradise

Over a quarter of a million people visit the gardens annually; many *cariocas* consider it their own backyard. Entire families, from the mightily high to the humble, can be seen at play and at rest. It is also a favored spot for wedding photographs, so the visitor should not be surprised to encounter a bride in full wedding regalia posing against a bamboo backdrop. Human statues, in the form of meditators, are not uncommon either.

The garden is best appreciated in the early hours of the morning and avoided, if possible, during the busy weekends. The minimal admission fee will seem a very small price to pay for a glimpse into paradise and the lungs of a city. If you're susceptible to mosquitoes, be warned that they are the only intruders in this Garden of Eden, so you should come prepared with insect repellent and something to cover your arms.

The Lagoa

People come from all over Rio to enjoy the **Lagoa Rodrigo de Freitas** ⑲. Neither the beach, nor exactly a park, it combines the wide-open spaces of both with the breathtaking backdrop of the Corcovado mountain and the rich green tapestry of the Floresta da Tijuca, Morro Dois Irmãos, and the distant tabletop of Pedra da Gávea. Around its winding 7 km (4½ miles) of shores joggers and walkers beat a steady path and cyclists whiz along, inspired by the very finest of Rio's mountain scenery. From sunrise to sunset, the colors of sky, water, and mountains shift and change, sometimes forming solid blues, grays, and greens, then splitting into rainbow streaks, or suddenly breaking into strange shapes and diverse colors.

The maintenance of the Lagoa has been an item on the agenda of almost every government since the 16th century, when it was the focus of an outbreak of tropical fever that struck the city. Since then, innumerable suggestions have been made as to how to preserve the purity of the

Map on page 122

The yellow blossom of the Ipê amarelo *makes a cheerful splash of color near the lake.*

BELOW: a cycling and jogging path around the Lagoa.

Margaret Mee

Amerigo Vespucci was disbelieving; Charles Darwin was overwhelmed; Rimsky Korsakoff was moved; Rudyard Kipling was dumbstruck; Stephan Zweig was mesmerized. Blame it on Rio, a city that excercises its magic on talented people in a multitude of ways.

Margaret Mee was an Englishwoman who came to Brazil to nurse a sick sister, and ended up staying for a lifetime. There were few corners of this vast land that did not receive her attention and her talent. A resident for many years of Rio's Santa Teresa district, she established a reputation as one of the 20th century's great flower painters.

Trained at the Camberwell School of Art in London during the dark days after World War II, she had no formal schooling in matters botanical. Such was her passion for the vegetation she encountered in Brazil that she picked up the tricks of the illlustrator's trade along the way. These included combining artistic sensibility with scientific accuracy, usually through the medium of watercolor, to produce a complete plant portrait. Seeds, stems, buds, withered leaves, and glorious flowers, all are portrayed in their most exact detail in one painting. Photography, however advanced, could never show these seasonal details in such a way. To achieve this level of competence, the artist must get to know the plant in its intimacy, in its minutest detail.

Margaret Mee's travels took her on 15 journeys on the River Amazon, often with just a local guide, and produced some of her most stunning work. But even a day out at Rio's Jardim Botânico was sufficient inspiration for this remarkable artist. One of her favourite subjects was the Lenten Tree, *(Tibouchina)*, whose gaudy purple blossoms cloak the hillsides when the Carnival costumes are put away for another year.

And on the subject of Carnival, not even in her fantasies could this soft-spoken English gentlewoman have imagined that her work would inspire one of Rio's premier samba schools, Beija Flor, to honor her with a heart-stopping parade. She was the first foreign woman to be so celebrated.

The devastation Margaret Mee encountered, year after year, on her trips to the Amazon caused her almost physical pain. She wrote infuriated letters to newspapers, mayors, and administrators, to refineries and charcoal factories, trying to put a stop to the damage. Eventually, she came round to the idea that education was the only way to stop the rot. If people could be made to understand our environment, and all its interconnected microsystems, they would stand a better chance of preserving the planet. To this day, scholarships are awarded in her memory to Brazilian students of environmentally important areas of study.

Considerably in advance of her time, Margaret Mee worried about ecology, long before it became a household word:

"The greatest tragedy would be the destruction of these superb Brazilian forests, a loss not only for the country, but for the entire world. After all, we, the human race, depend on the animal and vegetable kingdoms for our very existence, while they get along very well without us," she wrote, with great foresight, in 1958. ❑

LEFT: *Tibouchina*, one of Mee's favorite subjects.

water, which, despite now being overwhelmingly polluted, is home to thousands of fish. The Lagoa and the Bay of Guanabara are two sad examples of the local authorities' inability to manage tracts of water.

In spite of this blot on the horizon, and occasional fishy fumes in the air, the Lagoa remains dearly loved by *cariocas*.

Kiosks by the lake

In recent years the emergence of little bars, or kiosks, similar to the ones on the beachfront, have made the Lagoa a popular meeting point, either for an ice-cold *agua de coco* (coconut milk) after a strenuous workout, or in the evening for a meal and a chat. The three main areas where the kiosks are grouped are opposite the Jockey Club, near the heliport; on the Ipanema side near the naval club; and on the Copacabana side, known as Cantagalo. Most of the kiosks specialize in a particular type of food; there are lots of crêpes stalls, and you can choose among Arab, German, Japanese, Italian, and Brazilian

dishes, often accompanied by the music of a small band. This is a low-key but very pleasant way to spend all or part of an evening. Apart from this informal style of entertainment, there are also numerous restaurants and bars in the area worth trying *(see pages 152–3)*.

A night at the races

Nestling between the Lagoa and the Jardim Botânicol, The **Jockey Club** ⑳ (tel: 2512-9988) is serious business. Out-of-town visitors are welcome to spend a night at the races in the members' stand; there is no charge and no identification is needed. What the Jockey Club wants is to get visitors in there and placing their bets, so they make it easy for them. Visitors wearing sandals or beachwear will not be admitted, but the overall tone in this Louis XV-style palace is extremely casual. There are several bars and restaurants on site, so you can really make an evening of it. On Monday, the first race is at 6pm; Friday racing starts at 4pm. At weekends, the first race is at 2pm, the last at 7pm. ❑

Map on page 122

Agua de coca *is one of the most refreshing drinks imaginable.*

BELOW: refreshment kiosks by the lake are busy day and night.

RESTAURANTS & BARS

Restaurants

This is an area rich in choice, which will suit the most demanding of visitors. Don't overlook the kiosks on the Lagoa (see page 151) for even more options for informal eating in spectacular settings.

Alvaro's

Avenida Ataulfo de Paiva 500, Leblon. Tel: 2294-2148. Noon to late, daily. $$

Alvaro's is a Leblon institution, which is more dining room than restaurant. You will find hearty food and friendly service. Try the thinly sliced Parma ham as an appetizer; sharing is very much the done thing. here

Ataulfo

Avenida Ataulfo de Paiva 630, Leblon. Tel: 2540-0606. 9am–late, daily. $$

Plenty of variety in a welcoming, modern setting. Deli, buffet, knife-and-fork meals; good for a proper meal or a snack at any time. Great ice creams.

Boteco 66

Rua Alexandre Ferreira 66, Lagoa. Tel: 2266-0838. Noon to midnight, daily. $$

Oodles of character and informality set the tone in this delightful bistro. Sensible portions of well-prepared, imaginative dishes join old favorites on this attractive menu. Remember to save room for the trademark Troisgros passion-fruit crêpe.

Celeiro

Rua Dias Ferreira 199. Tel: 2274-7843. Closed Sun. L only Mon–Sat. $–$$

The name translates as The Barn, but this is anything but a barn. Owner-operated, tastefully decorated and always popular, it serves the best salads in Rio. Be there at noon if you don't want to wait for a table. The desserts are to die for. The Barn is one of Rio's enduring success stories.

Galeto

Rua Dias Ferreira 154, Leblon. Tel: 2294-3997. 11am–late, daily. $

Spit-roasted spring chicken with fries are the order of the day. No frills, but reliable food and friendly service in an excellent location.

Garcia & Rodrigues

Avenida Ataulfo de Paiva 1251, Leblon. Tel: 3206-4100. L & D daily. $–$$$$

An all-in-one food emporium, where you can buy freshly baked bread or freshly imported truffles. Very fine menu, ranging from delicious sandwiches to gourmet extravaganzas.

Gattopardo

Avenida Borges de Medeiros 1426, Lagoa. Tel: 2219-3133. D Mon–Thur; L & D Fri–Sun. $$–$$$

Modern setting for what many consider to be Rio's best thin-crust pizza. Lots of options on the menu, under a broadly Italian gastronomic umbrella. Gathering place for beautiful people.

Hipódromo

Praça Santos Dumont 108, Gávea. Tel: 2274-9720. All hours, daily. $

A stalwart on the local restaurant scene, Hipódromo is great for simple grills, steak cut into bite-sized morsels all washed down with icy-cold draft beer. The entertainment here is people-watching.

Jiló

Avenida General San Martin 1227, Leblon. Tel: 2274-6841. 6pm–late, Mon–Fri; noon to late Sat–Sun. $–$$

This is sophisticated take on a typical local bar. Cheeky and light-hearted, as you would expect from a bar named after a bitter vegetable that nine out of 10 people would refuse to eat if it was the last edible thing left on the planet.

Mistura Fina

Avenida Borges de Medeiros 3207, Lagoa. Tel: 2537-1844. Noon to late, daily. $$–$$$

Bar, restaurant, show house. Executives seal deals over lunch here, couples dine here, and musicians play here in the pocket theatre upstairs. A true all-rounder.

Nam Thai

Rua Rainha Guilhermina 95 shop B, Leblon. Tel: 2259-2962. 7pm–late Mon; noon–4pm, 7pm–late Tues–Sun. **$$$**

The dishes here have the refreshing zing of authentic Thai cuisine. Work your way through the menu for a string of delicious surprises. The dining area is on the small side, so it is a good idea to reserve a table.

Natraj

Avenida General San Martin 1219. Tel: 2239-4745. 7pm–late Tues–Sat; 12.30pm–midnight Sun. **$$–$$$**

You may not immediately think of an Indian meal when in Rio, but this is Indian cooking taken to its delicious extremes. You will find samosas, vindaloos, roghan ghost curry cooked in many different ways.

Olympe

Rua Custódio Serrão 62, Lagoa. Tel: 2539-4542. L & D Fri; D only Mon–Thur and Sat. **$$$$**

Chef of the year for many years running, Claude Troisgros melds quality local ingredients with the best in international food trends, a formula that makes for unforgettable eating. A good place to come for a special meal, well worth the extra expense.

Pizzeria Guanabara

Avenida Ataulfo de Paiva 1228, Leblon. Tel: 2294-0797. All hours, daily. **$**

This is a true Leblon institution, attracting many different kinds of customers. You will find retired people sipping a small beer before lunch, cab drivers popping in for a snack, and all through the night youth and the young at heart dropping in for a sizzling slice of freshly baked thin-crust pizza with a beer.

Sushi Leblon

Rua Dias Ferreira 256, Leblon. Tel: 2512-7830. L & D daily. **$$–$$$**

Popular with newspaper journalists working in the area. Come for sushi and sashimi, as well as quality grills with an oriental touch.

Zuca

Rua Dias Ferreira 233, Leblon. Tel: 3205-7154. D only Mon; L & D Tues–Sun. **$$$**

Enjoy creative combinations of contemporary food in a clean, minimalist interior.

Bars

Academia de Cachaça

(Rua Conde de Bernadote 26, shop G. Leblon). Open Tues–Sun, noon until late. Patriotism comes in a bottle here, a temple to *cachaça*, Brazil's sugar-cane firewater.

Appetizers are strictly regional, delicious morsels you've probably never come across before. No credit cards are accepted. If there is no space here, you will find plenty of other possibilities on same street.

Cobal (Rua Gilberto Cardoso, Leblon). Various bars and informal eateries have taken over part of this farmers' market. Very casual, neighborhood atmosphere and plenty of interesting people-watching. None of the outlets are likely to take credit cards, so be sure to come with cash. The Botafogo version provides more of the same.

Saturnino (Rua Saturnino de Brito 50, Lagoa). Open daily 6pm–late, this trendy young people's bar has

an eye for good design. Variations on the *caipirinha* theme keep the barman busy, and the kitchen produces some tasty, imaginative nibbles to accompany the beer.

Jobi (Avenida Ataulfo de Paiva 1166, Leblon). Open all hours. Back to basics at Jobi, if you can get in! This is a great favorite with bohemian types, simple and to the point. Order portions of tasty nibbles. It is also well located for other evening entertainment.

PRICE CATEGORIES

Prices for a two-course meal for two. Wine costs around $20 a bottle:

$ = under $35
$$ = $35–60
$$$ = $60–100
$$$$ = more than $100

SÃO CONRADO AND THE BARRA DA TIJUCA

Green, open spaces and uncrowded beaches make São Conrado an attractive proposition, while the new developments at Barra da Tijuca offer lots to do. But that may mean the crowds will soon be moving this way. Catch it while it's still quiet

As Rio started to outgrow itself, so it required more space. To one side were massive mountains, to the other, the sea, so westwards the city went to what is now **São Conrado** and, beyond that, the **Barra da Tijuca**.

To reach São Conrado, you leave Leblon via the scenic coast road, Avenida Niemeyer, which provides some stunning views of the ocean and mountains to one side, and disturbing insights into how the other half lives, to the other. Vidigal *favela* clings to the rocks here, but it isn't all shantytowns: some magnificent homes are located in this area, too, sharing the view with their less favored neighbors.

As you round the last curve on the coast road, the flawed idyll of São Conrado is before you, dominated by the massive square mountain called Pedra da Gávea, named for its resemblance to the topsail of a ship. (The other way to reach São Conrado is through a tunnel under the Two Brothers Mountain; though quicker and often safer, this route is quite charmless.)

São Conrado contrasts

The feeling of wide-open space in São Conrado is provided in large part by the storybook 18-hole **Gávea Golf and Country Club ❶**.

While membership to the club is exclusive and expensive, the general population benefits enormously from its being there. The lengthy tracts of well-kept lawns and good fences hint at a high quality of life in a neighborhood that is plagued by troubles, despite its natural beauty. The troubles can be imputed, in part, to its proximity to Rocinha, the *favela* with the biggest reputation, and population, for many miles around. While the huge majority of people living in Rocinha are law-

LEFT: Vidigal *favela* stretches up the hill behind São Conrado. **BELOW:** beachside accommodation at Barra da Tijuca.

abiding families, a few bad apples see to it that the neighborhood is never totally at ease.

São Conrado's other problem is the fact that all traffic from the Barra must pass through it to reach the south zone of Rio, and bottlenecks are legendary. In many ways, São Conrado is a perfect diorama representing the rest of Rio: stunning beaches, beautiful scenery, shanty-towns, magnificent homes, a delightful shopping mall – and some of the world's worst poverty and traffic conditions.

A lovely Sunday lunch can be enjoyed, however, in what would seem unlikely circumstances. Since 1700 a plantation house has occupied some premier territory in São Conrado, and sports a palm avenue planted by the Brazilian royal family. A favorite spot for weddings and corporate functions, the Villa Riso *(see page 161 for details)* offers a Sunday buffet in a delightful setting, with some art and history thrown in.

Flying down in Rio

An attractive road leading into the hills framing **São Conrado church** is the beaten track for hang-gliders, who take off from the promontory

Barrashopping: every consumer delight beneath one shiny roof.

of Pedra Bonita. Even people who have never hang-glided before seem to be overtaken by the urge when they get to Rio, and all degrees of experience can be accommodated. You can fly with a qualified instructor, and plenty of operators offer a reliable service *(see the Activities section, page 223)*.

Brave new world of Barra

On to the brave new world of **Barra**, reached via a truly cliffhanging overpass, beneath which the waves break noisily against the rocks. Barra is not only a place, is it a lifestyle, and people either love it or hate it. It is practically a self-contained city, offering all services, schools and shops to a point where residents of Barra rarely, if ever, need face the traffic or venture into what used to be the real Rio.

Being a product of a building boom only some 20 years old, Barra is not pedestrian-friendly, and although buses and cabs abound, it is not a particularly easy district in which to get around.

Shoppers' paradise

This area is truly a monument to consumerism, and large amounts of

Map on pages 156–57

cash change hands here daily. Many established retailers from other parts of Rio have set up branches in Barra, a reminder that this is where the money is.

Perhaps the most eloquent example of the Barra lifestyle is summed up in the monstrous **Barrashopping mall ❷**. There are 600 shops selling anything from doughnuts to dinner services; 18 cinemas, one of Rio's best bowling alleys, and dozens of restaurants, from fast-food joints to full, sit-down, à la carte options. Banks, a post office, bicycle repair outlets, it's all here.

When you think you've had enough and long for pastures new, you can jump on the free shuttle bus that will take you to its sister mall, the **New York City Center ❸**, which is guarded by a somewhat ludicrous replica of the Statue of Liberty. There are malls, large and small, all over Barra; some of them offer a free bus service from the hotels in Copacabana and Ipanema to attract the visitors in.

Endless beach

Each stretch of **Praia de Barra ❹** has its own characteristics; some parts are for families, some for sin-gles, some for surfers. There is even a stretch that is off limits, as it is a nature reserve. Along its 18 km (11 miles), the longest beach in Rio offers all manner of refreshments, facilities, and accommodation.

Beyond Barra itself is what is possibly Rio's most beautiful beach, **Prainha ❺**. Framed by mountains covered in tropical vegetation, it looks like a set for a movie portraying paradise. An especially active neighborhood association, consisting mainly of the surfing community, keeps progress and undesired development at bay.

A place to stay

The advent of new hotels of all categories in the Barra is very welcome, and a reflection of its ever-increasing role in the life of Rio de Janeiro. Hitherto, accommodation was restricted principally to motels, not intended for overnight stays, but rather for trysting – to put it politely. Some of these motels are ludicrously named: Sinless, Escort, and Love Land, for example. Barra's proximity to the massive convention centre at RioCentro is another reason for this relative boom in the hotel sector

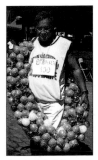
A colorful enticement to try your luck on the lottery.

TIP

RioCentro, where the 1992 Earth Summit was held, is the largest convention center in Latin America. Fully equipped with the latest in audiovisual and telecommunications equipment, it plays host to a huge variety of international events. It is really of interest only to visitors who are in Rio for conferences or conventions.

BELOW: musicians are among the figures depicted in the Museu Casa do Pontal.

On the down side, the evolution of Barra has been no exception in terms of the growth of shanties, which have more than doubled in the last decade.

A word of warning: there is a district in the north zone of Rio called Tijuca, landlocked and offering little to interest the visitor. Be sure you are aiming in the right direction for Barra da Tijuca and don't end up in Tijuca instead.

Natural education

Parallel to Barra Beach is a system of lagoons, which make for some wonderful scenery. They also make for some heated controversy, as plans to build tourist resorts, high-rise residential condominiums and even golf courses have been announced for the neighborhood. This area, a hub for the Pan American Games of 2007, is undergoing change at a fast rate, and not all of it is welcome.

The **Parque Chico Mendes** ❻ is named in honor of the murdered rubber-tapper, union leader, and environmentalist, whose death in

1988 produced outrage the world over, and drew international attention to destructive logging in the Amazon rainforest. The unusual Diurnal owl, hawks, kestrels, the Lesser anteater, guinea pigs and ferrets all make their homes here, as does the Yellow-bellied cayman. Plant life is exceptionally rich.

Casa do Pontal

There's much more to the Barra than surfing and shopping, if you look for it. You may need help finding the **Museu Casa do Pontal** ❼ (Estrada do Pontal 3295, Recreio, tel: 2490-3278; Tues–Sun 9.30am–5pm; admission charge), because it hides in an off-road area of Recreio in a rambling garden, but it is certainly worth a visit, and the admission charge is minimal.

The house is given over to an exhibition of popular Brazilian art, amassed over a period of 50 years by the late French designer and war hero, Jacques Van de Beuque, who came to Brazil in 1946.

In the words of M. Van de Beuque himself: "The Casa do Pon-

tal is dedicated to the country which took me in and allowed me to live my dream – a dream I hope to convey to our visitors. In a corrupt world, full of violence and hatred, it is a great comfort to be able to enter a universe created by the skilled hands of humble and honest artists."

And into this universe you go, visiting different areas of Brazil and peeking into local traditions and festivals. The entire population of this vast and diverse country seems to be present in the displays. The doctor, the lawyer, the policeman, country folk, saints and sinners: are all here. Materials used include sand, clay, papier maché, iron, wood, and textiles. The clay figures capture, with great humor in many cases, the simplicity of the lives of the artists who created them. The animated scenes are complex and fun for all ages. Even death is represented, in a poignant, darkened corner of this most professionally laid-out exhibition. Less gloomy is the collection of erotica, discreetly lodged behind a closed door so as not to offend those of delicate sensibilities.

You leave the Casa do Pontal feeling that you have visited Brazil not through the artificial lens of the glossy brochure, but through the very eyes of the people who live, work, and play in it.

Landscaper to the world

The former home of world-famous landscape designer Roberto Burle Marx (1909–94) is located in Guaratiba, the next district immediately after Barra. Distances are considerable, so taking a cab or hiring a car for the outing is a good idea. You need to phone in advance to book a tour at the **Sítio Burle Marx** ❽ (Tues–Sun tours 9.30pm and 1.30pm; admission charge); a knowledgeable guide will be your designated companion for the visit. Consider wearing long trousers and sleeves, and adding an extra layer of insect repellent, especially if the weather is humid.

Burle Marx was a leader of opinion, an all-round artist and an export-model Brazilian. With his abundant shock of hair, his flamboyant mannerisms, his adventur-

TIP

You don't have to join a large group for tours of the Sítio Burle Marx. They will run them with as few as two people, or as many as 35–40.

BELOW: a hang-glider soars over São Conrado Beach.

One of the sculptures in the fascinating Burle Marx garden.

Map on pages 156–57

BELOW: an ingenious use of odd materials at the Sítio Burle Marx.

ous approach to life, and his propensity for breaking into song at the slightest provocation, he was charisma itself. His fierce rages were legendary, too.

Burle Marx did much more than just design gardens; he transformed the way people looked at spaces, through his use of varied textures and unusual plant groupings.

Examples of his work can be seen in Flamengo Park, and on the famous sidewalks of Copacabana, whose hallmarks are the dancing paving stones in alternating colors. His work can also be seen in such far-flung places as Venezuela, California, Cuba, Belgium, Argentina, Chile, and Japan.

Bequest to the nation

The Sítio Burle Marx was the designer's home from 1949 to his death in 1994, whereupon it was bequeathed to the nation. He was an avid plant collector, and made numerous field trips into the wilds to find new plants, many of which were named after him. He became increasingly frustrated by his dependence on commercial suppliers in the gardening business, so he started to produce his own stock. His garden also became the nursery for the finds of other plant collectors, among them those of the English flower painter, Margaret Mee (*see page 150*).

In the plant department, there is plenty for the expert, and more than enough for the amateur: the jade vine is vast and, in season, almost surreal in its color, and the calabash tree is charm itself.

Burle Marx was a most daring collector of non-plant material, too, and displayed old doors from demolition sites, bowsprit figures, clay pots, and chunky rocks to incredible effect around his house.

This iconic figure is known as the landscaper to the world, and a wander though his home will transmit a vivid dose of his genius and charm to the visitor.

Refreshments or lunch may be in order after so many sights, and the Guaratiba area abounds in choice. Recommended restaurants are listed on the opposite page. ❑

RESTAURANTS

Restaurants

The restaurant scene in the Barra is mainly centered on the malls, all of which have countless options. The Rio Design Barra (Avenida das Américas 7777) concentrates some of the more upmarket eateries in stunning surroundings. There you are truly spoiled for choice.

Amir
Avenida das Américas 7777, Rio Design Barra, 3rd floor. Tel: 2431-1664. **$$–$$$**
A thousand and one nights, right on your plate. Huge variety on the Arab buffet, weekday lunches, and tempting gourmet options à la carte.

Bira
Estrada da Vendinha 68A, Barra de Guaratiba. Tel: 2410-8304. Noon–6pm Fri–Sat; noon–8pm Sat–Sun. **$$$**
No credit cards accepted, and limited hours. But the ups more than make up for the downs. Divine seafood consumed on a spacious leaf-shrouded veranda, with marmosets for company.

Borsalino
Avenida Armando Lombardi 633, Barra. Tel: 2491-4288. L & D Tues–Sun; L only Mon. **$$–$$$**
Delightful, stylish setting. Ostrich meat is a favorite, but the pasta options are plentiful and well prepared.

BibiSucos
Avenida Olegário Maciel 440, Barra. Tel: 2493-6168. All hours, daily. **$**
Juice, glorious juice, in all its forms, plus some great sandwiches. Chicken filet with melting Minas cheese on baguette is a winner. No credit cards.

Clube Chocolate
São Conrado Fashion Mall. Estrada da Gávea 688. Tel: 3322-1223. L & D daily. **$$$$**
Once you get over the shock of dining in a dress shop, you'll be fine. Très chic, and delicious, always innovative dishes. Not cheap, and nor are the dresses.

Fratelli
Avenida Sernambetiba 2916, Barra, Tel: 2494-6644. D only Mon–Fri; L & D Sat–Sun. **$$$**
A not-just-pasta Italian option, with an attractive wine list. The appetizers served before you order are special.

Joe and Leo's
São Conrado Fashion Mall, Estrada da Gávea 899, shop 203. Tel: 2422-0775. Noon to late, daily. **$$**
US sporting memorabilia adorns the walls of Rio's best-loved burger parlor. The Great American Dream lives on through the Di Maggio special and other variants.

Manekineko
Avenida Ayrton Senna 2150, CasaShopping, Barra. Tel: 2429-8033. L & D daily. **$$–$$$**
Contemporary oriental flavors. Sushi is big, but the rest is good, too.

Oasis
Estrada do Joá 136, São Conrado. Tel: 3322-3144. 11am–late, daily. **$$$**
Favorite with families, and can be noisy at weekends. It's eat-all-you-can-style, with service on a spit.

Tia Palmira
Caminho do Souza 18, Barra de Guaratiba. Tel: 2410-8169. 11.30am–5pm Tues–Fri; 11.30–6pm Sat–Sun. **$$**
Set menu that never ends. No frills, just fine fish dishes laid on the simple tables. No good if you don't enjoy fish stews.

Villa Riso
Estrada da Gávea 728, São Conrado. Tel: 3322-1444. Sun L only. **$$**
A former sugar-cane plantation is the setting for this buffet lunch, which emphasizes Brazilian cuisine. Unobtrusive live music. Reservations are essential.

PRICE CATEGORIES

Prices for a two-course meal for two. Wine costs around $20 a bottle:
$ = under $35
$$ = $35–60
$$$ = $60–100
$$$$ = more than $100

RIGHT: shady corner of the Tia Palmira.

FLORESTA DA TIJUCA

A forest in the middle of a city is a pretty rare thing, but that's what the Floresta da Tijuca is. Filled with birds, picnic areas and water courses, it is a peaceful place that also contains an interesting Art Gallery, the Museum by the Weir

Brazil is often accused of being one of the world's greatest destroyers of forests, but is rarely held up as an example of reforestation and reversing the damage done by man to nature. This, however, is exactly what happened to the Floresta da Tijuca, now officially the **Parque Nacional da Tijuca** , which occupies an enormous amount of land – 3,300 hectares (8,155 acres) – right in the middle of one of the most populous cities in the world.

BELOW: getting a drink from a forest fountain.

The first villains

The first villains in the story of the Floresta da Tijuca were, ironically, enough, Jesuit priests. While essentially known as the colonial world's educators, they were also farmers, after a fashion, and from about the 1570s they cleared great swathes of jungle in order to plant sugar cane. Sugar production flourished for two centuries, and by 1760 the magical crop of coffee had been introduced from what was then French Guiana. Farmers in the far northern state of Pará attempted to grow the crop, but failed; the climate was too hostile. A second attempt to grow coffee, this time in the Floresta da Tijuca, bore fruit, and precious, much-prized beans. Everybody was eager to cash in on the extremely lucrative coffee-growing business.

Destructive beans

The strain selected was called "bourbon," which first flowered in its third year of growth, and reached full production in a mere six years. This was a truly great little money-arner – but at a terrible price. The soil was gradually exhausted, forcing the entrepreneurs to find new locations for their coffee farms. If they had bothered to look back, they would have seen useless soil, on which little would grow. More

Map on pages 156–57

importantly, the soil had lost its capacity to hold and channel water for the fast-growing city below.

Reversing the damage

The year was now 1861, and the chronic water shortages indicated that urgent steps would have to be taken to restore the Floresta's function as a reservoir. Major Manuel Gomes Archer was chosen for the seemingly superhuman task of replanting this vast area.

At the height of the summer rains, in early 1862, Archer, accompanied by six slaves, started planting. The first saplings were transplanted from the nearby Paineiras forest, but before long the major was plundering his own land, towards the Green Coast in Guaratiba, for suitable seeds and shrubs to fill the seemingly endless emptiness. Estimates as to the astonishing rate of planting vary, but by 1887 more than 100,000 trees stood firm where sugar cane and coffee had once reigned.

Making their homes in these trees were those other industrious planters, the birds, who filled in the gaps left by nature by spreading seeds, which sprouted and, in turn, attracted forest creatures to nibble their tender shoots. A visible natural cycle had been established in a relatively short time, and persists to this day, with its own microclimates and specialized habitats for all the living things in the forest.

The Museum by the Weir

Some of the former coffee plantations in the Floresta da Tijuca have survived to the present day, and none is more attractive than the **Museu do Açude** (Museum by the Weir; tel: 2492-5443; Thur–Sun 11am–5pm; admission charge). It houses a fine display of artworks from all corners of the world, and is itself a glorious example of the neo-colonial style of architecture.

In 1913 this had become the country home of the Castro Maya family, fabulously wealthy industrialists with a taste for the glamor of the high life as well as for the peace of the forest.

The other home of Raymundo Ottoni de Castro Maya was the Chácara do Céu (Little House in the Sky), which holds a wonderful collection, and is fully described in the Santa Teresa chapter (*see page 104*).

Repaying society

Castro Maya repaid his high birth and privileged lifestyle with an active sense of civic responsibility. Answering the plea of his friend Henrique Dodsworth, mayor of Rio, he oversaw major works that were greatly to enhance the Floresta's potential as the playground for a fast-growing city. From 1943–7 Castro Maya saw to the dredging of lakes and the cleaning of rivers, as well as the installation of countless visitors' facilities, rest areas, picnic tables and benches. For this he received a token annual *cruzeiro*, the lowest coin in circulation. ❑

Follow the signs, and don't get confused by the similarity of the names.

BELOW: a fast-flowing waterfall in Floresta da Tijuca.

A Shrine to the National Obsession

Rio's Maracanã Stadium is one of the world's best-known venues for soccer. The game itself is a national obsession – nowhere more so than in Rio

The Maracanã Stadium was built in 1950 for that year's World Cup, a tame affair by contemporary standards, as many of the countries which would have taken part were still emerging from post-war chaos. The stadium's official name is Estádio Mário Filho, in honor of a sports journalist who was one of the driving forces behind its construction. The name Maracanã refers to the red-shouldered macaw which used to be populous in the Rio area.

Like the Sambadrome, the stadium was constructed in record time – two years – lending credence to the idea that if *cariocas* want something badly enough, they'll give their souls to make it happen. Attendance numbers for crowds at major matches read like the population figures for small countries: it is said that 195,513 people watched the Brazil v. Paraguay match in 1954. The classic 1953 confrontation between Flamengo and Fluminense, two hugely popular Rio clubs, is said to have been seen by 176,656 fans. Extensive refurbishment has left the stadium spanking new, with added safety features and increased comfort for spectators.

LEFT: football strips and memorabilia are on sale at the stadium and in shops and kiosks all over the city.

BELOW: young soccer enthusiasts demonstrate that you don't need expensive kit to play the game.

LEFT: football fans manage to create an atmosphere not unlike that of Carnival, especially when their team is winning.

A GREAT LEVELER

While many people perceive soccer (football) as one of Brazil's great export products, it is well to remember that it was originally an import. Charles Miller brought the game back with him to São Paulo when he returned from a stint in an English boarding school in 1894. From that day to this, soccer has been played with passion the length and breadth of this vast country.

From the prestigious world fixtures featuring the national side in their distinctive yellow kit – the canaries, they used to be called – to barefoot games on tracts of beaten earth in the slums, soccer is a sport that can be played at all levels of skill.

All around Rio, impromptu matches are played on all surfaces at all times of the day and night. The major clubs, with their mammoth followings are, among others, Fluminense, Vasco, and Botafogo – but Flamengo's fans far outnumber those of the other clubs.

Children play soccer from an early age – it is on the curriculum for most schools – but it is often those kids who are rarely in school who rise to stardom, and for many of them it is their greatest dream from the time they are very young.

ABOVE: soccer isn't the only thing to take place at the Maracanã: Pope John Paul II celebrated Mass here in 1980, and Paul McCartney holds the world record for the largest audience for a solo act (180,000) at a concert here in April 1990.

RIGHT: Ronaldinho (Little Ronaldo) is currently the biggest name in Brazilian soccer, and is the idol of many aspiring young players. He first played for the national team in 1999, at the age of 19, when he scored the winning goal against Venezuela.

BELOW: the beaches make ideal pitches, and soccer on the sand is practiced and played whenever the opportunity arises, sometimes drawing enthusiastic audiences.

EXCURSIONS

A guide to easy-to-reach places outside the city,
cross-referenced by number to the maps

Rio is the capital of the state of Rio de Janeiro, which is replete with attractions of its own. *Cariocas* flock to the hills or to the surrounding coast whenever they have a long weekend or a few days' holiday, and any visitors who have a few extra days to spare should try to follow their example.

The nearby Rio highlands are an attractive destination that can easily be visited on a day trip, by bus or private transport. The hills themselves shelter gourmet enclaves, and the Serra dos Orgãos mountain range is stunning, whether you are a serious walker, or just there for the views. The refreshing coolness of the resort towns of Teresópolis and Petrópolis will be as welcome to visitors as it was to Brazil's 19th-century royal family, for whom Petrópolis was built as an escape from the oppressive heat.

The coastline of the state of Rio contains formidable rivals to the city's beaches, but to appreciate them you should plan on at least an overnight stay. For many *cariocas*, the trendy beach resort of Búzios, to the east of the city, is unmatched anywhere in Brazil, while others insist that the gorgeous Costa Verde (Green Coast) to the west of Rio is unsurpassable.

From the archipelago of Angra dos Reis, ferries take visitors to the idyllic Ilha Grande, or numerous other, smaller tropical islands. And a short distance further along the coast the picturesque little colonial town of Paraty is a delight.

All these coastal treasures are within a few hours of Rio, and, like the highlands, are accessible by an efficent public transport service (detailed in the Transport section, *page 209*). ❑

PRECEDING PAGES: crystal-clear waters at Forno Beach, Búzios.
LEFT: Igreja Santa Rita church, Paraty.

PETRÓPOLIS AND THE RIO HIGHLANDS

Dom Pedro II started a trend in the 19th century when he fled to the hills to escape Rio's oppressive summer heat. Those in the know have been following his example ever since. For visitors, an excursion makes a pleasant contrast to the city

The practice of fleeing the heat of the Rio summers and their attendant fevers by taking to the hills was established by Brazil's emperors in the 19th century, and continues to this day. Dom Pedro II was especially keen on his summers away, and it was his interest in the vacation potential of **Petrópolis** ❶ that put it on the map in the first place.

During his 58-year reign he moved the court to Petrópolis annually, dragging along with it the various ministries of state, embassies, and other accoutrements of the monarchy. Pedro's summers were somewhat elastic, too, often starting in November and lasting through to June. The frequent imperial presence in Petrópolis has ensured that even today it has an air of nobility, and a grandeur of scale lacking in other neighboring resorts.

Getting away

Petrópolis is Rio de Janeiro state's leading mountain getaway, and makes an enjoyable day out for the visitor to Rio, provided the weather is fine. The Rio–Petrópolis highway, on which a toll is levied, is excellent, and provides some truly memorable views. There are plenty of lay-bys, so visitors can pull in and take photographs. The drive covers 70 km (45 miles) and takes approximately one hour and a quarter. The regular service from Rio's downtown bus terminal (Rodoviária Novo Rio) is efficient and reliable. Tourist information is available from several booths before you set off. One is in the historic city center at Praça dos Expedicionários (daily 9am–5pm).

Discovering Petrópolis

Petrópolis covers a huge area, accommodating palatial retreats, weekend apartments, and a resident population of more than 300,000

Map on pages 174–75

LEFT: Casa de Santos Dumont, home of an eccentric.
BELOW: a leisurely form of transport around the town.

*Trono de Fátima –
the views from it are
far more interesting
than the view of it.*

---

people. To get a feel for the terrain, and how the city's density is dictated by rivers and massive rocks, take a cab ride up a long, steep hill to the **Trono de Fátima** (Fatima's Throne; Rua do Bispo Dom José; open all the time; free access). Hang on to the cab, as you'll never get another one up there. This extremely nondescript monument is not what you're there for: you've come for the bird's-eye view of the city spread out below.

Petrópolis is increasingly serving as a dormitory town for Rio de Janeiro, as property prices and rents are lower and the quality of life better than in the capital itself; schools and medical care are cheaper, and the crime rate is far lower, too. Temperatures in Petrópolis are lower than in Rio as well, and the sweater-clad inhabitants of the city give it an autumnal air during the cool months.

A truly elegant way to get to know the imperial neighborhood is to take a horse-drawn buggy, which will enable you to peek over the walls into the gardens of the residents at a leisurely pace.

BELOW: the Museu Imperial, housed in the summer palace built for the monarchy.

Imperial summer splendor

The town's premier attraction is the **Museu Imperial** (Rua da Imperatriz 220, tel: (24) 2237-8000; Tues–Sun 11am–5.30pm; admission charge), housed in the original building that was built for and occupied by the monarchy. For the first 50 years of the last century it was leased out to a school, but has since been artfully restored to its former condition, and now constitutes one of the model cultural centers in the country.

In the gardens (open from 8am), noteworthy trees and plants are identified by plaques. For security reasons, only 300 people are admitted into the museum's principal building at any one time, so visitors are asked to be patient if there is a line to enter. The wait will have been worthwhile, however.

Visitors don felt overshoes on entry, which both protect and polish the dazzling hardwood floors. Imperial memorabilia is set out in every room: Sèvres china, Aubusson carpets, beautiful Brazilian carved wooden chests and tables. The tele-

phone and telescope serve as a reminder of the emperor's scientific bent. The crown jewels are always a success with visitors, as is the toucan-feathered imperial mantle. The collection of ladies' fans is fun, and the swords and armaments are evocative of times gone by.

Courtly portraits stare down from every wall; Édouard Vienot's 1868 portrayal of Dom Pedro II shows in a sympathetic and friendly light the face of the man who ruled Brazil during its longest period of growth and stability. Notwithstanding the obvious trappings of power on display, the visitor's lasting impressions of the occupants of the former palace are, perhaps surprisingly, of their essential simplicity.

Home at last

A few blocks away, at Rua São Pedro de Alcântara 60, is the French Gothic-style **Catedral de São Pedro de Alcântara** (tel: (24) 2242-4300; daily 8am–8pm; free). Its construction was commissioned at the time of the founding of the city of Petrópolis, but the semi-completed building was only inaugurated in 1929. Work then continued on it for another 40 years before the building was finally finished.

The carved Carrara marble is outstanding, especially that which adorns the imperial tombs. Dom Pedro II and his wife, Dona Teresa Cristina, both died in exile, and their bodies were only returned to Brazil in 1939, 19 years after the decree banishing the royal family was revoked. The remains of their daughter, the Princess Isabel, and her husband, the French Count of Eu, were not brought back from France until 1971.

Casa de Santos Dumont

A visit to the home of Alberto Santos Dumont is a peek into a brilliant but somewhat twisted and superstitious mind. The unusual, spooky **Casa de Santos Dumont** (Rua do Encanto 22, tel: (24) 2231-3011; Tues–Sun 9am–5pm; admission charge) is very much worth a visit. Alberto Santos Dumont, credited by Brazilians – and many Europeans – as the Father of Aviation, lived in

Dom Pedro II – still keeping an eye on the town he loved, and which was named after him.

BELOW: Gothic-style arches in the Catedral de São Pedro de Alcântara.

this strange abode, which he designed himself, from 1918 until his death at the age of 59 in 1932. In keeping with his superstitious nature, the street on which he lived is called Rua do Encanto – Enchanted Way.

The scion of wealthy Franco-Brazilian landowners, Santos Dumont moved to Paris in 1891, at the age of 17, to study engineering, and stayed for 20 years. Fascinated by the possibility of flight, it was there, in 1906, that he made the first fully documented flight in a heavier-than-air machine. (The Wright Brothers, whose names are more familiar, made an earlier flight, at Kitty Hawk, North Carolina, in 1903, but only produced documentation for it five years later.)

Tribute to eccentricity

Santos Dumont's home is a tribute to his eccentricity. The house has only one room; no tables, just shelves designed for various purposes, no bed (he slept on top of a chest of drawers) and no kitchen. He didn't need one, as his meals were all delivered by a local hotel. The house employs built-in ladders as staircases, one of which leads to a loft where his unusual sleeping accommodation is located.

However, it is the steps giving entry to the house that are the oddest of all, so designed that it is impossible for a visitor to use them other than with "his right foot first," which Santos Dumont regarded as essential to good luck. Tragically, the inventor committed suicide at a São Paulo beach resort after telling friends he was despondent over the use of the airplane in warfare.

Itaipava

The pretty plateau of **Itaipava** ❷, nestled between the peaks of the Petrópolis and Teresópolis mountains, and only 15 km (9 miles) from

Alberto Santos Dumont – a brilliant but troubled man who came to a sad end.

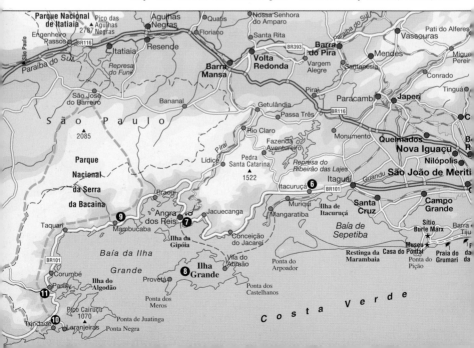

Map
on pages
174–75

the historic city center of the former, has always been a popular area, thanks to its excellent climate and pretty views. The countryside is littered with a mixture of palaces and bungalows, farms and modest condominiums. A lot of "new" money has been attracted to this area, as it provides space for ample properties within easy reach of civilization and urban comforts.

Eco-tours

There are a number of eco-tours in operation in the area, some of which take you into private homes to see working farms – some rearing sheep, Jersey cows, and thoroughbred horses, others growing mushrooms and fine herbs – which are open to the public, as part of the **Brejal Circuit**. Reservations are essential if you want to join a tour, and can be made by calling tel: (24) 2259-1562. Further information can be obtained from the information booth at Estrada União Indústria 8764 (daily 9am–6pm).

Conspicuous consumption

In direct contrast to historical Petrópolis, Itaipava is an icon not to imperialism but to consumerism. It would be impossible to say where the center of Itaipava is, as it is essentially one long road, called Estrada União Indústria, lined on either side with fun things to see and innovative ways to spend money.

The building boom in and around Itaipava has ensured that the antique dealers, and those who trade in bric-a-brac and junk, have flocked to the area. Fifties memorabilia is always a good seller, and Betty Boop still has her fans. **Garage Salles** at number 14999 Estrada União Indústria specializes in old wooden furniture, while at number 13291 the **Antiquário Daquele Tempo** (Tues–Sun) is a mixture of antiques shop and art gallery. A favorite with visi-

TIP

The herb-producing farms offer opportunities to buy dried herbs as well as oils, soaps, and other herb-scented produce.

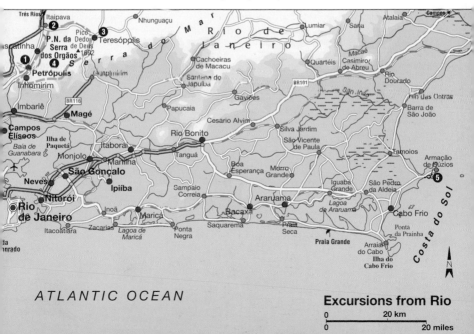

ATLANTIC OCEAN

Excursions from Rio

| 0 | 20 km |
| 0 | 20 miles |

Souvenirs for sale. The Brejal market has local crafts of all kinds, as well as fresh produce.

BELOW: sweetcorn, straight from the field to the cooking pot.

tors and residents alike since the 1950s, **Luis Salvador** produces high-quality, Portuguese-style pottery at 10577 Estrada União Indústria. Full dinner services, oversized serving dishes, cups and saucers, candlesticks, table lamps, and umbrella stands make walking through the shop a hazard with a child in tow – or for a clumsy adult. A riot of color decorates all these pieces, which can be made to order and exported.

Right next door, **Gregory Somers** carries on the family pewter business, based in São João del Rei in Minas Gerais, with a stunning line of tableware, often allying pewter with glass and, most impressively, with warm Brazilian wood. Another good place to stop is the **Arteiro**, on the same street, at No. 11407. It is as much a living museum and display of contemporary crafts as a shop, and happy hours can be spent poking into its over-filled corners.

Headdresses, cooking utensils, and musical instruments made by indigenous Brazilian tribes fight for space with amusing woodcarvings of angels and imps in the baroque style of Minas Gerais. Coconut, burity palm, and bromeliad fibers are cunningly woven into baskets, mats, and decorative items. An adjoining shed houses the loom where carpets of all sizes are produced; the garden is a quaint minefield of tiny frogs spouting water, strange statues, and precious plants.

The people's market

Although most foreign visitors are unlikely to need to buy tomatoes, aubergines (eggplants), and lettuces, a stop at the **Horto Mercado do Brejal** (Fri–Sat all day, Sun am) on Estrada União Indústria is always worthwhile. Here, local farmers gather to sell their freshly picked, first-class produce. If you find some of it irresistible, you could always put together a picnic.

The market's car park is also a great gathering point for local craftspeople, who offer anything from a Model T Ford car made of varnished, twisted twigs, to delicate, embroidered dish towels. In all

Map on pages 174–75

instances, whether you are just looking around or actually buying, the Brejal market provides great insight into what the local people buy, and why. In a small way, it's like visiting their homes, however vicariously, and getting some idea about how they live.

The gourmet highlands

If Búzios was the gourmet capital of the state of Rio some years ago, that spot has been firmly taken over by the Petrópolis/Itaipava area. The various shopping centers along the Estrada União Indústria all have their food halls, where tasty snacks or a meal can be had throughout the day, but there is also a plethora of owner-operated gourmet restaurants. In common with all other resort destinations in the state of Rio, *pousadas* (inns) are plentiful. Some are tiny, some are hidden in the jungle-clad mountains or sit by streams, while others are on the main road.

Among the starred-hotel options are the **Locanda della Mimosa** in the Vale Florido area, which towers above the competition in every way, including price. Here, the best of sophisticated Italian cuisine can be appreciated, as well as a truly outstanding wine list, and six exquisite guest rooms are available.

The **Pousada Tankamana**, in the Vale do Cuiabá area, is almost in the same league, though much more relaxed, providing good restaurants with hotel facilities. But possibly the prizewinner in terms of charm is the stunning **Pousada Alcobaça** in Correias; it is hard to say whether top prize should go to the garden, the food or the welcome *(see page 215 for details of all these hotels).*

Hydrangea Way

The 53-km (33-mile) drive from Petrópolis and Itaipava to Teresópolis follows a wondrously convoluted, steep mountain road, and can be done in about an hour, complete with hairpin bends and belvederes where you simply have to stop to admire the view. This road was originally called the Estrada das Hortensias (Hydrangea Way), and the walled mansions of the seriously

Visitors may be used to seeing Busy Lizzies in pots at home, but here they run riot over the hillsides.

BELOW: taking in a view of the highlands.

The area has a number of broccoli farms, and the produce is sold at local markets.

BELOW: giant bromeliads thrive on the bare, rocky slopes.

wealthy give way to patches of hydrangea bushes, their polished leaves picking up every glimmer of sunshine, their blossoms lush and exotic when in season.

Between the house walls and the hydrangeas, there is seemingly endless nothingness: ancient trees, proudly wearing their epiphytic beards of Spanish moss, tower over smallholders' farms, clinging bravely to the slopes (epiphytic plants are those that grow on others, and take their nutrients from the air and rain). Banana plantations abound, and broccoli farms are especially noticeable, the slightly bluish tones of the broccoli leaves blending with the predominant greens and browns. Giant bromeliads crown the massive bare rocks that dot the slopes.

Teresópolis

Unexpectedly, after a long downhill stretch, there is **Teresópolis ❸**. Private homes of all styles announce the cultural confusion of a town that has received immigrants from many countries. None of them has left a dominant mark, although each has contributed something. If anything, a Tyrolean influence persists.

Great green swathes herald the Teresópolis Golf Club, a nine-hole course that welcomes visitors at all times. On into the town, and rows of billboards, odd architecture, and the general feel of a mixed esthetic brand the place as nondescript, in terms of what man has to offer. Nature, on the other hand, more than makes up for this.

The first hotelier

The town is named in honor of Dom Pedro II's wife, the Empress Dona Teresa Cristina, although there is no record of her actually visiting the place. Among its earliest settlers was George March, an Englishman who was so taken with the area in the early 1800s that he established a huge farm, covering most of what is now downtown Teresópolis. He bred horses here and farmed vegetables for the Rio market.

March also did a great deal of entertaining: botanists and other specialists from all over the world

George Gardner

George Marsh wasn't the only British adventurer attracted to this area in the 19th century. In 1836 the aptly named Scottish botanist, George Gardner, arrived in Rio, and made a number of excursions into the Serra dos Orgãos, where he collected a wide variety of plants and seeds, including orchids, which he sent back home to Scotland. Gardner stayed in Brazil for five years, and although many of his trips took him into the interior of the country, he retained a fondness for the Orgãos mountains and a lively interest in their vegetation. Once back home in Scotland, Gardner wrote a book called *Travels in the Interior of Brazil*.

Map on pages 174–75

trekked up the mountains with their mule packs to visit him and to study the plants and wildlife of the region. This was a period when explorers and botanists from northern Europe had become fascinated with exotic flora and with the possibilities of transplanting some of it to their own colder climates. When his house could accommodate no more guests, March started to rent out small chalets to his visitors, making him the first, although possibly unwitting, hotelier in Teresópolis.

After his death, his lands were divided and snapped up by frantic *cariocas*, in search of somewhere cool and healthy to spend the scorching summers. The current population of some 130,000 people still doubles in the summer months. Off-season, every square kilometer accommodates 166 people, half of Rio's density.

Health and plenty

Teresópolis has little or no tradition in the formal hospitality area, but new *pousadas* are springing up all the time, catering to every taste, and some of them are extremely attractive. The first hotelier certainly started a trend.

If you decide to spend the night in the area, make inquiries in advance before leaving Rio, rather than hoping to find somewhere when you get here. Look for somewhere with a fireplace if you come in the winter, as central heating is unknown, and it can get very chilly. Restaurants, too, spring up in unlikely settings; some survive and flourish, but the vast majority do not.

One favored area in which to stay is Quebra Frascos, which translates as Broken Bottles, so called because the climate here was said to be so good that early residents broke their medicine bottles, having no further need for them.

An alternative (and less healthy) origin for the name Broken Bottles has George March and his guests picnicking in the area, and, after a few drinks, dropping and breaking their bottles of whisky as they negotiated, unsteadily, the rocks and boulders of the mountain streams. Very bad behavior for botanists.

BELOW: bananas flourish against a rocky mountain backdrop.

TIP

Climbers and trekkers should contact local mountaineering organizations for permission to scale the peaks of the Serra dos Orgãos. Try Rio Hiking, tel: 2552-9204, or consult the local tourist office.

BELOW: the Dedo de Deus, seen from Teresópolis.

The climate that was recommended for visitors is certainly healthy for orchids, as can be seen at **Aranda** (Rua João Daudt de Oliveira, tel: (24) 2742-0628; Mon–Sat 9am–4.30pm, Sun 9am–1pm; free). This is one of the country's major orchid producers, and the blooms are a wonderful sight all year round.

Bargains

The shops of Teresópolis are much more basic than in upmarket Itaipava, but the town is now famous for its market, or Feirinha, which is held every weekend and public holiday, weather permitting, in the Praça Higino da Silveira, better known as the **Praça do Alto**. Cheap clothing for sale in an attractive setting is pretty much the sum of it, and people arrive by the bus-load to take advantage of the bargain prices. Also available are hand-made goods in leather, lace and basketwork; the elaborate babies' outfits are a sight apart. Food stalls, amateur musicians, and people selling puppies keep the place lively.

Serra dos Orgãos

Like Itaipava, Teresópolis seems to consist of one long road, even if it does change names five times along the way. At the Rio end of town is the great treasure of Teresópolis, the **Parque Nacional da Serra dos Orgãos ❹**, created in 1939 to protect an area of rich biodiversity, and covering 11,000 hectares (27,000 acres). An overview of the park can best be appreciated from the **Soberbo Belvedere** at the top of the Rio–Teresópolis highway. Contrary to what one might imagine, the Serra dos Orgãos (Organs) mountain range and park are named not for their clear anatomical allusions, but for their resemblance to the pipes of a church organ.

As has been mentioned before, the Empress Teresa Cristina never actually visited the town named after her. But she is here for ever now: an impressive statue of a stern-looking lady in Victorian dress marks the top of the highway, where the view is at its best. She is looking out to distant Rio, and seems almost to be in motion. Note that she is

carrying an umbrella. This is no mere artistic embellishment, but a necessity in this area which is not called "rainforest" for nothing.

Natural wonders

The national park may only be entered through the official entrance points, at Teresópolis, Petrópolis, and Guapimirim, where you get tickets (small charge). At the main Teresópolis entrance there is a visitor center. The park is open to visitors from 8am–5pm, but it is also possible to camp overnight, for a small fee, providing this is booked in advance (tel: (21) 2642-1070). Obviously, visitors should not pick plants, light fires, or drop litter, and are also asked not to make noise that would disturb the birds or animals.

The park provides a show of the natural world that would be hard to beat. Underfoot, the carpet of fallen leaves on the forest floor, decomposing and ready to be reabsorbed into an endless cycle; and above, a canopy of green, harboring hundreds of species of birds – more than 265 species according to the park's

official statistics. There are also around 60 species of animals. Walking trails, waterfalls and swimming areas make it a delightful place to spend a day.

The Finger of God

The Soberbo Belvedere provides an unforgettable vista: the **Dedo de Deus** (Finger of God), perennially pointing upwards. Rising to over 1,692 meters (5,500 ft), the finger is but one of the peaks that make up this range, other notable ones being **Pedra do Sino** (Bell Mountain) at 2,260 meters (7,400 ft) (a difficult, four-hour climb) and the **Nariz do Frade** (The Friar's Nose), with its optional extra (sometimes called "the pimple") balanced on the top.

The view over Rio is stunning, especially after a holiday weekend, when the furnaces of industrial Rio have been switched off for a few days and the air is cleaner. Sugar Loaf and Corcovado can be seen, lording it over the bay. It is obvious why the early settlers thought they had entered a river; and equally obvious why they stayed. ❑

Map on pages 174–75

TIP

At Guapimirim, to the south of the park, you can visit the Von Martius Museum, named after German naturalist Carl Friedrich Von Martius (1794–1868), another visiting European naturalist, who was sent here on a mission in 1817.

RESTAURANTS

Locanda della Mimosa
Alameda das Mimosas 30, Vale Florido, Tel: (24) 2233-5405. L only Fri; L & D Sat–Sun. **$$$$**
Here we have haute cuisine in the highlands of Rio. Danio Braga is considered to be one of Brazil's best chefs, and with good reason. The fact that his restaurant is situated off the beaten track doesn't deter his fans, who would gladly follow him even further afield. Six

stunning guest rooms are provided for the lucky few *(see also under Accommodation, page 213).*

Majorica
Rua do Imperador 754, Petrópolis. Tel: (24) 2242-2498. 11am–late, daily. **$$**
Majorica is a traditional steak house which spurns modern trends such as buffets. Excellent rump steak remains the menu's best-seller, but there are dishes with sauces,

and some good fish options, too, in case non-carnivores drop by.

Pousada Alcobaça
Rua Dr Agostinho Goulão 298, Corrêas, Petrópolis. Tel: (24) 2221-1240. 8am–late, daily. **$$$**
This delightful guest house situated on the outskirts of Petrópolis could be called a little piece of heaven. It provides simply prepared home cooking of the highest standard. Most of the vegetables served are home grown *(see also under Accommodation, page 213).*

Solar do Imperio
Avenida Koeler 376, Petrópolis. Tel: (24) 2103-3000. L & D daily. **$$**
Wonderfully located in grand downtown Petrópolis, the restaurant of this relatively recent hotel is beautifully appointed. It offers an attractive menu, including a good-value *prix fixe* lunch during the week.

● ● ● ● ● ● ● ● ● ● ●
Prices for a two-course meal for two. Wine costs around $20 a bottle. **$$$$** *= more than* $100, **$$$** *= $60–100,* **$$** *= $35–60,* **$** *= under $35.*

BÚZIOS AND THE SUN COAST

Búzios has been transformed from a quiet fishing village into an international resort. Out of season it is still peaceful, and its clear waters and idyllic beaches make it a tropical paradise all year round

According to history books, **Búzios 5** was discovered by the Portuguese at the start of the 16th century. Local people, however, know better. Búzios was actually discovered in 1964, by Brigitte Bardot. Convinced by an Argentine friend to visit this tropical paradise, Bardot enjoyed two well-documented stays in Búzios, parading her famed bikini-clad torso along its incomparable beaches and, in the process, spreading the fame of Búzios across the globe.

The memory of Bardot may have faded, but the little town hasn't been the same since. A life-sized bronze of Bardot sitting by a battered suitcase and staring sightlessly at the Rua das Pedras, the town's buzzing main street, pays testimony to her far from unanimously welcomed role as "discoverer." It mysteriously disappeared for a while in 2005, but has since been returned.

Hedonism in the sun

Búzios was once a tranquil fishing peninsula fronting the lapping waters of a bay. Its name is a reference to the formerly plentiful conches used by fishermen to communicate with each other. The town's full name, in fact, is Armação de Búzio – Armação means "trap," an allusion to the whale traps that were set along its beaches. Praia dos Ossos (Bones Beach) is where the whale carcasses where dragged once their precious oil had been extracted. But a name is only a name, and after Bardot, Búzios came to represent everything that splendor in the tropics is supposed to be – endless, unspoiled beaches, palm trees and coconuts, beautiful people, and a relaxing, intoxicating lifestyle of serious hedonism beneath an unceasing tropical sun.

Map on pages 174–75

LEFT: keeping a watchful eye on things in Búzios.
BELOW: the Fishermen's Union in Rua das Pedras.

*Brigitte Bardot,
immortalized in
bronze.*

BELOW: hire a beach
buggy to get the most
out of the coast.

The Sun Coast

Located 190 km (115 miles) to the east of Rio, along what is known as the **Sun Coast** (Costa do Sol), Búzios is a sophisticated, international resort that nine months of the year just manages to retain the air of a tranquil fishing village. The high season, however, is another matter: from December until after Carnival (in February) Búzios is overrun by tourists, its population of 20,000 multiplying sixfold. Even the die-hard true resident community finds "the season" just a little bit too busy.

The village occasionally lacks the infrastructure to receive and cater for everyone who wants to visit it, and systems break down: water can become scarce and traffic comes to a standstill. However, it is hoped that in the medium term this will change, as Búzios has achieved its long-awaited political emancipation from neighboring Cabo Frio, and the local people will now have more say in how their tax money is spent.

The fashionable homes that dot the Búzios beachscape for the most part blend in with the picturesque fishing village. Many new arrivals have purchased homes from the fishermen. Architectural harmony has been retained, however, as they remodel them on the inside while the outer shells look no different from their traditional neighbors.

Improved communications

People who have been coming here for years tell tales of nightmare car journeys from Rio lasting anything up to 12 hours, but these have now been relegated to the history books. Major roadworks, following the privatization of the highway linking Rio to Búzios, have reduced traveling time significantly, and the scenic drive can now be done easily in two-and-a-half hours. Holiday weekends still see massive traffic jams, however, and should be avoided if at all possible. Visitors should beware of the "sleeping policemen," or speed bumps, that punctuate the approach to the city, and succeed in slowing down the traffic.

Although Búzios now has a small airport, this principally serves privately owned aircraft and charter flights. However, regular flights by TEAM Airlines link Rio and São Paulo with Cabo Frio, some 23 km (15 miles) away by road. Comfortable buses run between Rio and Búzios at regular intervals and are a good way of getting here, especially in the high season and on holiday weekends, when a car can become a real handicap.

Certainly, having your own vehicle gives you flexibility, but visiting all the beaches by land is not only tiring but unnecessary, as the fishermen of Búzios have become part-time tour operators, and visitors can rent boats by the hour or day for cruises along the beaches. Sailboats, as well as cars, dune buggies, bikes, motorcycles, and horses may also be rented, as may all the equipment needed by diving enthusiasts.

Hospitality

Búzios is a fickle market, vulnerable to the whims of inconstant patrons, the local labor force's relaxed approach to work, and the weather; running a business there is something of a challenge. Perhaps this is why many service outlets – bars, restaurants, *pousadas* – are owner-operated. People running their own businesses will always put in the requisite number of hours and pay attention to details. Until the international chain operators move in, personal attention will remain the hallmark of Búzios hospitality.

This hospitality can be enjoyed at many of the *pousadas*, the small inns that dot the landscape: Le Palmier on Praia da Ferradura (Horseshoe Beach), the Martin Pescador on Manguinhos Beach, and Le Relais de la Borie on Geribá all share a long-standing reputation for excellence.

There are literally dozens of others, and it is quite in order for visitors to ask to see a room, check the view, inspect the tariff, and then, if they are not satisfied, move on to something more suited to their style. This is not considered impolite. Noise, or the lack of it, should feature in your choice of accommodation, as Rua das Pedras really does go all night, and light sleepers will be non-sleepers.

Trolley tours

There's no better way to get your bearings than by taking the Búzios Trolley *(see margin for details)*. Specially adapted trucks carry 35 passengers per trip, protected from the sun by a canopy but open on the sides to the cooling breezes. They set off at their appointed time regardless of the number of passengers. Tours leave at 9am, noon, and 3pm and last for two hours, and are the best way to get an overview of Búzios, its beaches and neighborhoods, all with their different characteristics. If you're early for the trolley, you can have a quick nine holes at the minigolf course.

You start the tour on the Orla Bardot, the seaside road and path named in honor of Búzios's illustrious 1960s visitor. Your next land-

Map on pages 174–75

Búzios Trolley tours start from Praia da Armação (tel: (22) 2623-2763). They cost about US$15, which includes fruit, soft drinks, and snacks.

BELOW: Olho de Boi – one of Búzios's many lovely beaches.

TIP

A reliable tour operator, which runs a full-service agency for all local attractions, is Mister Tour, Rua das Pedras 21, tel: (22) 2623-2100 and (22) 2623-1022. The Búzios Trolley Company offers a similar service *(see previous page for contact details)*.

BELOW: a boat full of refreshments means you don't have to go far for a drink.

mark will be the Yacht Club and the port area, where massive cruise ships dock and disgorge hundreds of visitors all through the season, for Búzios is very much on the cruise-ship trail these days.

You will notice that the fishing origins of the village are commemorated here with a clever *trompe l'oeil* group of sculpted fishermen eternally hauling in their catch: their hats provide a great perch for the frigate birds.

You then head off in the direction of the northernmost point of the peninsula, toward João Fernandes Beach. Sumptuous summer homes line the roads, and the occasional windsock indicates that some of the homeowners are true high flyers, accustomed to using helicopters to beat the traffic.

Doubling back on itself, the trolley climbs up to a lookout spot, high above **Praia Brava**. The next stop reveals the stunning views of **Praia do Forno** and **Praia da Foca**. As it goes southwards, it takes you to the always popular **Praia Ferradura** (Horseshoe Beach).

The beaches

In all, you visit 12 beaches on the trolley tour, just over half of the 23 beaches in the Búzios area, some of them fronting onto quiet coves and inlets, others onto the open sea. The main distinction, though, is accessibility. Beaches close to the town, such as Ossos, which is especially beautiful at sunset, Geriba, and Ferradura are easily reached on foot or by car. Not surprisingly, the "best" beaches – as in most parts of the world – are those that require the most effort to reach.

Outdoor excitement

Apart from beach-hopping in water taxis and generally soaking up the sun, there are plenty of fun excursions to be made from Búzios. It makes sense to use one of the professional tour operators, who know the ropes and take the guesswork out of things *(see margin note)*. Cabo Frio is the nearest large town, and really quite missable.

Arraial do Cabo, some 30 minutes south by car from Búzios, is worth a visit for its crystal clear,

greenish-blue waters which make it very popular with divers. The views from the Pontal do Atalaia are especially spectacular. **Sana** and **Casemiro de Abreu** are both within easy distance of Búzios, and make use of the incredible scenery and the best the natural world has to offer in terms of leisure activities. Whitewater rafting, rappeling, country walks, horseback riding, and showering in cool, clear waterfalls are all available, offering a pure adrenaline rush in storybook surroundings.

Back closer to Búzios, if you feel overdressed in a fig leaf, the Praia Olho de Boi (Bull's-Eye Beach) is the place for you: this tiny beach, reachable only by foot from Praia Brava on the northeastern coast of the peninsula, is an officially designated nudist beach.

Lazy days, late nights

Days start late in Búzios, probably because the nights go on and on. *Pousadas* serve buffet breakfasts until 10.30am, after which people start to drift about the place. Most head for the beaches, others wander along **Rua das Pedras**, a thriving commercial center, albeit over ankle-breaking cobbles, where some of the most attractive shops in Brazil have branches. Before noon, there is a definite air of "the morning after" on this street, silent and still after the revels of the night before.

Life after dark

Búzios comes alive at night, with people from all backgrounds rubbing shoulders down the main street. Headquarters for the noise and hubbub is often outside Chez Michou, a huge crêperie serving freshly sizzled, filled crêpes, cold beers, and loud music.

When it comes to knife-and-fork food, Búzios is a good place to be. Its culinary past is probably more august than its future. Among those who came to Búzios in its days of culinary glory in the 1970s and 1980s was Claude Troisgros: he moved the gastronomic goalposts slightly closer together. Now resident in Rio, he is the undisputed master of the amalgam of French cooking and Brazilian ingredients.

This tribute to the former slave colony in Hasa may give visitors pause for thought.

BELOW: oysters don't come much fresher than this.

Emerências Reserve

An organization called IEBMA (Búzios Atlantic Forest Ecological Institute) organizes ecological walks through the Emerências Reserve. The walks usually start from Caravelas Beach on Monday, Wednesday, and Friday during the high season. Tracks lead through stretches of practically untouched Atlantic Forest, with flora and fauna typical of the region. If you are lucky (and quiet), you may see endangered Golden lion tamarin monkeys along the way. Wear sensible shoes, cover yourself in sunscreen, and take plenty of drinking water. For details, contact IEBMA at Km 5, Estrada Velha de Búzios (Old Búzios Road), tel: (22) 2623-2200.

Map on pages 174–75

A local handicraft shop offers all kinds of gifts and souvenirs.

BELOW:
the always-popular
Praia Ferradura
(Horseshoe Beach).

However, excellent meals can also be enjoyed at Le Cigalon, Don Juan, and Brigitta's, all on Rua das Pedras. A little further on, in the direction of the Bardot bronze, is Satyricon, a branch of the upmarket Ipanema fish restaurant.

Informal snacks of all descriptions can be had from any vendor on any corner; multicolored, knock-out cocktails are whizzed up in a blender there and then, and poured into an ice-filled, plastic cup. It is not for nothing that the English-speaking residents call the village "Booze-ious".

Plenty of action

When Bacchus gives way, once more, to breakfast, there is plenty to do in Búzios. Watersports are easily catered for, and traditional schooners cruise the waters on full- and half-day jaunts. Visitors can hop into a water-taxi and simply point to the beach of their choice.

If you want to do the beaches in style and be looked after, you could take a (fairly expensive) trip on one of the many schooners that tour the area. *Caipirinhas* (those lovely, but sometimes lethal, *cachaça*-based drinks), fresh fruit and soft drinks are all included in the price, and the crew keep an eye on children and non-swimmers.

Back on dry land, Búzios is putting itself on the golfing map with a challenging, links-type 18-hole course, designed by Peter Dye. Visitors pay a green fee, and are always welcome. In fact, they are more likely to get a tee time here than in any of the members-only clubs of Rio itself *(see page 223).*

Búzios magic

What makes Búzios so special? Is it the stunning scenery? Is it the searing sunshine? Is it the happy mix of nationalities – Brazilians, Argentinians, French, Dutch, Americans – all at play together? Or the brilliant bougainvillea, winding its searching purple fingers through walls and fences? It is true that Búzios is showing signs of wear and tear. It is no longer the idyllic fishing village of yore, but a thriving resort. Despite this, it is still special. ❑

RESTAURANTS

Restaurants

The number of restaurant options in Búzios is staggering, but it is a fickle market, especially in the outlying beach areas, and many establishments don't make it past their first season. We have selected the stalwarts of the market that have stood the test of time, but this list is very selective. Poke your nose into, or wander through, any restaurant that takes your fancy; all tastes and pockets are catered for in Búzios.

Bar do Zé
Orla Bardot 382, Center. Tel: (22) 2623-4986. D only daily. $$$
Despite its unprepossessing name, this is a fine eatery, serving gourmet fare. The menu varies according to what's fresh in the market on the day – always a good sign.

Boom
Rua Manoel Turíbio de Farias 110, Center. Tel: (24) 2623-6254. L & D daily. $–$$
Boom is a cheerful, practical self-service eatery spread over several floors. You can choose your own grilled meat right off the barbecue, and fill up on fries, vegetables and all sorts of salads from a wide selection on offer.

Brigitta's
Rua das Pedras 131, Center. Tel: (24) 2623-6157. 5pm–late, daily. $$$
Unmissable on the stony street, Brigitta's is a real and long-lasting landmark, celebrating life. Shrimp and lobster figure prominently on the menu, but there are less expensive choices to be had, and they are all very good.

Chez Michou
Rua das Pedras 90, Center. Tel: (22) 2623-2169. 5pm–late, daily. $
A Búzios monument and meeting place for local people and visitors alike. They specialize in inexpensive crêpes, filled in imaginative ways, and there's always lots of noise. No credit cards accepted at the time of writing.

Cigalon
Rua das Pedras 265, Center. Tel: (22) 2623-6284. 6pm–late Mon–Sat; 1pm–late Sun. $$$
Enterprising menu in a sophisticated setting. Many of the dishes have a French touch, and the desserts are very fine indeed.

Estância Dom Juan
Rua das Pedras 178, Center. Tel: (22) 2623-2169. noon to late, daily. $$$
A themed Argentine restaurant serving melt-in your mouth beef. It's a delightful setting, and it's occasionally livened up by a tango evening.

Guapo Loco
Rua das Pedras 233, Center. Tel: (22) 2623-2657. 6pm–late, daily. $$
If you crave chili, this is the place to come. Here you can savor tacos, burritos, re-fried beans and all things Mexican. Guapo Loco also has branches in Niterói and Rio (Leblon), which are also recommended for those who like fiery food.

Sawasdee
Orla Bardot 422, Center. Tel: (22) 2623-4644. 6pm–late Thur–Tues. $$$–$$$$
A touch of Thai: plenty of ginger and tamarind, in the happy company of freshly caught seafood and a great atmosphere.

S´Essa Rua Fosse Minha
Rua das Pedras 133, Center. Tel: (22) 2643-2261. 1pm–late Fri–Sun; 3pm–late Mon, Tues, Thur. $$
A new kid on the block, which opened in 2004 in a former art gallery. There's a lovely veranda overlooking the ocean and Canto Beach, and they specialize in seafood; lots of variety on the menu.

PRICE CATEGORIES

Prices for a two-course meal for two. Wine costs around $20 a bottle:
$ = under $35
$$ = $35–$60
$$$ = $60–$100
$$$$ = more than $100

RIGHT: strolling past Chez Michou on Rua das Pedras.

FLORA AND FAUNA

No matter what time of year you visit Rio, there's always something in flower, in fruit, or simply stunningly beautiful

Among the whirl of buses and hooting taxis in downtown Rio, flowering trees bloom enthusiastically, and the odd bunch of bananas ripens in a garden. On the seafront, smart buildings have luxuriant little gardens overflowing with exotic plants; and hundreds of humble Busy Lizzies, *impatiens*, are everywhere, even sprouting from cracks in the walls of derelict buildings.

Public planting is taken seriously here, mainly due to the influence of landscaper Roberto Burle Marx *(see page 159)*; bold use of contrasting leaf colors and plenty of pebbles make for some striking displays. Spiky plants, such as the Crown of Thorns, are often used to preserve parks and gardens from the attentions of pedestrians; and the palms, with their trunks bedecked with necklaces of jewel-like seeds, are a real treat, especially for visitors from cooler climes.

ABOVE: there's no better place to see nature in action than the lake in the Jardim Botânico. Get there early to see toucans leap from palm to palm, and watch the hummingbirds dart from bloom to bloom.

ABOVE LEFT: carmine hibiscus, egg-yolk-colored allamandas, cherry-pink crêpe myrtles, all colors thrive in these perfect conditions, even white.

BELOW: bromeliads are self-contained little worlds, home to tiny frogs and all manner of insects. This huge botanical family contains some real treasures – including the pineapple. Some bromeliad fibers are strong enough to be woven into hammocks and other household items.

RIGHT: turtles sun themselves beside the pond at the entrance to the Jardim Botânico, then plunge back into the pond for a cooling dip. What a life!

FAUNA

Ornithologists will find plenty of interest at the zoo, but they may not find it necessary to make that trek, as any quiet square will be visited by a staggering variety of birds. First on the scene may well be the Yellow-breasted great kiscadee, which looks somewhat sinister, as if he is wearing wraparound sunglasses. The Rufous-bellied thrush might be next: he resembles a robin, but is at least three times the size of anything that appears on a frosty Christmas card. Harmless and huge lizards are best observed on the warm rocks at the top of the Corcovado mountain, and on the Claudio Coutinho walk in Urca. But for many, the stars will be the mischievous marmosets, as they perform their acrobatics on the overhead electricity cables, as if rehearsing for some simian circus.

ABOVE: the Masked water tyrant is a frequent flier here. Swift and acrobatic, it positively dances about the place.

LEFT: a distant relative of the heliconia *(below)* is the Emperor's staff, actually a native of Asia, though you wouldn't guess this from the enthusiasm with which it blooms in the Rio area. It is especially attractive to butterflies and birds

RIGHT: heliconias, often growing alongside gingers, stand proud, and intrigue horticulturalists and casual observers alike with their strength and symmetry.

ABOVE: looking rather like a cross between a pig, a dog, and a cartoon-sized rat, is the agouti, a placid, herbivorous rodent. The place to see it is the Campo de Santana in downtown Rio, where it lives in apparent oblivion to the swirling traffic and surrounding mayhem.

RIGHT: the elegant iguana is cool and green. Look but don't touch: he's not crazy about humans, and may turn nasty.

COSTA VERDE

Relaxation and unspoiled tropical beauty, along with a fascinating history, are among the pleasures offered by the Costa Verde, an area within easy reach of Rio, by public as well as private transport

Map on pages 174–75

LEFT: Angra dos Reis (Kings' Cove) was once a vital port.
BELOW: smooth rock formations on Santo Antonio Beach, Ilha Grande.

The Costa Verde stretches 260 km (160 miles) southwest from Rio to the São Paulo state border. It is nature at its best: a splendid tropical mix of mountains, rainforest, beaches, and islands. Not for nothing is it called the Green Coast, for green, in every imaginable shade, is everywhere.

Visiting the area is easy and enjoyable on coastal Highway BR101, known as the Rio–Santos highway, for the two port cities it connects. An excellent service operates punctual and comfortable buses linking Rio and the area. The drive is breathtaking in places, as the road rises high up a mountainside for a wide, unobstructed view, then drops and winds steeply down to the shoreline.

Danger signs

A word of caution: if you're renting a car, don't drive at night. Not only do you miss all the scenery, but also in the dark, the highway – with its sharp curves, unmarked hard shoulders and the odd crater – can be extremely dangerous. The road passes fascinating, contrasting extremes: a national park, a nuclear power plant, tourist resorts, fishing settlements, tanking stations, cattle ranches, a shipyard, and Paraty, a quaint, colonial village. The most popular attractions are, naturally

enough, the beaches. Some are small, encased by rocky cliffs, with clear, tranquil lagoons. Others stretch uninterrupted for miles, and are pounded by rough surf. The whole area is a haven for sports enthusiasts, offering everything from tennis, golf and boating to surfing, deep-sea fishing, diving, hiking, and river rafting.

The area is also a haven for mosquitoes, so insect repellent is a must. It's also advisable to take light cotton trousers and shirts or blouses with long sleeves for evenings.

Schooner trips

After leaving Rio on Avenida das Américas through Barra and Recreio, the highway turns inland past Santa Cruz and returns to the coast some 60 km (40 miles) later at **Itacuruçá 6** (pop. 3,500), where the Costa Verde really begins. From the town's harbor, schooners, which take up to 40 people, leave every morning at around 10am on one-day excursions to the nearby tropical islands (there are 36 of them) in the surrounding Sepetiba Bay.

These trips are well-planned and good value, and include stops for swimming and snorkeling and a seafood lunch on one of the islands. Reservations can be made in advance through a Rio tourist agency or your hotel.

Angra dos Reis

"At times I was transported by the aroma of the trees and flowers, and the flavors of the fruits and seeds, so much so that I thought I had reached an earthly paradise. How can I describe the number of birds, the colors of their feathers and their song, how many there were, and how beautiful? I won't go on, as I doubt anyone will believe me."

These are the words of Amerigo Vespucci, a member of the expedition that first ventured into the tropical paradise of the bay of Ilha Grande on January 6, 1502 – Dia dos Reis, or the Day of Kings in the Church calendar.

Originally just a small settlement built around a church, over the next century the town that would eventually become known as **Angra dos Reis 7**, or Kings' Cove, grew in importance, largely due to the strategic location of its port, in a sheltered bay on a peninsula. The first produce from the area was sugar cane, and later Angra port was used in the shipment of gold coming from Minas Gerais.

In the 19th century it was at the hub of the coffee boom, and enjoyed rapid physical and economic growth until the abolition of slavery in 1888, the failure of the coffee crops in the state of Rio, and the construction of new roads and a railway link between São Paulo and Rio. All this progress left Angra somewhat abandoned and unnecessary. Today, the region looks mainly out to sea for its sustenance as, apart from the banana plantations inland, fishing and tourism have taken over as the main source of income.

Weekend escape

The beautiful beaches and sheltered bays of Angra, plus its accessibility from the city, make it a favorite weekend spot for stressed *cariocas*, many of whom have bought into the numerous condominiums in the area or built sumptuous houses. Some of the super-wealthy own whole islands, like the internationally famous plastic surgeon, Ivo Pitanguy, and a helicopter pad is de rigueur for many. But the region caters for all kinds of people and

TIP

On New Year's Day Angra dos Reis hosts a huge maritime procession of beautifully decorated boats, many hosting on-board parties.

BELOW: fishing boats in Itacuruçá harbor.

bank balances, and every type of accommodation is available, from campsites through bed and breakfasts *(pousadas)* to luxury hotels.

The city – unprepossessing at the best estimate – sprawls over several hills at the beginning of a 100-km (60-mile) long gulf that contains 365 islands, 2,000 beaches, seven bays, and countless coves. The water is warm, clear and calm, a perfect sanctuary for marine life. Spear fishing along the rocky shores is a popular activity, as is fishing in deeper waters. Hiring a boat to take you to one of the island beaches is essential in order to appreciate fully what the region has to offer. Angra is, essentially, a stepping-stone to some earthly paradises, although the town itself is entirely missable.

Eating and sleeping

The Costa Verde is not renowned for its gourmet restaurants, but that does not mean to say you will not eat well. Local seafood is abundant and varied, and some of the most delicious food is to be had in the most unexpected places.

There are numerous *pousadas* in the Angra area, and their prices and quality vary, but there is plenty of accommodation to be had in the clean, comfortable, and reasonably priced category.

There are several good resort hotels in the area. Located on a beach 7 km (4 miles) outside town, the Blue Tree Park *(see Accommodation, page 216)* is a comprehensive resort hotel and convention center, offering watersports, pools, spa facilities, and tennis alongside the natural beauty of the region. The rooms are comfortable and well appointed, and there is a good choice of restaurants and bars.

The Frade Hotels Group was a pioneer in the area with the Hotel do Frade *(for details, see Accommodation, page 216)*; they also run the only golf course in the area. The 325-room Club Med is another resort option, located near Mangaratiba, on the Rio–Santos highway. The hotels will arrange transport from Rio if required, and have their own catamarans which tour the nearby islands.

TIP

There are fast-track ferries that run passengers in small boats from Ilha Grande to Mangaratiba, where buses wait to deliver them to Rio hotels or direct to the airport. Information on the harbor front in Abraão.

BELOW: boarding the island ferry in Mangaratiba.

In Vila do Abraão, even the shopping malls are pretty.

Ilha Grande ~~Island~~

...nety minutes by boat from Angra ...Mangaratiba is the paradise island of **Ilha Grande** ⑧ (Large Island), partially covered by dense Atlantic forest, and with mangroves reaching down to the water. Ilha Grande can be reached by inexpensive ferries which run daily from Mangaratiba and Angra dos Reis.

The schedule is as follows: Mangaratiba to Ilha Grande departs at 8am, with an extra ferry on Friday at 10pm. Return from Ilha Grande to Mangaratiba is at 5.30pm. From Angra dos Reis to Ilha Grande, ferries depart at 3.30pm during the week, and at 1.30pm at weekends. Return to Angra is at 10am, throughout the week. The cost of the trip is approximately US$3 on weekdays, double that amount at weekends.

The 300-sq. km (115-sq. mile) island is blessed with some spectacular fauna and flora, with waterfalls and limpid pools, and some of the country's most beautiful tropical beaches – there are said to be 106 of them in all.

BELOW: floating restaurant at Mangues Beach.
BELOW RIGHT: walking across the island to Lopes Mendes Beach.

The pristine state of an island so close to Rio is due to the existence, for many years, of a high-security jail – Cândido Mendes – which housed both hardened criminals and political prisoners, and from which there were some sensational escapes. It was only after the unit was closed, and the building blown up, in 1994, that tourism took off and visitors began to arrive, first in a trickle, then in greater numbers. At present, the infrastructure is still fairly basic, and there is a glorious absence of high-rise modern hotels.

The islanders used to live mainly from fishing, and from canning and smoking the catch, but the fishing fleet has now dwindled, and the island is faced with the dilemma that affects many beautiful but economically deprived parts of the world. Tourism is the industry that may save the economy, but tourism, if badly handled, could ruin the natural beauty and ecology of the island.

Fortunately, this threat is being taken seriously. The whole island is a protected area, divided into three specific regions: a state park (cre-

ated in 1971), a marine state park, and the biological reserve of Praia do Sul, created in 1981. Most of the agencies that bring tourists to Ilha Grande specialize in "eco-tourism" and stress the need to protect and preserve the natural attributes and traditional values of the island.

Abraão

Vila do Abraão, the "capital," has about 500 permanent inhabitants, and is the largest of the three settlements on the island. It is the landing point for visitors from the mainland – as well as for most of the supplies needed to keep the inhabitants and tourists fed, watered, and comfortable. It has just two streets running parallel to the sea and five narrow lanes crossing them, all lined with wooden-shuttered buildings painted in bright primary colors.

An increasing number of simple hotels are opening up, but they are all in traditional two- or three-story buildings, most of them family homes converted to simple *pousadas* along the palm-lined beachfront. This is an expanding market,

Map on pages 174–75

and visitors are encouraged to research accommodation in advance of arriving in Rio, especially over long weekends and holidays. There are quite a few restaurants, too, serving excellent seafood.

The 21st century has arrived in the form of a couple of internet cafés, but public phone boxes are still the only places from which you can telephone the mainland. There are no cars on the island – apart from an ambulance and a police car, which seems to troll up and down without much to do – and visitors' luggage is conveyed from the harbor to their hotel on trolleys or wheelbarrows.

Praia Preta

A short walk leads to **Praia Preta**, west of Abraão, and the site of the Lazareto, an old quarantine facility built in the mid-19th century, that is misleadingly known as O Leprosário (Lepers' Home). In fact, it was used to quarantine immigrants, who were kept here for 40 days to determine whether they were carrying any infectious diseases after

The tower of Abraão's little white church.

BELOW: sarongs and hammocks for sale in Vila do Abraão.

their sea voyages. This became the site of the first prison, before the high-security facility was built at the other side of the island, in Dois Rios. The Lazareto building was then imploded, and only the dank ruins remain.

Ruins of an old aqueduct that supplied the Lazareto are still standing near by, and you can wander down to what is known as the slaves' pool. A large rock protruding from the middle, with iron hooks still embedded, is said to have been used to attach the slaves' chains, so they could bathe, but not escape.

Exploring the island

Abraão has a pretty little beach of its own, where you can watch the gaily colored boats bobbing in the harbor, but if you want even better beaches and even more tranquility, there are other idyllic sandy stretches within easy walking distance along wooded paths; or you can hop on one of the vessels running a sort of water-bus service at hourly intervals. Alternatively, you can rent a small boat to take you to some of those slightly further afield, such as secluded **Saco do Céu**, surrounded by mangroves.

You can walk across the narrowest part of the island to **Lopes Mendes Beach** on the Atlantic side. The walk is delightful, and, if you do it early enough in the morning, is a great opportunity for birdwatching or even hearing the calls of howler monkeys, but it takes about two hours, and can be tiring in the heat of the day. Wear strong shoes and take plenty of water.

The long stretch of Lopes Mendes Beach, with white sand so fine it squeaks beneath your feet, is completely devoid of any buildings or commercial enterprises, apart from a few beach vendors selling cold drinks from cool bags.

Said to be the most beautiful beach in Brazil, Lopes Mendes is a popular spot for surfing, but currents in the clear turquoise waters can be extremely strong, and it is essential that surfers and swimmers stay in designated areas and obey the whistles and shouts of the ever-vigilant lifeguards.

TIP

There are *capoeira* classes held in the Casa de Cultura in Abraão. Visitors are welcome to join in, although the energetic mix of dance and martial arts may defeat all but the very fittest.

BELOW: the wide white sands of Lopes Mendes Beach.

If you fancy the beach but not the walk, you can get a boat from Abraão to Mangues Beach, from where it's only a 20-minute walk. Enjoy the breaking surf at Praia de Santo António, spectacular for its scenery, on the way. Small boats are not equipped to venture round the tip of the island into the gusty Atlantic waters.

Adventures on the island

For the adventurous, there's a longer hike across the island to **Praia da Parnaioca**, a lovely beach close to an almost deserted fishing community – the inhabitants fled after being terrorized by escaped prisoners from Cândido Mendes.

Or you could climb the 960-m (3,150-ft) peak called the **Bico do Papagaio** (Parrot's Beak), which resembles its name. If you do so, take water and mosquito repellent, and make sure somebody knows where you've gone. It's not a particularly difficult climb if you're fit, but the weather can change rapidly, and clouds and mist descend in no time, which can be disorientating.

Picturesque villages

Tear yourself away from paradise and return to the mainland, where there are more treats in store. A short way to the west of Angra dos Reis lies the picturesque village of **Mambucaba** ❾. The houses are built right on the wide, sandy beach, and a large white church in the town center faces out to sea. The simple little colony attracts a bohemian crowd, including a number of musicians who help maintain a lively atmosphere. The waves here are also very popular with surfers.

Continue down the coast past Paraty *(see page 201)*. Due south of the town is one of the coast's most carefully guarded treasures, the tiny fishing village of **Trindade** ❿. Once a haven for pirates, Trindade has some spectacular beaches with clean, clear waters. One of them, Cachadaço, is known for its large, natural pool formed by smooth volcanic rocks; while Cepilho is the surfers' favorite.

All in all, the Costa Verde has a lot to offer, and none of it very far from Rio. ❏

The road from Rio is a good one, which means you can be in paradise in no time at all.

RESTAURANTS

The pit stops on the BR-101, the Rio–Santos highway, are not noteworthy, with the exception of the Morro do Côco, Frade Hotel's restaurant. Ilha Grande offers plenty of choice, most eateries being extremely informal. Many are merely the homes of fishermen, whose wives don their aprons to provide for the visitors. Being owner-operated, they offer friendly service. Don't expect linen tablecloths, just some terrific seafood. However, there are a few smarter places as well.

Casarão da Ilha
Praia de Abraão, Ilha Grande. Tel: (24) 9987-3032. **$$**
Great food, right by the beach.

Lua e Mar
Praia do Canto. Tel: (24) 3361-5113. **$$**
Delicious fish served at tables set out on the sand. Try the *moqueca*, a rich, Bahian-style fish stew that involves coconut milk and palm oil, along with fresh fish and prawns, and, of course, a dish of rice.

Morro do Côco
Hotel do Frade, Km 513, Rio–Santos highway. Tel: (24) 3369-9500. L & D Fri–Sun. **$$$**
Upmarket international cuisine in a spectacular setting, overlooking the bay and the hotel's own palm plantation.

O Pescador
Praia de Abraão, Ilha Grande. Tel: (24) 3361-5114. **$**
The very best of Brazilian cookery, in a superb setting. Also an excellent *pousada*.

Restaurante Recreio da Praia
Praia de Abraão, Ilha Grande. Tel: (24) 9987-3055. **$**
Well-prepared food in a storybook setting, with friendly service. If you want to stay the night, there are rooms to rent.

● ● ● ● ● ● ● ● ● ●
Prices for a two-course meal for two. Wine costs around $20 a bottle. **$$$$** = *more than $100,* **$$$** = *$60–100,* **$$** = *$35–60,* **$** = *under $35*

PARATY

Designated a UNESCO site of historical importance, Paraty is the jewel of the Costa Verde, a beautifully preserved colonial town with its own beaches that does a thriving trade in *cachaça*

The star of the Costa Verde lies some 100 km (60 miles) past Angra and a three-and-a-half-hour drive from Rio. **Paraty** ⑪ (pop. 32,500) is an attractive town of historical importance which in 1966 was designated an international monument by UNESCO. It's charm, bohemian reputation, and historical connotations have made it a favorite among visitors, both local people and those from overseas.

Paraty was founded in the early 1600s in the heart of the booming sugar cane-producing area, and, like Angra dos Reis, acquired great importance during the 18th century as one of the ports from which gold, diamonds, and precious stones from the state of Minas Gerais were shipped back to Portugal.

Constant attacks by pirates, coupled with the same factors that influenced the decline of Angra *(see page 194)*, meant that at the end of the 19th century Paraty lost its strategic position and went back to being a fishing village and a respected producer of *cachaça*, the strong cane spirit that forms the base of the *caipirinha*.

A forgotten town until the middle of the last century, Paraty managed to resist redevelopment, and is considered one of the finest examples of colonial heritage in Brazil.

Colonial area

The best way to get a feel for Paraty is to walk around the historic city center. You don't have to watch out for cars as they are prohibited in this part of town, but keep a careful eye on the bicycles and horse-drawn buggies. The large, shiny, uneven paving stones are a true test of balance. In a further challenge to your equilibrium, the roads slope in towards the center and down towards the sea to drain off heavy rains and flooding tides.

Map on pages 174–75

LEFT: the Casa de Cultura, picturesque without, fascinating within. **BELOW:** Paraty's churches have been repainted snowy white.

TIP

If you are wondering whether Parati or Paraty is the correct spelling, join the club. The letter "y" was excluded from the alphabet in Brazilian Spelling Reform in 1943, but the exclusion was not widely adopted. Quite appropriately, the literary festival followed the rules, and sticks to the modern spelling of Parati.

BELOW: a corner café sets tables out on the cobbled street.

Paraty is known for its extreme tides, with the water sometimes receding several hundred meters, leaving all the local fishing boats and dinghies stranded like abandoned toys. Conversely, at the full moon, the rising sea floods the streets near the port. Locals claim this cleans the streets, but often the dirt that is washed away is replaced by rotting seaweed.

Apart from the simple beauty of the architecture, visitors may notice the Masonic influence in the geometric designs that adorn some of the houses. Commercial activity in the 18th century attracted a strong Masonic contingent, whose influence can also be seen in the layout of the roads. Many are at odd angles to one another, the official reason being that these angles created a windbreak, and also allowed a more even distribution of sunlight among the houses.

Hidden treasures

Take your time as you wander around the town, browsing through the many galleries and handicraft stores, and peeking (politely) through the doorways of *pousadas* and private houses that open onto boldly landscaped courtyards decked out with ferns, orchids, rose bushes, and begonias.

Other treasures are produced by artists, who are drawn to the town as if by magnets. They keep an open-door policy, and you'll soon find their tiny homes, open to those who wish to wander in, filled with their work: papier mâché, wood-carvings, oil paintings, and mosaics.

The Rua do Comércio is bustling with restaurants, *pousadas* and shops selling local crafts, which include straw and woodwork, but do check out the old fish market, which is now an attractive craft market. It was built beside the port, but thanks to the Brazilian habit of appropriating bits of the sea through landfills, it is now several blocks inland.

Paraty's loveliest church is the **Igreja de Santa Rita** (1722), a classic example of Brazilian baroque, which houses a Museum of Sacred Art. Next to it, in what was once the town's prison, is a tourist informa-

Literary Festival

The Festival Literario de Parati (FLIP) was one of those ideas that started small and daring and has become huge and is still daring. To stage a literary festival in a town where probably less than 20 percent of the population has ever read anything other than a Bible takes quite a lot of daring. This is a quality that the mentor of FLIP, Liz Calder, has shown she possesses in no small measure. Her meteoric rise in the publishing world is one of the most impressive success stories of recent times. She has always trusted her instincts, and her friends have always trusted her. The result has been this annual madness which induces the likes of Paul Auster, Salman Rushdie, Margaret Atwood, Julian Barnes and Eric Hobsbawm to wander down the cobbled streets of Paraty and turn it into a world literary production, every act of which is watched by the international press.

Calder's involvement with Brazil, a country she loves, goes back a long way, stemming from the years she spent in São Paulo in the mid-1960s, working as a model. In 2004 she was awarded the Order of Merit for services to Brazilian culture.

tion office. **Nossa Senhora dos Remedios** is the oldest church in the town, having started life as a mud construction in 1646. By 1712 it was replaced with a grander place of worship made of stones stuck together with whale oil. By 1873 it was too modest to accommodate the faithful, and was replaced by the current structure, in neo-classical style.

Local culture

Paraty and its people have a great sense of identity, and this is never better displayed than in the stunning **Casa de Cultura** (Sun–Mon and Wed–Thur 10am–6.30pm, Fri–Sat 1–9.30pm; minimal admission charge), located at the intersection of Rua Dona Geralda and Rua Doutor Samuel Costa. This is a monument to Paraty and to its people, their simplicity and dignity. On the ground floor are a bookshop, souvenir shop, and café; upstairs is a permanent exhibition that is vibrant, full of personality and visually astonishing. We won't ruin it for you by going into detail; just make sure you visit the Casa de Cultura.

The Gold Trail

A recent and highly successful initiative has retraced the routes taken by the gold prospectors of the 1700s from the mines in Minas Gerais to the port of Paraty. This has provided yet another leisure option in the area, one which combines history, nature, adventure, and some fabulous scenery. Specially adapted open trucks take visitors to the village of **Penha**. From here there is a 2½-km (1½-mile) hike, accompanied by a most useful creature, the *frigo-burro* (cooler-donkey). This innovative beast of burden carries iced drinks for refreshment along the way. On arrival at the farmhouse, lunch awaits, as well as any number of outdoor activities, including just sitting around soaking up the historic surroundings. Departures are from the Teatro Espaço at Rua Dona Geralda 327 in the old town of Paraty (Wed–Sun 10am, returning by 4 or 5pm). Further information can be had on tel: (24) 3371-1575. The cost of the outing is approximately US$10, with a further US$US5 for lunch. ❏

Map on pages 174–75

Paraty produces cachaça, *and in shops all over town you will see shelves lined with bottles of all shapes, sizes, and colors.*

RESTAURANTS

Paraty is one of those places where you wander around and stop when a bar or restaurant takes your fancy. There are numerous places to go for a drink and a small plate of something, before moving on to more of the same somewhere else. Below are listed the top-of-the-range knife-and-fork options for when you want a full meal.

Banana da Terra
Rua Doutor Samuel Costa 198. Tel: (24) 3371 1725. D Mon, Wed, Thur; L & D Fri–Sun. $$–$$$
Seafood partnered with basic local ingredients. Some brave combinations can make for memorable meals.

Bartholomeu
Rua Doutor Samuel Costa 176. Tel: (24) 3371-5032. D only. $$–$$$
A touch of class. Fine dining in an 18th-century setting. Comfortable and very well appointed. Prime Argentine beef is a house specialty.

Merlin o Mago
Rua do Comércio 376. Tel: (24) 3371-2157. D only Thur–Tues. $$$
A touch of magic and whimsy at Merlin's, where the emphasis is on the freshness of ingredients and respect for their preparation. Very special, housed in a 1780s building.

Porto Entreposto Cultural
Rua do Comércio 14. Tel: (24) 3371-1058. L & D daily. $$–$$$
A spot of refinement.

Creative menu, and an attractive setting.

Refúgio
Praça da Bandeira 1. Tel: (24) 3371-2447. L & D daily. $$$
Nicely decorated, comfortable surroundings in which to enjoy some fine fish and other dishes. Lots of shrimp, which pushes the price up. One of the area's traditional restaurants.

● ● ● ● ● ● ● ● ● ● ● ●
Prices for a two-course meal for two. Wine costs around $20 a bottle. **$$$$** = *more than $100,* **$$$** = *$60–100,* **$$** = *$35–60,* **$** = *under $35*

TRANSPORT

GETTING THERE AND GETTING AROUND

GETTING THERE

By Air

An ever-increasing number of airlines offer international services to and from Rio de Janeiro with a variety of routes, but most incoming flights head for São Paulo first. Depending on where you are coming from, there are also direct flights to Rio de Janeiro and Brasília, Salvador, Recife, and Manaus on the Amazon River – all of which have air links with Rio. If Rio is your sole Brazilian destination, do try hard *not* to have to travel via São Paulo, as this is time-consuming and an added irritant to what is, for most people, already a long journey.

Direct international flights connect Rio with both the east and west coasts of the United States, as well as with Canada, major cities in Europe and South America, Japan, and several African cities. The flight to Rio from New York takes nine hours; from Miami it is slightly less, and from Los Angeles 12 hours; flights from Europe average 11–12 hours (but you may hang around in São Paulo for an hour if you can't fly direct). Many international flights are overnight, so you arrive in the early morning.

Rio international airport, tel: (21) 3398-4526 or 2155

Some international airlines' phone numbers are:
Aerolineas Argentinas, tel: 0800-7073313
Air Canada, tel: 2220-5343
Air France, tel: 3212-1818
Alitalia, tel: 0800-7040206
American Airlines, tel: 0300-7897778
British Airways, tel: 0300-7896140
Continental Airlines, tel: 0800-7027500
Iberia, tel: 0800-7707900
Lufthansa, tel: 4503-5000
Swissair, tel: 0800-7074750
TAP, tel: 0800-7077787
United Airlines, tel: 0800-162323
Varig, tel: 4003-7000
Local carriers include:
GOL, tel: 0300-7892121
TAM, tel: 4002-5700

By Sea

Cruise traffic through the port of Rio is on the increase, especially during the northern hemisphere's winter months. An increasing number of cruise ships sail up and down the Brazilian coast between October and

AIR PACKAGES

Rio being the premier destination that it is, many travel packages are available, to suit every interest group and pocket. Whether you travel with your young family, with a same-sex partner, or with a senior, all can be accommodated. Travel that will include Carnival and/or New Year's Eve should be booked well in advance, as these periods are in great demand, and priced accordingly. Realistically, you can expect to pay double for a trip to Rio which includes Carnival or New Year's Eve.

Air travel within Brazil is expensive, so if you plan to visit other places as well as Rio, look into the Brazil Air Pass. This is a multiple-product program that enables you to visit from four to nine cities at considerably reduced rates. All flights must be pre-booked before departure from your home country, and although a series of restrictions apply, this is still a very good deal. It also saves you the trouble of booking internal flights once you get there.

TO AND FROM THE AIRPORT

By Cab
To get from the airport and into Rio, the preferred form of transport is a taxi. You buy your fixed-price ticket (sample fare: airport to Copacabana is approximately US$20) within the terminal building itself, and so are safe from any unscrupulous drivers lurking outside the building.

By Bus
Inexpensive air-conditioned buses leave the airport at half-hourly intervals, starting at 5.30am; the last one leaves the airport at 11.10pm. The final destination of the bus is the Alvorada Terminal in Barra. Santos Dumont domestic airport in

downtown Rio is the first stop. From there, the bus follows the coast along Flamengo, Botafogo, Copacabana, Ipanema, Leblon, Vidigal, São Conrado and on to Barra.

This route is altered during the morning rush hour, 7–10am, when all lanes of the coast road lead into the city. The bus is then obliged to take the next road inland from its usual route. For the return journey, the first bus rom the Alvorada Terminal in Barra leaves at 5.30am, the last at 11.10pm. Passengers must flag this bus down, as there are no official stops. Allow plenty of time, in case of traffic jams.

discouraged from using them, since the incidence of hold-ups and pickpocketing is high. If you do decide to catch a bus, avoid the rush hour, when passengers are packed in shoulder to shoulder. Don't carry any valuables, keep your camera inside a bag, and hold shoulder bags or rucksacks in front of you.

By Cab
Rio is exceptionally well served by cabs, which are, on the whole, reliable, comfortable, and inexpensive. They all have meters, which should always be switched on when you start your journey. Cabs are painted yellow with a blue stripe down the side. Regular cabs are permitted to charge a higher fare, shown by the number 2 appearing on the meter, after 9pm any day, on Sunday and holidays, and in December.

As an example of the sort of rates you can expect to pay, from Leblon to Centro the fare is unlikely to exceed US$12. Good service is provided by:
Central de Taxi, tel: 2593-2598
Coopsind, tel: 2589-4503
JB Radio Taxi, tel: 2501-3026

In the "visitor" areas of Leblon and Ipanema, **Rio Service Taxi**, tel: 3890-0573, provides an excellent service.

April. You could consider traveling to or from Brazil by luxury liner, or even joining a cruise for a few days. Popular ports of call are Manaus, Fortaleza, Recife, Salvador, Rio de Janeiro, and Florianópolis. A great many ships call in to Rio for New Year's Eve and at Carnival time.

By Road

Comfortable, on-schedule bus services are available to all parts of Brazil from Rio de Janeiro, and to major cities in neighboring South American countries. There are direct lines to Asunción (Paraguay), Buenos Aires (Argentina), Montevideo (Uruguay), and Santiago (Chile). For the foreign visitor, buses are inexpensive. While undoubtedly a good way to see the countryside, remember that distances are enormous, and you will be sitting in a bus for several days and nights. You might prefer to break a long journey with a stop along the way.

Various comfort levels are available on these buses. On the six-hour ride between Rio de Janeiro and São Paulo, for example, you can either take the regu-

lar bus, with upholstered, reclining seats, or the more expensive *leito* (sleeper), with wider and fully reclining seats with foot rests. There is also a toilet, and coffee and soft drinks are available on board. If you're not in a hurry, traveling by bus can be an interesting adventure.

At busy times like public holidays, buses on the Rio–São Paulo line depart at the rate of one per minute. On other routes, there may be one bus a day (such as the Rio–Belém route, a 52-hour trip) or just one or two per week.

By Rail

Except for overcrowded urban commuter railways, trains are not a major form of transportation in Brazil, and rail links are not extensive.

GETTING AROUND

Within Rio

By Bus
The regular city buses are very cheap, but visitors are usually

BELOW: city bus

TRANSPORT

ACCOMMODATION

ACTIVITIES

A – Z

LANGUAGE

Flagging a cruising cab on the street is not difficult; there are usually plenty of them. Technically, on a one-way street the cabs are supposed only to pull over to the left-hand sidewalk, the right-hand side being reserved for buses.

Rio's radio taxis are more expensive than yellow cabs, but extremely professional and reliable. If you wish to pay by credit card, advise them when you make your reservation. Numbers to call are: Coopertramo Radio-taxi tel: 2560-2022; Transcoopas, tel: 2590-6891.

Be wary of car services stationed outside the five-star hotels, or other possibly "pirate" forms of transport, as they charge what they will, and it's difficult to argue with them, especially if you don't speak Portuguese.

By Metro

Rio de Janeiro has an excellent, though not extensive, subway service, with bright, clean, air-conditioned trains. The metro is one of the easiest ways for a tourist to get around without getting lost, although, of course, it doesn't familiarise you with the the city landmarks. Maps in the stations and in each train help you find your way without having to communicate in Portuguese.

Lines run out from the city

center, and the service is extended by bus links, with train-bus combination tickets. The service operates Monday–Saturday from 5am–midnight, and on Sunday from 7am–11pm. Information can be obtained by calling tel: 0800-595-1111, Monday–Saturday 8am–8pm.

Line 1 links Copacabana (Estação Siqueira Campos) to Praça Saens Peña in Tijuca. This line is the most useful for visitors as it runs from Presidente Vargas, via Uruguaiana, Cinelândia, Glória, Catete, and Carioca and stops at Botafogo, Flamengo, and Largo do Machado.

Line 2 is of less interest, as it serves the suburbs, which have little to offer the visitor.

There is just one price for a single *(unitário)* ticket, even if you transfer from one line to another. There are round-trip *(ida e volta)* and multi-fare tickets, as well as combination tickets for use on buses as well *(metrô-ônibus)*. Tickets are sold in the stations and on the *integração* buses, and prices are clearly posted. Note: *entrada* = entrance; *saida* = exit.

By Bicycle

Rio has, in theory, a 132.5-km (82-mile) cycle track that is intended to cover most of the city. It goes from the Marina in Glória out to the Barra, sharing

space with roads on occasions. Bicycles can be rented for short trips from any number of suppliers along the beach.

If you take your cycling seriously, consider renting a bike from **Special Bike**, Rua Visconde de Pirajá 135, Ipanema, tel: 2521-2686, www.specialbike.com.br, who will deliver your machine direct to your hotel.

Driving

For the faint-hearted, Rio's driving may well be their most vivid memory of the city. That all this seemingly undisciplined behavior on the roads requires considerable skill doesn't seem such an obvious fact while your cab oozes across the fast-moving lanes of traffic from the far left-hand lane to make a right turn a mere hundred meters/yards ahead of you. Street markers in the form of painted lines are often treated as an affront to a driver's independence, and "keep clear" marks painted on intersections are frequently invisible, as an enterprising driver decides there's room for just one more car: their own.

Bus drivers are especially tyrannical, and sticking in their own designated right-hand lanes is something they just won't do, any more than they will stop to let non-fare-paying seniors and uniformed school children board. Worse even than the bus drivers are the van drivers, who zoom around the streets in their over-full, under-maintained people-carriers on their regular routes. This form of transport should be avoided by the visitor.

Stopping at a red light after dark in Rio is considered lunacy; most drivers slow down, look both ways and run the light. Sadly, this isn't simply a sign of drivers' impatience, although there's plenty of that, but a reflection of the amount of crime that takes place at traffic lights. Much traffic-related crime involves motorcycles, so special care should be taken if a motorcycle or two

BELOW: cycling is one way to go.

starts to become intimate with the car in which you are traveling.

During the day, however, it is usual to stop at a red light, and there is plenty of entertainment when you do. People selling biscuits, fruit, and car accessories cruise up and down between the idling cards, and junior acrobats go through terrifying gymnastic routines hoping to grab your attention and some small change. Advertising leaflets are squeezed through car windows. All very entertaining, but keep your doors locked, and don't be distracted, as some of the people wandering around might have their eye on an unguarded bag on your back seat.

Parking

Parking is another problem, as the city is poorly supplied with car parks. People called *flanelinhas* – after the flannels they invariably wave, suggesting that they are going to clean your windscreen – are employed by the municipality to take your parking fee in exchange for a ticket which you then display on your windscreen. Mysteriously, they have often "run out" of tickets, but you have to pay anyway.

In places where parking is not regulated there are no signs, and within seconds a freelance car "guard" will appear, either offering to keep an eye on your car in the hopes of receiving a tip or actually demanding payment in advance for his (dubious) vigilance. The equivalent of US40–50 cents is sufficient. It's best to pay this small sum, or you risk finding some slight damage to the car upon your return.

Pedestrians

Things are not that much easier for the pedestrian. Even if you are trying to cross a one-way street, you should always look both ways: Rio's cycle path is cunningly embedded in the sidewalk in places, and you can easily be wiped out by a fast moving, perfectly law-abiding cyclist. Be sen-

ABOVE: Rio's bus station.

sible and go that extra half-block to cross at the traffic lights.

Car Rental

If, knowing the hazards, you do choose to drive, or need a car for excursions outside the city, vehicles are easily rented in Rio, although car rental is not particularly cheap. **Hertz** has offices in Copacabana at Avenida Princesa Isabel, tel: 2275-7440; at the international airport, tel: 3398-4338; and at Santos Dumont airport, tel: 2262-0612. **Avis** operates out of Avenida Princesa Isabel in Copacabana, tel: 2543-8481; the international airport, tel: 3398-5060; and Santos Dumont airport, tel: 3814-7378.

Outside the City

By Air

There are flights connecting Rio to all Brazil's main cities, including Brasília, São Paulo, Belo Horizonte, Porto Alegre, Salvador, and Florianópolis *(see page 206 for airline phone numbers)*.

GOL is the newest carrier, and offers a no-frills, low-cost service in competition with the "giants" in the sector. It began in 2001, and is the fastest-growing airline in Latin America. It

flies to all the above cities, except Salvador.

By Bus

Long-haul buses, which go to all the places mentioned in the Excursions section, are efficient, safe, and reliable. Call the **Rodoviária Novo Rio** (bus station) on tel: 3213-1800 for information. Búzios is served by the 1001 bus company, tel: 2625-1001/2625-0577. The Costa Verde company connects Rio to the western coast, Angra dos Reis and Paraty; tel: 2233-3809. Petrópolis is served by two companies, Fácil and Única, both on tel: 2263-8792.

By Boat

Paquetá island can be reached from the boat station (Estação das Barcas, Praça XV de Novembro, tel: 2533-7524/2532-6274) in downtown Rio. The regular ferry takes 70 minutes; the hydrofoil does the journey in 20 minutes. Fares are low, with the hydrofoil costing just a little more than the ferry.

Ferries to Ilha Grande run from Mangaratiba every morning and Angra dos Reis every afternoon (journey time: 90 minutes). Fares are very low – even at weekends, when they double the weekday amount. The boats are fairly basic, but there are refreshments and toilets available.

A CCOMMODATION

SOME THINGS TO CONSIDER BEFORE YOU BOOK THE ROOM

Choosing a Hotel

Rio hotels follow a fairly straight-forward pattern: they tend to be large high-rise buildings, with varying degrees of luxury and facilities. Designer and boutique hotels are much talked about, but these characterful inns and hostelries are not yet a major feature of the Rio hotel scene.

HOTEL AREAS

The highest concentration of hotel rooms is in Copacabana. These range from the loftiest possible international standards of the iconic beachfront Copacabana Palace to some ordinary, noisy properties several blocks from the beach, done up in dubious taste. Ipanema and Leblon, hitherto almost hotel-free areas, are very slowly catching up with Copacabana in terms of numbers, with a similar range of accommodation. Hotel accommodation in the Barra was, until very recently, in very short supply, but this, too, is changing. Remember, though, that Ipanema and Leblon can be a long and boring car ride away from the Barra in the rush hour. Non-mainstream tourist areas include Flamengo and Glória,

which can offer very good value for money.

Home from Home

Apart from conventional hotel rooms, Rio is rich in serviced apartments, called "apart-hotéis" or "hotel residências." These properties usually provide a one- or two-bedroomed apart-ment with a small kitchen. Maid service is available, and a var-iety of other on-site facilities, such as laundry rooms, bars, and restaurants. If you are trav-eling with children, or are pre-pared to do a little food prepara-tion yourself, and are staying more than a week, they can be just the ticket.

You should be very careful about reserving an apartment from sometimes not-quite-legal operators. Their internet ads show attractively done-up proper-ties, but most make misleading use of a wide-angle lens and are not representative of the accom-modation you may think you are getting. If in doubt about the legitimacy of any accommoda-tion offered to you, it pays to check with Riotur, the city's tourism bureau, before parting with any credit-card numbers.

Bed and Breakfast options (Cama e Café), available only in the Santa Teresa district, are fully explained in the section

dealing with accommodation in that area *(see page 212)*.

Seasonal Rates

Apart from the instrinsic facili-ties and level of luxury offered, the time of year you plan to visit Rio is crucial to establishing the price of accommodation. The high seasons of Carnival and New Year's Eve see prices almost doubled, especially in the beachfront hotels. During low season, short-break vacations can be attractively priced. Discounts, however, may not apply if there is a major inter-national convention being held in the city, or even an important sporting event. Proximity to the beach is a major price determi-nant, and you can save a consid-erable amount of money by stay-ing three blocks away from the beach instead of across the road from it.

Some hotels include breakfast during low seasons, but not dur-ing peak booking times. Rates are far from set in stone, and a certain amount of negotiation is in order. Consequently, the price ranges given below are for your guidance only. The best advice is to do your research properly. Sometimes a flash "special offer, limited availability" can put a usually out-of-range hotel within financial reach.

CENTRAL RIO

All the hotels in this section are in the Flanengo area. Some readers might find it odd that there are no hotels listed for the downtown district of Rio, but there is good reason for this omission. Downtown is not a good area to be in after dark, and the area truly only functions during the daytime. There may be rooms to let and even a couple of un-starred hotels in the area, but they are unlikely to meet the standards of even the most undemanding international visitor, and would certainly not be recommended.

Hotel Argentina
Rua Cruz Lima 30, Flamengo
Tel: 2558-7233
Fax: 2285-4573

BELOW: Hotel Glória's snowy-white façade.

www.hotelargentina.com.br
Budget accommodation in Flamengo. The décor is somewhat suspect, but it makes a good base. After all, you haven't come to Rio to look at the four walls of your hotel room. Breakfast is included. **$**

Flórida Hotel
Rua Ferreira Viana 81, Flamengo
Tel: 2195-6800
Fax: 2285-5777
www.windsorhoteis.com.br
The Flórida Hotel has nothing to do with Florida. Located in a residential area of Rio, and practically adjacent to the Palacio do Catete, the hotel provides adequate accommodation and attentive service. The pool and leisure areas offer great views. One of the reliable Windsor hotel chain. Breakfast is included. **$$**

Hotel Glória
Rua do Russel 632, Glória
Tel: 2555-7272
Fax: 2555-7282
www.hotelgloriario.com.br
Vast, unmissable, monumental white palace on the Parque do Flamengo. Its 630 rooms offer all styles of accommodation, from luxury down to the bare essentials. Front-facing rooms have wonderful views of Sugar Loaf and the Bay. Two swimming pools, bars and restaurants. Handy for downtown Rio and the metro. Breakfast is included. **$$**

Golden Park Hotel
Avenida Rua do Russel 374, Flamengo
Tel: 2556-8150
Fax: 2285-6358
E-mail: gparkrio@pontocom.com.br
Functional accommodation. The superior rooms on the upper floors have views of Flamengo Park and/or the sea, while some lower rooms have no views at all, although they all cost the same. There's a small rooftop pool. Breakfast is included. **$$**

Hotel Novo Mundo
Praia do Flamengo 20, Flamengo
Tel: 2105-7000
Fax: 2265-2369
www.hotelnovomundo-rio.com.br
The Novo Mundo (New World) is a genuine Rio landmark, with spectacular views of Sugar

Loaf mountain. It offers graciously appointed accommodation at attractive rates, although there's no swimming pool. Because of its proximity to the former seat of government, the hotel had its glory days in the 1950s, when Rio was still the capital of Brazil. Breakfast is included. **$$**

Hotel Rondônia Palace
Rua Buarque de Macedo 60, Flamengo
Tel: 2556-0616
Fax: 2558-4133
www.hotelrondonia.com.br
Set in a quiet location just off Parque do Flamengo. There are 62 rooms; they don't have views, but they are clean, comfortable, and air-conditioned, and many of them have a sauna or a jacuzzi. You should check this when booking, as the price may be the same, with or without. **$$**

SANTA TERESA

This bohemian area of Rio, with its charming, winding roads and its famous tram, has its own self-contained association of Bed and Breakfast establishments. A true pioneer in a city known for its impersonal high-rise hotels, the Cama e Café circuit consists of 50 houses whose owners are properly trained and offer accommoda-tion with a difference. Prices vary as much as the type of accommo-dation offered, starting as low as about US$20.

Accommodation varies from a room in a delightfully decorated apartment to a suite in a gabled art deco treasure. The human element is equally diverse: from artists through intellectuals, all the hosts are natu-rally gregarious, invari-ably befriend their guests, and share their first-hand knowledge of the city with them.

It pays to research your choice of Bed and Breakfast accommoda-tion with care; some things you may take for granted, such as a hair dryer or a private bath-room, may not be avail-able. On the other

hand, you might think waking up to the sound of marmosets playing in the trees outside your windows more important.

www.camaecafé.com.br.

COPACABANA AND LEME

Copacabana Palace Hotel
Avenida Atlântica 1702
Tel: 2548-7070
Fax: 2235-7330
www.copacabanapalace.orient-express.com
Right on the beach-front. The Palace by the Sand, richly appointed, is steeped in tradition, and yet competitively modern. Luxury is the keynote, from the fan-tastic flower arrange-ments to the in-room amenities. Pit stop for the kings and queens of all sectors of soci-ety, from rock stars and movie queens to real-life royals. There are two restaurants: the Pérgula, for infor-mal dining by semi-Olympic-sized swim-ming pool; and the Cipriani, the best of the best. Breakfast is not included. **$$$$**

Excelsior Copacabana Hotel
Avenida Atlântica 1800
Tel: 2195-5800
Fax: 2257-1850
www.windsorhoteis.com
Beachfront. Part of the Windsor Group, which operates a small but successful chain of hotels which caters mainly to the business traveler, and thus often provides good cost-benefit ratios. Rooftop

pool. Breakfast is included. **$$$**
Grandarrel Ouro Verde Hotel
Avenida Atlântica 1456, Copacabana.
Tel: 2543-4123
Fax: 2543-4776
www.dayrrell.com
Beachfront. This trad-itional Rio hotel has changed hands, and received a lick of paint. The façade is in art-deco style, the rooms are generously propor-tioned. Rates for back-facing rooms make it a good deal. Breakfast is included. **$$**
Hotel Copa Sul
Avenida Nossa Senhora de Copacabana 1284
Tel: 2106-0442
Fax: 2287-7497
www.copasul.com.br
On one of the busiest streets in the world,

BELOW: Rooftop pool with a view.

the Copa Sul offers simple, no-frills accommodation in a perfect location for those who want to be at the hub of the action. Buffet-style restaurant. No pool, but only a block away from the beach. Breakfast is included. **$**

J. W. Marriott Hotel
Avenida Atlântica 2600
Tel: 2545-6500
Fax: 2545-6555
www.marriott.com
Beachfront. Warmly appointed throughout, with plush upholstery and an air of casual chic, this Marriott hotel meets all the demands of the business traveler, and is also a favorite with families. The lack of local color inside is made up for by its excellent location. Breakfast is not included. **$$**

Le Meridien Copacabana
Avenida Altântica 1020, Leme
Tel: 3873-8888
Fax: 3873-8883
www.lemeridien-copacabana.com
Beachfront. Striking, elegant building on the street that separates the bustle of Copacabana from the relative peace of Leme. Bold use of color livens up many of the rooms, which range from the comfortable standard through to the height of luxury in the suites. Eating options within the hotel are especially attractive. Terrace pool. Very convenient for Rio Sul shopping mall. Breakfast is included. **$$$**

Luxor Regente
Avenida Atlântica 3716, Copacabana
Tel: 2525-2070
Fax: 2267-7693
www.luxor-hoteis.com.br
Beachfront. The Luxor Group has three hotels in Copacabana, and has always offered good value for money. The other two are the Luxor Copacabana ($$), also beachfront, and the Luxor Continental ($$), one block from Leme Beach. Not exactly packed with local color, they nonetheless provide a comfortable, well-organized base for vacationers. Breakfast is included. **$$**

Miramar Palace Hotel
Avenida Atlântica 3668, Copacabana
Tel: 2195-5500
Fax: 2521-3294
www.windsorhoteis.com
Beachfront. Another member of the Windsor Group. No pool. Spacious rooms, gym, and sauna. Breakfast is included. **$$**

Pestana Rio Atlântica
Avenida Atlântica 2964
Tel: 2548-6332
Fax: 2255-6410
www.pestana.com
Modern, 18-floor hotel with stunning beach views. Well designed and comfortable, it caters to both business and tourist clients. Excellent breakfasts, a heath club and a rooftop pool and bar. **$$$**

Plaza Copacabana
Avenida Princesa Isabel 263, Copacabana
Tel: 2275-07722
Fax: 2257-1850
www.windsorhoteis.com
Well located on the avenue that separates Copacabana from Leme. The modern décor and attention to detail make this a good value for money choice. Guests from Japan receive special attention. Rooftop pool. Breakfast is included. **$$**

Portinari Design Hotel
Rua Francisco Sa 17
Copacabana
Tel: 3288-8800
www.hotelportinari.com.br
Rio's first design hotel, with each of its 11 floors individually designed. Its just one block back from the beach, and there's no pool, but it's a great place to stay, and there are stunning views from the Restaurante Brodowski on the top floor. **$$$**

Rio Copa Best Western
Avenida Princesa Isabel 370, Leme
Tel: 3875-9191
Fax: 3875-9192
www.riocopa.com
Midway between Leme and Copacabana, an efficient, smoothly run hotel, catering for business as well as leisure travelers. "Café Le Soleil" offers attractive menus. Breakfast is included. **$**

Rio Internacional Hotel
Avenida Atlântica 1500, Copacabana
Tel: 2546-0000
Fax: 2542-5443
www.riointernacional.com.br
Beachfront. There's an uncluttered, modern feel to this extremely efficiently run hotel. Well suited to both the business and leisure traveler, it is conveniently located, just 10 minutes by taxi from downtown Rio. There's a pleasant rooftop pool and bar. Breakfast is included. **$**

Rio Othon Palace
Avenida Atlântica 3264, Copacabana
Tel: 2525-1500
Fax: 2522-1967
www.hoteis-othon.com.br
Beachfront. The Othon Group of hotels offers an enormous range of hotels in Rio de Janeiro and other Brazilian cities. Top of the line is the gigantic Othon Palace, right in the thick of things on Copacabana Beach. This massive hotel, with its 586 rooms, offers every type of accommodation, from a back-facing single to the presidential suite. The rooftop Skylab bar and restaurant provide a high-in-the-sky view of Copacabana Beach. Heated rooftop pool. Breakfast is included. **$$$**

Windsor Palace
Rua Domingos Ferreira 7, Copacabana
Tel: 2545-9000
Fax: 2549-9373
www.windsorhoteis.com.br
The Windsor Palace is not right on the beachfront, but it is only a short walk away. There are only 74 rooms in this modern, functional hotel, and they all face the front. There's a rooftop pool and bar. You get the kind of friendly, attentive service that you would expect from a small hotel. Breakfast is included. **$$$**

PRICE CATEGORIES

Price categories are for a double room with or without breakfast, as indicated:

$$$$	over US$300
$$$	US$200–300
$$	US$100–200
$	under US$100

TRANSPORT   ACCOMMODATION   ACTIVITIES   A – Z   LANGUAGE

IPANEMA

Arpoador Inn
Rua Francisco Otaviano 177
Tel: 2274-6995
Fax. 2511-5094
At the Copacabana end of Ipanema beach, in an extremely pleasant location. Especially attractive for surfers, whose preferred beach is right outside. Rooms without a sea view are a bargain. Breakfast is included. **$**

Caesar Park
Avenida Vieira Souto 460
Tel: 2525-2525
Fax: 2521-6000
www.caesar-park.com.br
Beachfront. Located at one of the hot spots of Ipanema beach, the Caesar Park combines plush sophistication with all the casualness that tipifies Ipanema. The rooms are elegantly furnished. The Galani rooftop restaurant offers both wonderful views and excellent cuisine. Breakfast is not included. **$$$$**

Everest Park
Rua Maria Quitéria 19
Tel: 2525-2200
Fax: 2521-3198
www.everest.com.br
Small, and just around the corner from the Everest Rio (see below). Guests at the Everest Park may use the larger hotel's facilities, including the pool. No pool on site. Breakfast is included. **$$**

Everest Rio
Avenida Prudente de Morais 1117
Tel: 2525-2200
Fax: 2521-3198
www.everest.com.br
One block from the beach. Conveniently located in the heart of Ipanema, a stone's throw from both the beach and serious shopping, the Everest has long been a favorite for families. Socializing takes place on the roof, 23 stories above Ipanema, where

the pool is located, drinks and snacks are served, and the Grill 360 restaurant is situated. Breakfast is included. **$$$**

Ipanema Plaza
Rua Farme de Amoedo 34
Tel: 3687-2000 or 3687-2121
Fax: 3687-2001
www.ipanemaplaza.com.br
A member of the Golden Tulip hotel group. Excellent location in Ipanema and an easy walk to the beach, great shops, and some of Rio's finest restaurants. Rooms decorated in pleasing contemporary design, with the emphasis on the practical. There's a beautiful rooftop pool. Breakfast is included. **$$**

Mar Ipanema
Rua Visconde de Pirajá 539
Tel: 3875-9191
Fax: 3875-9192
www.maripanema.com
A modern hotel, situated right in the heart of Ipanema shopping

country, just two blocks from the beach. Rooms are rather basically furnished and decorated. There's no pool, but it's a great location for fun-seekers. Breakfast is included. **$$**

Sol Ipanema Best Western
Avenida Vieira Souto 320
Tel: 2525-2020
Fax: 2247-8484
www.solipanema.com.br
Beachfront. The hotel has a brilliant location, even if the rooms are sparingly decorated. The decor is more than compensated for by the staff, who are well known for their friendliness and excellent service. Breakfast is included. **$$**

LEBLON

Leblon Palace Hotel
Avenida Ataulfo De Paiva 204
Tel: 1-877-477-5817
A tall, glass structure that offers all the usual mod cons: air conditioning, 24-hour room service, cable TV, access to internet, efficient service, restaurant, and swimming pool. **$$**

Marina All Suites
Avenida Delfim Moreira 696
Tel: 2172-1001
Fax: 2172-1010
Beachfront. An aura of freshness pervades

this stylish hotel, where design shares center stage with personal service. The Bar and Café d'Hôtel have become hotspots in their own right, and the beautiful people gather there. Rooftop pool and bar. Breakfast is not included. **$$$**

Marina Palace
Avenida Delfim Moreira 630
Tel: 2172-1000
Fax: 2172-1010
www.hotelmarina.com.br
Beachfront. Sober, streamlined decoration

and very well-appointed rooms. Well located for the village feel of Leblon. The Azulino restaurant serves a clever mix of local ingredients treated with international flair. Breakfast is not included. **$$**

Sheraton Rio Hotel and Towers
Avenida Niemeyer 121
Tel: (21) 2274-1122
Fax: (21) 2239-5643
www.sheraton-rio.com
All 560 rooms have balconies with views of beaches or lush moun-

tain scenery, plus all the amenities you would expect from a hotel in the Sheraton chain. The 15 meeting rooms and state-of-the-art business center make it popular with business travelers. **$$$**

SÃO CONRADO AND THE BARRA

Entremares Hotel
Avenida Erico Veríssimo 846,
Barra
Tel/Fax: 2494-3887
No-frills basic accom-
modation, two blocks
from Barra Beach. No
pool. Public areas are
over-furnished, while
actual room are sparse-
ly so, but it's good
value for the price.
Breakfast is included. **$**

Hotel Inter-Continental
Avenida Prefeito Mendes de
Morais 222, São Conrado
Tel: 3323-2200
Fax: 3322-5500
Nothwithstanding the
slight shadow cast
upon it by its proximity
to the Rocinha *favela*,
this is still a nice hotel
in an almost idyllic set-
ting. All you expect

from a hotel of this
standing. Once the
headquarters for major
happenings in Rio, and
temporary home to –
among many others –
Manchester United
Football Club, the
Formula One motor-
racing circus and the
Brazilian national soc-
cer team! Breakfast is
included. **$$**

Ocean Drive
Avenida Sernambetiba 6900,
Barra
Tel: 2239-4598
Fax: 2259-2191
www.redeprotel.com.br
Beachfront. The Protel
group manages a num-
ber of all-suite hotels,
mainly in the Barra
area. All have fully
equipped kitchens, as

well as complete hotel
services, which makes
them very good options
if you are traveling with
children. This sort of
property is known as a
Hotel Residência or
Apart-Hotel. Breakfast
is included. **$$**

**Sheraton Barra Hotel
and Suites**
Avenida Lúcio Costa 3150,
Barra
Tel: 3139-8000
Fax: 3139-8085
www.sheraton-rio.com
Beachfront. Possessing
all the facilities you
would expect from an
international resort
hotel, and located
about half an hour by
taxi from Ipanema.
Breakfast not included
in the rate. **$$$**

**Transamerica Flat
Barra**
Avenida Gastão Senges 395,
Barra
Tel: 2123-7000
Fax: 2123-7151
www.transamerica.com.br
Modern, functional
hotel in the heart of
Barra, close to the
shopping centers.
Some apartments have
galley kitchens, which
can be an advantage if
you are traveling with
children. Breakfast is
included. **$$**

PETRÓPOLIS AND THE RIO HIGHLANDS

Pousada Alcobaça
Rua Agostinho Goulão 298,
Correas, Petrópolis
Tel: (24) 2221-1240
Fax: (24) 2221-3390
www.pousadadaalcobaca.com
Tucked away just out of
sight and sound of
Correas, a busy little
outlying district of
Petrópolis, is a little
piece of heaven on
earth. Eleven suites
are available in this
European-style house,
surrounded by some of
the best-tended gar-
dens for many miles
around. The food is
exquisite, and attracts
diners from near and
far. Owner-operated,
and truly special, this
pousada is very much
worth a visit. Breakfast
is included. **$$**

Locanda della Mimosa
Alameda das Mimosas 30
Tel: (24) 2233-5405
Fax: (24) 2233-5405
www.locanda.com.br
Owner Danio Braga's
name is synonymous
with fine dining and,
especially, fine wines.
At this jewel of an inn,
he and his wife Lilian
entertain special
guests with outstanding
class and hospitality.
Only six rooms are
available, so advance
booking is essential.
The cuisine is essen-
tially regional Italian,
but always dynamic and
innovative. The only
member of Les
Grandes Tables du
Monde in Brazil.
Breakfast and tea are
included. **$$$**

Pousada Tankamana
Estrada Julio Capua, Vale do
Cuiabá, Itaipava
Tel: (24) 2222-9181
The accent is firmly on
the environment at the
Pousada Tanamana.
Sixteen chalets, each
with a fireplace and all
modern necessities
(kettle, fridge, etc.),
are set in spectacular
mountain scenery.
Horseback riding,
archery, and hiking
can all be arranged.
The excellent restau-
rant specializes in
trout, fished from the
pousada's own farm.
There's a minimum
two-night stay.
Breakfast is included.
$$

Hotel Village Le Canton
Estrada Teresópolis–Friburgo

Km 12, Vargem Grande,
Teresópolis
Tel: (21) 2741-4200
Fax: (21) 3643-6000
www.lecanton.com.br
If the tropics get too
much for you, you can

PRICE CATEGORIES

Price categories are for
a double room with or
without breakfast, as
indicated:
$$$$ over U$300
$$$ US$200–300
$$ US$100–200
$ under US$100

steal away to the mountains and enjoy a more European approach. Le Canton offers a wide range of accommodation options, and is especially welcoming to children. The young ones are royally taken care of by trained staff, and can take part in all manner of sports and activities. The room rate includes three meals per day, which is convenient, as Le Canton is somewhat off the beaten track, and nearby alternatives might be hard to come by. **$$$**

BÚZIOS

Casa Brancas
Morro do Humitá 10
Tel: (22) 2623-1458
Fax: (22) 2623-2147
www.casasbrancas.com.br
Lording it in more ways than one over the hustle and bustle of Rua das Pedras is one of the most charming hotels in the area. A boutique hotel with everything going for it: unbeatable views, carefully decorated apartments and a first-class restaurant. You can pamper yourself with all manner of massage and body treatments at the in-house spa. Visa is the only card accepted. Breakfast is included. **$$$**

La Soberana
Rua I-II, Ferradura
Tel: (22) 2623-4508
Overlooking the spectacular Ferradura Bay. The décor at La Soberana can be described as modern rustic, though the bedrooms are more classically appointed. Very well located, and within easy reach of Rua das Pedras. Visa is the only card accepted. Breakfast is included. **$$**

Le Palmier
Rua J VI 14, Ferradura
Tel: (22) 2623-2032
Fax: (22) 2622-1339
www.lepalmier.com.br
Sixteen suites, each with their own theme and personality, set in a lush tropical garden, 800 m/yds from Ferradura and an easy walk to the nightlife on Rua das Pedras. All major credit cards are accepted, and breakfast is included. **$**

Pousada do Martim Pescador
Enseada do Gancho, lote 15A
Tel: (22) 2623-1449
Fax: (22) 2623-2547
One of Búzios's most respected *pousadas*, which has stood the test of time, and still remains fresh. There are 18 well-appointed rooms in a slightly off-the-beaten-track location, offering wonderful views and plenty of peace. Only Visa cards accepted; breakfast is included. **$$**

Le Relais de la Borie
Rua dos Gravatás, Praia de Geribá

Tel: (22) 2620-8504
Fax: (22) 2623-2303
www.laborie.com.br
It is easy to relax in this tastefully appointed and traditional Búzios *pousada*. It's all very tropical, but with an added touch of European efficiency. There are special packages available, including ones with green fees for golfers. Major credit cards accepted, and breakfast is included in daily rate. **$$$**

COSTA VERDE

Blue Tree Park
Estrada Vereador Benedito Adelino 8413, Angra dos Reis
Tel: (24) 3379-2800
Fax: (24) 3379-2801
www.bluetree.com.br
A resort on the grand scale, in an exclusive, guests-only setting. More than 300 guest rooms, all tastefully decorated in light, tropical tones. Wonderful beaches within easy reach by boat. Hotel offers all manner of entertainment and sports, for all ages. Price includes breakfast and dinner in buffet-style restaurant. Minimum two-night stay. **$$$**

Club Med
BR101, Km 445.5, Mangaratiba
Tel: (21) 2688-9191
Fax: (21) 2688-3333
www.clubmed.com
The Club Med experience can be tasted to the full at its Costa Verde mega-premises. Perfect if you're traveling with children, as the fun never stops. Whatever you're in the mood for, the Club Med will organize it for you. All meals included. **$$**

Hotel do Frade
BR101, Km 513, Angra dos Reis
Tel: (24) 3369-9500
Fax: (24) 3369-2254
www.hoteldofrade.com.br
Pioneers of hospitality in the area, the Frade group's friendly approach and the warm welcome offered to

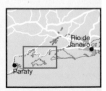

families makes this a great spot to enjoy the fantastic beaches in the Angra area. The golf course is stunning. Rates and minimum stays are much affected by holidays (New Year and Carnival), so you need to do your research. **$$$**

Pestana Angara
Estrada Benedito Adelino 3700
Tel: (24) 3364-2005
Fax: (24) 3365-1909
www.pestana.com
Close to Angra, but hidden away in lush gardens, the Pestana has attractive, individual bungalows set around a pool. There are great views across the bay.
$$$

Pousada do Canto
Vila do Abraão, Ilha Grande
Tel: (24) 3361-5115 or (11) 3284-2999

The brightly painted Pousada do Canto is a five-minute walk from the center of Abraão and the ferry dock. It is right on a section of the beach called Praia do Canto. Family-run and friendly, the little *pousada* has a small swimming pool and a children's pool. Two of the 11 rooms have sea views and verandas. All are en suite and have ceiling fans. Furnishings are fairly basic but adequate, and there are laundry

facilities. Breakfast is included. **$**

Pousada Manacá
Vila do Abraão, Ilha Grande
Tel: (24) 3361-5404
Situated on the beach about 44 meters/yds from the center of Abraão, this is a simple, attractive place, with just five spacious guest rooms, and wide verandas furnished with hammocks – and there's a sauna. French-owned, the Manacá also has a good restaurant,

serving fish straight from the sea. Breakfast is included. **$**

Pousada O Pescador
Vila do Abraão, Ilha Grande
Tel: (24) 3361-5114
A simple little place, right on the beachfront, and absolutely charming. O Pescador offers all you could possibly need in the glorious nature reserve of Ilha Grande. It also has what is currently one of the best restaurants in the area. Breakfast is included in the room rate. **$**

PARATY

Pousada Aconchego
Rua Domingos Gonçalves da Abreu 1
Tel: (24) 3371-1598
www.aconchegohotel.com.br.
Aconchego is a word that summons up a feeling of coziness and warm welcome. That is what awaits visitors at this traditional *pousada*. Hammocks swing in the verandas, and bonsai trees lord it over the patio. Attractive swimming pool. Own parking; breakfast is included. **$**

Pousada do Cais
Travessa Santa Rita 20
Tel: (24) 3371-1200
www.pousadadocais.com.br
Neighboring the postcard-perfect church of St Rita, the Pousada do Cais occupies a colonial building, carefully restored to maintain its historic features intact while at the same time offering fine levels of comfort. Family-run. Breakfast is included. Visa cards only. **$**

Coxixo
Rua do Comércio 362
Tel: (24) 3371-1460
www.hotelcoxixo.com.br
Dominated by the charm of proprietress Maria Della Costa, a big name in Brazilian theatre, the Coxixo offers comfortable accommodation with modern facilites. Bedrooms tastefully furnished. No children under 12. Pool; private parking. Breakfast is included. **$**

Pousada da Marquesa
Rua Dona Geralda 99
Tel: (24) 3371-1012
www.pousadadamarquesa.com.br.
A rambling collection of small buildings around a spectacular atrium garden, with pool and lounging areas. Rooms are basic but comfortable. Watch out for celebs during the Literary Festival. Breakfast included. **$**

Mercado de Pouso
Largo de Santa Rita
Tel: (24) 3371-1114
www.mercadodepouso.com.br

Twenty-four guest rooms in this restored inn dating back to colonial times. Uncluttered and well located beside St Rita church and the dock. The *pousada* has its own boat, great for cruising the beaches. Breakfast included. **$$**

Pousada Pardieiro
Rua do Comércio 74
Tel: (24) 3371-1370
www.pousadapardieiro.com.br
Neat as a pin, with a stunning garden, the Pardieiro takes the hospitality business seriously. The historic city center is at your feet. No children under 15. Pool; breakfast is included. **$$**

Pousada Picinguaba
Rua G, 130, Vila Picinguaba
Tel: (12) 3836-9105 or 3832-9013
Fax: (12) 3836-9103
www.picinguaba.com
Sits above a peaceful bay, half an hour's drive south of Paraty. Ten spacious, rustic-style rooms. Excellent

seafood. Prices include private transport from Rio or São Paulo. **$$$**

Pousada Porto Imperial
Rua Ten. Francisco Antonio s/n
Tel: (24) 3371-2323
Fax: (24) 3371-2111
www.pousadaportoimperial.com.br
A beautiful colonial mansion with 52 pleasant double rooms on two floors around a central courtyard. Small pool and pretty garden. Breakfast is included. **$$**

TRANSPORT ACCOMMODATION ACTIVITIES A – Z LANGUAGE

ACTIVITIES

THE ARTS, NIGHTLIFE, FESTIVALS, SHOPPING, AND SPECTATOR SPORTS

THE ARTS

Museums

We have mentioned the premier museums and art venues in the downtown and Santa Teresa chapters of this guide (see pages 87 and 105). But Rio abounds in unexpected esthetic surprises, many of them quite specialized. A word of warning: museums sometimes close unexpectedly for restoration for long periods – often several years. Check with the tourist office (or via your hotel reception) to make sure a museum is open before traveling long distances.

A few of the museums that were not included in the relevant chapters of this guide, but are still worth a look if you have time to spare, are as follows:

Museu do Indio (Indian Museum), Rua das Palmeiras 55, Botafogo, tel: 2286-8799 (Tues–Fri 10am–5pm, Sat–Sun 1–5pm). Handicrafts, utensils, photographs, sound recordings, and text give an insight into the rich creativity of the indigenous people of Brazil. A life-sized replica of a Guarani home and a collection of festival masks and headdresses are among the high-

lights. There is a good gift shop, too. All artifacts are certified as "legal" by the forestry and indigenous people's government departments.

Fundação Eva Klabin, Avenida Epitácio Pessoa 2480, Lagoa, tel: 2523-3471 (Wed–Sun, 1–5pm). Former home of fanatical collector Eva Klabin, this home-museum showcases objects of beauty from all lands and periods. Egypt, Greece, England, and Holland have produced the treasures on display. Guided tours may be booked in advance on the phone number above. Evening concerts are occasionally held in this delightful setting.

Brazil's first export to Hollywood – the Lady in the Tutti-Frutti Hat – is commemorated at the **Carmen Miranda Museum**, on Parque do Flamengo, across the road from Avenida Rui Barbosa 560, Flamengo, tel: 2299-5586 (Tues–Fri 10am–5pm; Sat–Sun noon–5pm).

Folklore is the focus of the **Museu Edson Carneiro**, at Rua do Catete 179, Flamengo, tel: 2285-0441 (Tues–Fri 11am–6pm; Sat–Sun 3–6pm). Grouped according to five themes – Life, Technology, Religion, Feasts, and Art, the 1,400 objects here make this a feast of folklore.

Classical Music

Unlikely though it may seem in what many perceive as chiefly a resort destination, culture vultures are well served in Rio. Every week a huge range of "classical" culture is consumed by avid cariocas, and the musical menus are unusually rich. Many of these performances of classical music are free, and part of the city's Music in Museums and Music in Churches programs. Not only is the standard of local performers very high, but Rio is on the circuit for many international ensembles as well. Of the local performers, Deborah Colker's ballets and Nelson Freire and Arnaldo Cohen on the piano are unmissable. Full listings of what's on can be found at www.vivamusica.com.br, as well as in the local press.

NIGHTLIFE

Rio comes alive at night. People go out to eat, to dance and to listen to music regularly, as there is a great deal on offer, and most of it is modestly priced. The younger you are, the later the action starts. Entry policy is fickle; some places will not welcome large groups of young men, as dawn post-nightclub confrontations have become an unattractive feature of some of the racier venues.

Many places will charge an inexpensive *couvert artístico*, which goes to pay the performing musicians. Others establish a *consumação mínima*, which means you are billed for a pre-set and known amount, whether you consume anything or not: good sense dictates that if you are going to pay for it anyway, you might as well get something – drinks or snacks – in return. It is common practice to be issued with a card on which your bill is kept; it gets marked up every time you order something. Don't lose this card, as the cash penalty for doing so will probably cover a couple more nights out on the town.

The Real Thing

Authentically Brazilian evenings out can be enjoyed in a part of Rio the visitor might not other wise visit, the Lapa district. This is the neighborhood in downtown Rio at the feet of the great aqueduct that marches across the city. The emphasis here is on Brazilian music, especially the *choro*, which is a fast-moving genre of makes-you-want-to-dance music.

The Lapa has such a concentration of night spots that at practically all times there will be something happening and some fun to be had. Obviously, Monday and Tuesday nights are slower, but the rhythm picks up later in the week. Try to phone ahead to find out what time the live action starts. If you have a smattering of the language, the site www.samba-choro.com.br is useful.

Carioca da Gema
Rua Mem de Sá 79, Lapa
Tel: 2221-0043
Well located for other bars and restaurants, variety is on the musical menu of the Carioca da Gema. No credit cards accepted.

Céu Aberto
Rua do Lavradio 170, Lapa
Tel: 2508-9466
A great setting for some great music, a vision of old Rio as it used to be.

Estrela da Lapa
Rua Mem de Sá 69, Lapa
Tel: 2507-6686
This mega-show house is modern and luxurious, by Lapa standards, with fierce air conditioning. It hosts shows by well-known performers at the weekends.

Flor de Coimbra
Rua Teotônio Regadas 34, Lapa
Tel: 2249-9138
What makes this old-fashioned bar special is the fact that it was the childhood home of artist Cândido Portinari *(see information box, page 91).*

Manoel & Juaquim
Praça João Pessoa 7, Lapa
Tel: 2232-3755
The Lapa branch of the hugely successful Manoel & Juaquim brand of bars is charm itself, and the history of Brazilian popular music is told in the giant mural.

Rio Scenarium
Rua do Lavradio 20, Lapa
Tel: 2233-3239 or 3852-5516
Part antique shop, part bar, part restaurant, part dance hall. Household odds and ends provide the setting for some excellent music.

Export Model Samba

The **Churrascaria Plataforma**, at Rua Adalberto Ferreira 32, Leblon, tel: 2274-4022, hosts one of Rio's traditions, the samba show, which is performed nightly in the upstairs theater. Downstairs is the Plataforma *churrascaria,* offering a varied menu as well as huge portions of beef. Adjacent is the 350-seat Bar do Tom, named in honor of its late, great patron, Antonio Carlos Jobim. While it may not be the most adventurous way to see the lovely ladies in feathers, it is safe, well-organized and punctual. The show goes on at 10pm

and lasts approximately one hour and a half; the cost is around U$35 per person at current (2006) rates.

Samba School

Attending a samba school rehearsal can be a memorable experience. Rehearsals often take place in out-of-the-way areas, and it is recommended that you go in an organized group, with transport to and, most importantly, back to your hotel at the end of the night, all booked in advance.

You won't see any costumes, of course, as these are often ready only hours before the big parades. What you will see is hundreds of *cariocas* letting their hair down, and dancing madly as they try to learn the words for next year's parade themes. Dress down, and be prepared for a sweaty, exhilarating experience. (For more detail, see separate entry for Carnival, *pages 65–71* and the Samba picture spread, *pages 100–1.)*

Dancing and Discos

Below is a selective list of night spots; credit-card policy is constantly changing, so do phone ahead to make sure your card wil be accepted.

Casa da Matriz
Rua Henrique de Novaes 107, Botafogo
Tel: 2266-1014
Multipurpose late-night destina-

DANCING IN THE SKY

Check local listings or call the Sugar Loaf (tel: 2546-8400) to see if there will be any parties or events held on the Morro da Urca, the first stage of the cable-car ride to the top of the mountain, during your visit. For many people, dancing on Sugar Loaf could be a dream come true.

tion with two loud dance floors and plenty of interest. Open until the wee hours.

Melt
Rua Rita Ludolf 47, Leblon
Tel: 2249-9309
Every night is different at the Melt disco, where a variety of DJs impose their personal style on the dance floor. Before about 10pm, it functions as a lounge bar, but as the night wears on, things liven up.

Nuth Lounge
Avenida Armando Lombardi 999, Barra
Tel: 3153-8595
A skilful mix of natural, decorative elements make a sophisticated backdrop for this hotspot, which offers a variety of ambiences and a restaurant.

00
Rua Padre Leonel Franca 240, Gávea
Tel: 2540-8041
Lively, well-appointed dance spot housed in Rio's Planetarium. Music runs the gamut from funk through samba and jazz.

Sky Lounge
Avenida Borges de Medeiros 1426, Lagoa
Tel: 2219-3132
From Wednesday to Sunday, from 10pm onwards, all types mix to dance to the selection of music chosen by the house DJs.

CARNIVAL

It is often said that you either come to Rio, or you come to Rio's Carnival. During Carnival, the unexpected can always happen: museums and galleries close down, streets are closed to traffic, and bus tickets to neighboring resorts are hard to come by, as is accommodation if you do manage to reach the resorts. Prices soar sky-high.

One of the high points of Rio's Carnival is the famed Samba School Parade, held in the purpose-built Sambadrome. This involves thousands of people

who are in fierce, sometimes cutthroat, competition for the first place in this annual championship. The parade is held over two nights, the Sunday and Monday of Carnival. Who parades when is decided by lot. The Sambadrome is actually in use from the Friday night of Carnival, hosting parades by much smaller, humbler schools and bands of revelers. These minor parades are very much in the "also-ran" category, and lack the glitter and glamour of the Sunday and Monday parades.

All sorts of seating is available at the Sambadrome, from ringside tables to hard-concrete overview locations. The boxes are bought, often at huge expense, by companies and then decked out with all modern conveniences such as air conditioning and private bathrooms. Private buffet services are contracted, and the booze flows. For the local people, the shenanigans in the boxes provide almost as much interest as the parades themselves, with movie and rock stars rubbing bare shoulders with politicians and the captains of industry.

Tickets for the parades must be bought in advance; already very highly priced, they are even more expensive when they have been through the hands of a couple of touts or black marketeers. Tourists are traditionally accommodated in Sector 9 of the Sambadrome, where the cheapest tickets cost about US$225. Ticket prices in other sectors of the Sambadrome start at about US$100. Ticket prices in Sectors 6 and 13 are much cheaper, at about U$5 each; this is because you only see the tail end of the school, and from quite a distance. The best stands from which to experience the parade are in Sectors 7 and 9, as the bateria stops when it gets about halfway down the avenue and reverses into a special recess between these sectors. Spectators there have an excellent view

CAPOEIRA

Capoeira is a uniquely Brazilian activity. It has been kept alive chiefly in Salvador, Bahia, but there are also academies in Rio de Janeiro, where tourists can either observe or take part in classes. The best-known of these is the Associação de Capoeira Mestre Bimba, Rua das Laranjeiras 1, Terreiro de Jesus.

Originally a form of ritual fighting practiced by African slaves, *capoeira* has evolved into a stylized fight-dance, with its own accompanying rhythms and music, using the feet a great deal to strike out, and requiring graceful agility.

Presentations are included in folk dance or samba shows – inquire at your hotel.

– but may also be deafened, as the *bateria* then performs in front of the judges' box while the rest of the school streams past them. A box for 8 people in a premier location can cost up to U$16,000, and that's before the cost of kitting it out for comfort. Tickets and further information can be obtained from the Samba School League, at www.liesa.com.br, tel: 21-2233-8151.

An evening at the parade is more than an evening: it is a whole night out. Whatever happens, don't get to the Sambadrome too early, as the crowd doesn't really get going until after midnight. Try to last until dawn, as watching the sun rising over thousands of frantic revelers is something quite special.

Another way to experience the parade is actually to join a samba school. This is not as outlandish as it sounds. Each section of the samba school is run by its own president, whose job it is to fill the ranks. Selling a costume over the internet to someone in London or New York is just another way of doing this. For the costume you may be asked to provide nothing more than your shoe and head sizes. There are annual grumbles at the number of "gringos" attempting to do the samba for a couple of hours straight, sticking out like sore thumbs from the rest of the school.

Carnival finds voice all over Rio, not just at the Sambadrome, and recent efforts to revive street carnivals have paid off. The Banda de Ipanema, with its hilarious drag queens and over 10,000 followers, kicks off the season by parading on the Saturday two weeks prior to Carnival itself. It musters in the Hippie Square (Praça General Osório) at about 4pm. Other outings by this historically irreverent and fun-loving bunch take place on Carnival Saturday and Tuesday, at about the same time. Each neighborhood has its own *banda* or *bloco*, and times and places can be found in the local press.

Travel light for these outings, of course, and drink plenty of water, so you don't get dehydrated. Don't dress up, or you will feel silly: Carnival costumes are pretty much restricted to children and the black-tie balls, and, of course, the outrageous crossdressers, with balloon bosoms and loads of lipstick.

ABOVE: choosing a bikini from a vast array on offer.

SHOPPING

Rio is a paradise for shoppers. The shopping malls provide a huge range of retail outlets all under one roof, with plenty of pit stops along the way, or places to sit and people-watch if any members of your party are not retailminded. The always creative *cariocas* make their shop windows look stunning. Opening hours are generally Monday to Saturday from 10am–10pm; Sunday food halls and movie houses only, usually from 3–8pm. Bargaining is not really a feature. Do not expect a discount if paying

with a credit card; a token amount may be knocked off the price if you are paying in cash. The monstrous Barrashopping is described in the São Conrado and Barra chapter *(page 157)*.

What to Buy

Conventional souvenirs, such as soccer shirts, little bottles filled with Ipanema sand, *caipirinha*-making kits, and cheeky beach towels are for sale everywhere, but the discriminating shopper will find much, much more.

A word of warning on what not to buy: fakes! Copyrights are not always respected, and pirated goods are a major headache in Brazil. Just because a soccer shirt says "Nike" doesn't mean that Nike made it. If it is too cheap, it is not a bargain, but a fake, and may well fall apart in its first wash. Not surprisingly, lingerie is a big seller in Rio; Nova Friburgo, 150 km (93 miles) away in the highlands, is considered the world capital of lingerie. Frills, ruffs, and naughty and nice underwear can be bought at attractive prices.

Jewelry

H. Stern's vast empire of gems and luxury jewelry is described in the Ipanema chapter *(pages 134–5)*. He can be found at Rua Garcia D'Avila at the corner of Rua Visconde de Pirajá. While Mr Stern is the mightiest in the business, many other creative designers have uniquely Brazilian, and not necessarily expensive, jewelry for sale.

One such is **Pepe Torras**, Catalan by birth but *carioca* by persuasion. His delicate, carefully crafted pieces use an assortment of Brazilian woods to produce stunning and extremely unusual pieces. He can be seen at work in his office at Avenida Ataúlfo de Paiva 135, shop 209, tel: 2274-5046.

Another interesting designer is **Tereza Xavier**, whose shop in front of the Copacabana Palace Hotel is worth a visit. She makes highly creative use of seeds, feathers and fibers to celebrate the contribution of the Brazilian Indians to the cultural scene.

For an important jewel for a special occasion, ring **Flavio Guidi** on tel: 2220-7285. He and his family have a tradition of combining painstakingly worked, 18k-gold with the chunkiest of Brazilian stones: very special.

Antonio Bernardo is another well-respected jeweler, whose unusual designs are popular with the young. His work can be seen at the São Conrado Fashion Mall and the Shopping da Gávea.

Handicrafts

The traditional leader in the handicrafts business is **Pé de Boi** at Rua Ipiranga 55 in Laranjeiras, tel: 2285-4395 (Mon–Fri 9am–7pm, Sat 9am–1pm). Owner-operated Pé de Boi seeks out handicrafts from the northeast of Brazil and the state of Minas Gerais, and also carries produce from other South American countries. Lacework, basketry, woodwork, feather art, and ceramics produce a display of the best in Brazilian popular art. Bulky pieces can be exported.

In the heart of the Ipanema shopping district, typically Brazilian goods can be found at the **Empório Brasil,** in a bijou mall at Rua Visconde de Pirajá 595, shop 108. The emporium has a huge range of tastefully displayed products, from feather and bead art through woodcarving to jewelry.

Havaianas

For those of you who think that flip-flops (rubber thong sandals) are utilitarian beach footwear, and all much of a muchness, think again. Havaianas, made in São Paulo, are internationally known, worn by movie stars and supermodels and, yes, they are better than your average thong. You can buy them everywhere, and prices don't vary much from store to store.

Cachaça

The strong cane spirit that is the basis of Brazil's national drink, the *caipirinha,* is a popular gift or souvenir to take home. Paraty, where it's made, is a great place to buy it, as there are numerous stores stocked with bottles of all shapes and sizes, but it is widely available wherever you go. **Lidador**, at Rua da Assembléia 65 and in Botafogo Praia Shopping, sells around 30 varieties of *cachaça,* and is also good for olives, nuts, and dried fruits.

The Malls

Botafogo Praia Shopping

Praia de Botafogo 400, Botafogo
Eight floors of the former Sears department store offering a good range of shops, plus excellent food outlets and a dazzling view thrown in for nothing.

Downtown

Avenida das Americas 500, Barra
This mall-with-a-difference consists of hundreds of gaily painted townhouses, and its landscaped gardens make it a pleasant place to visit. Many major retailers have outlets here, and there is also a movie complex. There are plenty of places to stop for a drink and a snack.

Rio Design Barra

Avenida das Américas 7777, Barra
This monster mall in Barra caters to the high-spending end of the market, and prides itself on having gathered under one stupendous roof the branches of some of Rio's best restaurants.

Rio Design Leblon

Avenida Ataúlfo de Paiva 270, Leblon
Formerly devoted to home decoration and furniture shops, and consequently of little interest to the visitor, the Rio Design has broadened its scope with the addition of many designer clothing stores and some excellent food outlets.

Rio Sul

Rua Lauro Muller 116, Botafogo
The first of the malls really to take off, the huge Rio Sul bustles with activity. All self-respecting retailers are represented at this mall, which spreads over four floors. Good for clothing.

São Conrado Fashion Mall

Estrada da Gávea 899, São Conrado
This is the Ritz of Rio's malls, located at the Leblon end of São Conrado beach. Top-of-the-line shops, and first-rate restaurants in a delightful garden-like setting.

Shopping Cassino Atlântico

Avenida Atlântica 4240, Copacabana

Adjacent to the Sofitel Hotel, this is the headquarters of the "antique" business, although that definition should be taken loosely. It is fun to see what's considered an "antique": teacups and Parker pens fight for space with ornate chandeliers, and heavy farmhouse furniture.

Shopping da Gávea

Avenida Marquês de São Vicente 52, Gávea
Plenty of interest in this traditional mall, which has a high concentration of art galleries. The pastries from Chez Anne on the ground floor are prize-winners.

The Hippie Fair

One thing you won't see here is a hippy, but the market dates back to the 1970s when such creatures existed. Huge range of handicrafts, artwork, leather goods, clothing, and knick-knacks are available at this Sunday-only market, which is a magnet for foreign visitors. It is held at Praça General Osório in Ipanema. A poor relation of the Hippie Fair – but still quite entertaining – is held nightly on the central reservation of Copacabana beachfront, at the intersection with Rua Djalma Ulrich. Soccer shirts, beach towels, handmade trinkets and costume jewelry are available.

SPORT

Participant Sports

Bodyboarding, climbing, hang-gliding, hiking, kite surfing, rafting, rappel, wakeboarding, and windsurfing are among the many outdoor activities the fit visitor might want to try while in Rio or the Rio area. Suppliers of equipment, training, or guidance in all these activities are legion, and the number grows as the popularity of these activities increases. Here is a partial listing of some respected operators in this area *(also see Adventure Tourism, next column)*:

Aribira Aventuras
Tel: 2235-3716 or 3204-9313
www.aribira.com.br
Rock-climbing in and around Rio, and hiking in the surrounding area. They also run rock climbing classes for climbers at all levels, and for children.

Arte Radical
Tel: 2210-1342
www.arteradical.com.br
Climbing on Morro da Urca and in the Floresta de Tijuca among other activities.

KlickRio
Tel: 2548-4974
www.klickrio.com.br
Organizes climbing, diving, rafting, and sailing excursions.

On the Rocks Adventures
Tel: 2529-8476 (Leblon) or 2491-9725 (Barra)
www.ontherocks.com.br
Hiking, kayaking, and climbing.

Rio Hiking
Tel: 2552-9204
www.riohiking.com.br
Hang-gliding, scuba-diving, horseback riding, and surfing as well as hiking and climbing

Hang-Gliding
The urge to hang-glide overtakes many people when they reach Rio. One of the best ways to organize a flight is to turn up at São Conrado's Praia do Pepino, where the hang-gliders land, and get yourself fixed up. The telephone number for the **Brazilian Association of Hang Gliders**, which is headquartered at the Pepino Beach, is 3322-0266.

Golf
There are two golf courses in the city of Rio, Gávea Golf and Country Club and Itanhangá Golf Club, both open to members only. However, certain hotels have arrangements with the clubs which enable guests to pay green fees and play during the week.

However, visitors are always welcome on the excellent, 18-hole course designed by Colorado-based Peter Dye at the **Búzios Golf Club** (tel: (22) 2629-1240 or (22) 2629-1338).

Spectator Sports

Soccer is *the* spectator sport as far as many *cariocas* are concerned. A major game at the **Maracanã Stadium** *(see picture story, pages 164–5)* is always a memorable occasion, and should not be missed. Beach volleyball has a large following, and occasionally a temporary stadium may be built on Copacabana Beach to house finals of important championships.

TOURS

Boating
Marlin Yacht Charters (tel. 2225-7434) and **Saveiros Tour** (tel: 2225-6064) both offer a full range of boating services, from sunset cruises to overnight outings to islands off the coast. Both have offices at the Marina in Glória. More personal service can be obtained from a number of independent operators, among them **Heitor** (tel: 9222-2026, www.sailing-in-rio.com).

Adventure Tourism
Indiana Jungle Tours (tel: 2484-2279, www.indianajungle.com.br) and **Jeep Tours** (tel: 2589-0883, www.jeeptour.com.br) are two highly reputable operators in the competitive market of adventure tourism. They offer everything from chasing butterflies to tree-climbing, from forest adventures to deep-sea diving.

Rio Adventures (tel: 2705-5747, www.rioadventures.com). Trips to Serra dos Orgãos National Park and Serra da Bocaina National Park, as well as rafting, scuba diving, hiking, and hang-gliding in and around Rio.

Ecological Tours
IEBMA (Instituto Ecológico Búzios Mata Atlântica/Buzios Atlantic Forest Ecological Institute; tel: (22) 2623-2200 or (2) 2623-2446). IEBMA organizes ecological walks through Emerências Reserve just outside Búzios *(see page 187).*

Motor Cycle Tours
Ayres Adventures (toll free tel: 1-877-275-8238, www.ronayres.com) runs motor-bike tours.

Favela Tours
The pioneering operator in this sector of the market is **Marcelo Armstrong**, who is well loved by the communities to which he takes his visitors, and by many satisfied customers. He can be reached on tel: 3322 2727 or www.favelatour.com.br. *(See Favelas, page 132.)*

View from Above
If money is not a problem, taking to the skies is a wonderful way to see the city's views and layout. **Helisight Tours** (tel: 2411-2141 weekdays, 2259-6995 weekends; www.helisight.com.br) runs an extremely reliable series of tours, for a minimum of three people at a time. Tours last anything from six minutes (about US$70 per person) to one hour (US$400 per person). Their helipads enjoy prime locations at Morro da Urca, the first stage in the Sugar Loaf cable-car system; and Lagoa, in the Parque dos Patins area, near the Jockey Club. **Gold Trail** *(see page 203).* Departures from Teatro Espaço, Rua Dona Geralda 327, Paraty, tel: (24) 3371-1575. Other guides can be contacted at the Sebrae office (tel: (24) 3371-1783).

BELOW: see Rio from the skies.

A – Z

A HANDY SUMMARY OF PRACTICAL INFORMATION, ARRANGED ALPHABETICALLY

A dmission Charges

Many exhibition sites, museums, and galleries do not charge any admission at all, and few of them charge more than a modest US$2, at current rates. The price for visiting Sugar Loaf and for taking the train up Corcovado can come as bit of a surprise, especially if you are traveling as a family, as they both cost more than US$10 per person.

Nightclubs featuring live music will often have an "artistic cover charge," which is sometimes deducted from your drinks bill. Whenever possible, phone ahead (or ask your hotel reception to help you do so) to find out how much an outing is going to cost, to avoid unpleasant surprises.

Airport Taxes

The airport tax at Rio international airport is considered high, at approximately US$36, so ensure that you keep back enough cash (reais or US dollars) to pay this on your way out. To find out the exact value at the time you travel, call the information section of the airport, tel: 2298-4525.

B udgeting for Your Trip

Rio de Janeiro is no longer the bargain holiday destination it may have been in the past. Accommodation runs the range from basic hostels to the world's finest hotels, and is priced accordingly. Eating out is relatively inexpensive, however; portions are huge, and sharing is not frowned upon. Decent wine is not cheap, and can add silly money to your restaurant bill, but perfectly drinkable table wine is reasonably priced. Beer and spirits are cheap. Spirit measures are huge: if you ask for all the components of your favorite tipple to be served separately – gin, tonic, and ice – you could easily make one tot do for two drinks. (But sharing of drinks is not done!) Informal eateries such as the stand-up juice bars provide wholesome, hearty snacks, so one sit-down meal a day will probably suffice for many.

CLIMATE CHART

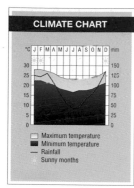

☐ Maximum temperature
■ Minimum temperature
— Rainfall
   Sunny months

Taxis are reasonable, a ride from Copacabana to Centro never costing more than US$10. However, beware of taxis lined up outside the elegant hotels, as they have very different rates and a ride can be just that: a rip-off. City buses are very inexpensive, but ride them at your own risk. Long-haul buses are very reasonable; Rio to Petrópolis, for instance, costs about US$10 for more than an hour's journey time. The metro is cheap, but limited in its reach. One thing not to stint on in planning your trip is health insurance. Private health care is very, very expensive in Brazil, so make sure you have adequate cover.

Business Hours

Business hours for most offices are Monday to Friday 9am–6pm. The lunch "hour" may last considerably longer than 60 minutes. Banks open Monday to Friday 10am–4pm. Some banks keep shorter hours for foreign exchange, though, so it may be best to try to change money in the middle of the day. Stores are mainly open 9am–6.30 or 7pm, but may stay open much later, depending on their location. The shopping centers are open Monday to Saturday 10am–10pm, and Sunday 3–10pm, although not all the shops inside keep the same hours. Most supermarkets are open 8am–8pm, although

some stay open later. Unlike many other Latin countries, there is no "siesta", and shops and office do not close down completely for a lengthy lunch.

C limate and Clothing

Rio de Janeiro, located just north of the Tropic of Capricorn at a latitude of 22.5° south, is at the southern extreme of the tropical zone. The climate, due to its location on the Atlantic coast, is humid tropical. In fact, the humidity can be quite crippling, and many women will find themselves wondering why well-behaved hair has suddenly turned into an untamable mane.

Temperatures in summer (December–March) are hot, from 29° to 35°C (84° to 95°F) on average, but can climb up to a sweltering 40°C (104°F). Winter weather (June–August) is a comfortable 20–21°C (68–70°F), occasionally dipping down to 18°C (65°F). The summer months are marked by rains, and, because the city is at sea level and surrounded by mountains down which the rainwater streams, streets often become rivers within minutes.

The climate in the mountain cities outside Rio (such as Petrópolis, Itaipava and Teresópolis) is slightly cooler than that of the coast. In these areas, the rainy summers and dry winters are more pronounced. In winter, although there is no danger of frost, the mountain air is nippy.

What to Wear

While they are very fashion conscious, Brazilians are actually quite casual dressers. Brasília and São Paulo tend to be dressier than Rio; and small inland towns are more conservative than the cities. If you are going to a jungle lodge as part of your trip to Brazil, you will want sturdy clothing and perhaps boots. If you come on business, a suit and tie for men, and suits,

skirts or dresses for women, are the office standard. Rarely are a suit and tie obligatory in restaurants, although obviously in a sophisticated establishment you are expected to dress appropriately, and you will feel better if you blend in.

There are plenty of opportunities for women to dress up, but try to avoid ostentation, and don't wear jewelry that will attract more attention to yourself than you may want.

Shorts are acceptable for both men and women in most areas, especially near the beach or in resort towns, but they are not usually worn in the downtown area. Bermuda shorts are comfortable in hot weather. In recent times, there has been an incomprehensible crackdown on people wearing thong sandals (flip-flops) in restaurants. Air conditioning can be fierce, so a shawl or wrap can be useful.

Some churches and museums do not admit visitors dressed in shorts, and the traditional *gafieira* dance halls will not admit men in shorts, either. Jeans are acceptable dress for men and women, and are worn a great deal in Brazil – but they can be pretty hot.

Obviously, you should not forget to pack a swimsuit. Or you could go mad and buy a tiny, local version of the string bikini, called a *tanga*, for yourself or someone back home – there are many stores that sell nothing but beachwear. New styles emerge each year, in different fabrics and colors, exposing this part or that. They seem to get smaller every year, but somehow they never disappear completely. The tiniest pieces are called *fio dental*, or dental floss.

In Rio nothing will be considered too trendy or outlandish. In smaller towns, although the local people may dress more conservatively, they are accustomed to outsiders, including Brazilian tourists from the big cities. Somehow, no matter how foreign tourists are dressed, Brazilians always seem able to spot them a mile away.

If you are coming for Carnival, remember that it will be very hot, and you will probably be in a crowd and dancing non-stop. Anything colorful is appropriate. If you plan to go to any of the balls, you will find plenty of costumes for sale or rental – you might want to buy just a feathered hair ornament, flowered lei, or sequined accessory to complete your outfit. Many women wear no more than a bikini and make-up, and sometimes even less. Most men wear shorts. Costume is by no means obligatory at Carnival balls, unless specifically stated.

You will need rain gear. Because of the heat, Brazilians use umbrellas more than raincoats. Something light that folds up small and can be slipped into your bag is best. Sunglasses are another essential item. Seaside hotels will provide you with sun umbrellas and beach towels.

As on any trip, it is sensible to bring a pair of comfortable walking shoes: there is no better way to explore than on foot. Sandals are comfortable in the heat. Beach thongs (flip-flops), even if you don't plan to wear them for walking around the streets, are very convenient for getting across the hot sand from your hotel to the water's edge. If there's one thing that gives Brazilians the giggles, it's the sight of a gringo going to the beach in shoes and socks.

Brazilian women often wear high-heeled shoes and show special agility on the sidewalks – which can be veritable obstacle courses of holes, stones, beggars, vendors and garbage cans, and are often completely taken over by parked cars. You may want to buy shoes or sandals while you are here – leather goods are still something of a steal in Brazil.

A sturdy but unobtrusive shoulder bag carried or tucked securely under your arm (not slung behind you in city streets)

is a practical item. Use it to carry your camera discreetly. Better still, copy the Brazilians and wear a small, rucksack-type bag, slung in front of you instead of on your back. Toss in a foldable umbrella, a guidebook, and map, and you're ready for a day's outing.

Although clothing made of synthetic fibers may be convenient – they are easy to wash and don't need ironing – these fabrics do not breathe or absorb perspiration as natural fibers do, and will make you feel twice as hot. There is no better fabric to wear in the heat than cotton.

Crime and Safety

There's no denying that Rio de Janeiro is a dangerous city, but perhaps no more so than many other major capitals with comparable populations. Foreign visitors are, of course, prime targets for petty thievery, so take nothing out of the hotel with you that you are not prepared to part with. The beaches are ripe territory for thieves. Carry cameras, if you must, discreetly. Leave valuables in the hotel safe, along with a list of your credit card and other document numbers. You could also leave your passport there, having previously made a photocopy to carry with you.

In restaurants, don't be surprised if a seal is placed on your handbag, attaching it to your chair. Brazilians believe that if you leave your handbag on the floor, all your money will fly away – which well it might if a thief gets hold of it!

Never accept a drink from a stranger.

The horrible crime that hits the international headlines and gives Rio such a bad reputation is not directed at the foreign visitor. Gang warfare, kidnappings, and shootings are, in the main, a local issue involving residents, usually connected to drug traffic. Notwithstanding, at the slightest sign of a scuffle or trouble, move away fast.

ABOVE: Tourist Police office.

Rio's Tourist Police has a special station for dealing with visitors. It is at Avenida Afrânio de Melo Franco 159, Leblon, tel: 3399-7171. If you are involved in an incident, it makes sense to report it, however inconvenient this may seem, as by doing so you may help prevent a fellow visitor suffering the same fate.

Customs and Duty Free

Arrival Cards and Accompanied Baggage Declarations must be filled in, usually on the aircraft before landing, and handed to local authorities on arrival. Customs officials spot-check the baggage of approximately 50 pecent of incoming "nothing to declare" travelers. This can be explained by the fact that Brazil is, unfortunately, a key player in the international illegal drugs market.

Furthermore, years of trade barriers between Brazil and the outside world gave rise to an efficient contraband system. If you are arriving as a tourist and bringing articles for personal use, you will have no problem. As in most countries, food products of animal origin, plants, fruit, and seeds may be confiscated. In addition to items for personal use, you are permitted to bring in to the country US$500-worth of goods acquired at the extremely well-stocked Duty Free Shops, located on the arrivals side of most international airports in Brazil. The limits on specific items (such as 24 bottles of alcohol per passenger) are well posted, staff are helpful, and any credit card or foreign currency is accepted, but reais are not.

Visiting commercial missions should seek prior exemption from any import duties that might apply to samples or equipment needed for their business purposes. The nearest Brazilian consulate should be able to advise on how to go about this.

The checked-in baggage of passengers departing from Brazil may be subject to inspection by customs and the federal revenue authorities. Carry-on baggage will be inspected by airlines for security reasons. Any attempt to export animal skins, birds, or ornamental fish illegally will be viewed very seriously by the local authorities. Departing passengers are also permitted to spend US$500 in the Duty Free Shops, but they must, naturally, respect the import restrictions of their country of destination. Left over reais are of no use in the Duty Free shops, as mentioned above. However, there is no shortage of good shops (including Bee, selling excellent T-shirts) where you can get rid of those last bits of local currency.

D isabled Travelers

Increased social awareness and the enforcement of appropriate legislation have ensured that most hotels and public places have facilities for travelers with disabilities, but if this an important issue for you, it is wise to phone ahead to check.

E lectricity

The current in Rio de Janeiro is 110 volts, 60 hertz, and two-pin plugs are used. Good hotels will have a 220-volt outlet in the bathroom. Most of the better hotels will also have a hairdryer in the bathroom.

Embassies & Consulates

Brazilian Embassies

Brazilian Embassies Overseas
Australia
19 Forster Crescent, Yarralumla, Canberra, ACT 2600, tel: 61-2 6273 2372; fax: 61-2 6273 2375; www.brazil.org.au
Canada
450 Wilbrod Street, Ottawa, Ontario, K1N 6M8, tel: 613-237 1090, fax: 613-237-6144; www.brasembbottawa.org
Eire
Europa House, 5th floor, Harcourt Street, Dublin 2, tel: 353-1 475 6000; fax: 353-1 475 1341; www.brazil.ie
Mexico
Calle Lope de Armendariz 130, Colonia Lomas Virreyes, CP 11000 Mexico, DF; tel: (5255) 5201-4351; fax: (5255) 5520 4929; www.cebmexico.org.mx
South Africa
201 Leyds Street, Arcadia; P.O. Box 03269 Pretoria, Code 001, tel: (12) 341-1712/341-5566; fax: (12) 341-7547; e-mail: braspret@cis.co.za
United Kingdom
32 Green Street Street, London W1Y 4AT, tel: (020) 7499 0877; fax: (020) 7399 9100; www.brazil.embassyhomepage.com
Consulates in the US
Boston: The Stattler Building, 20 Park Plaza, Suite 810, Boston, MA 02116, tel: (617) 542-4000; fax: (617) 542-4318; www.consulatebrazil.org
Chicago: 401 North Michigan Avenue, Suite 3050, Chicago, IL 60611, tel: (312) 464-0244/464-0245; fax: (312) 464-0299; e-mail: central@brazilconsulatechicago.org
Houston: Park Tower North, 1233 West Loop South, suite 1150, Houston, TX 77027, tel: (713) 961-3063; fax: (713) 961-3070; www.brazilhouston.org

Los Angeles: 8484 Wilshire Blvd, suites 711–730, Beverly Hills, CA 90211, tel: (323) 651-2664; fax: (323)-651-1274; www.brazilian-consulate.org
Miami: 80 SW 8th St, Miami, FL 33130, tel: (305) 285-6200; fax: (305) 285-6229; www.brazilmiami.org
New York: 1185 Avenue of the Americas, 21st Floor, NY 10036, tel: (917) 777-7777; fax: (212) 827-0225; www.brazilny.org
San Francisco: 300 Montgomery Street, Suite 900, CA, 94104, tel: (415) 981-8170; fax: (415) 981-3628; www.brazilsf.org
Washington, DC: 3009 Whitehaven St NW, Washington, DC 20008, tel: (202) 238-2700; fax: (202) 238-2827; www.brasilemb.org

Foreign Consulates

Addresses and telephone numbers for some consulates in Rio de Janeiro are listed below. It's a good idea to call before visiting. Diplomatic missions frequently do not keep normal business hours, and some are not full consulates, merely honorary.
Australia
Avenida Presidente Wilson 231, 23rd floor, Centro, tel: 3824-4624; fax: 2262-4247; honconau@terra.com.br (Honorary Consul)
Canada
Avenida Atlântica 1130, 5th floor, tel: 2543-3004; fax: 2275-2195, www.dfait-maeci.gc.ca/brazil
South Africa
Rua David Campista 50, tel: 2527-1455 (Honorary Consul); Avenida Paulista 1754, 12th floor, São Paulo, tel: 11-3285-0433; fax: 11-3284-4862 (Consulate General), www.africadosulemb.org.br
United Kingdom
Praia do Flamengo 284, 2nd floor, Flamengo, tel: 2555-9600; fax: 2555-9672; www.uk.org.br
USA
Avenida Presidente Wilson 147, Centro, tel: 3823-2000; fax: 3823-2003; www.embaixada.americana.org.br

TRANSPORT ACCOMMODATION ACTIVITIES A – Z LANGUAGE

Emergency Numbers

Police: 190
Ambulance: 192
Fire brigade: 193

Entry Regulations

Visas and Passports

Brazil follows a reciprocity policy regarding visas: thus an entry visa must be obtained before arrival in Brazil by citizens of countries which require Brazilian visitors to present visas. US citizens must arrive with a visa in order to enter Brazil; EU and Mercosul citizens need it. Ensure you get the proper visa information by contacting the appropriate authorities before buying your ticket.

A visitor's visa is valid for 90 days from the date of entry into the country. This visa does not permit you to work. Temporary visas are issued to foreigners who will be employed in a specific activity in Brazil (for which they may stay longer than a tourist visa would allow), or who will be working or doing business in the country. This is usually the case for a student, journalist, researcher, or multinational company employee. If this is your situation, contact a Brazilian consulate well before you plan to travel, as it can be difficult to change the status of your visa once you are in the country. If you arrive with a tourist visa, you may have to leave the country to obtain and return on another type of visa.

An Extension of Stay visa may be obtained from the Federal Police in Brazil, if requested at least 30 days prior to a visa's expiry, for a total stay of up to 180 days per year. To obtain such an extension, you must go to the immigration sector of the federal police, located at Avenida Venezuela 2 (downtown, near Praça Maúa), tel: 2291-2142 ext. 1136. Opening hours: Monday to Friday 10am–5pm. This procedure can be a bit baffling for someone who has not mastered the language, and requires patience.

Etiquette

Social customs in Brazil are not vastly different from those in "western" countries, but Brazilians can confuse foreigners by being both awkwardly formal and disarmingly offhand. Surnames are little used. People start out on a first-name basis, but titles of respect – *senhor* for men and *dona* or *senhora* for women – are used out of politeness to strangers, but also to show respect to someone who belongs to a different age group or social class.

Handshaking is common practice on introduction, but it is not unusual to greet not only friends and relatives but also complete strangers with a kiss. This "social" form of kissing consists usually of a kiss on each cheek. While men and women greet each other with kisses, as do women among themselves, men rarely kiss each other, but shake hands while giving a pat on the shoulder with the other hand. If they are more intimate, men will embrace, thumping each other on the back. Although this is the general custom, there are subtleties, governed by social position, about who kisses whom. If you are in doubt or do not want to be kissed, proffer your hand to initiate a handshake. Visitors will notice that Brazilians seem quite unabashed about expressing affection, or, indeed, any emotion, in public.

Brazilians are generous hosts, ensuring that guests' glasses, plates, or coffee cups are never empty. Besides the genuine pleasure of being a gracious host, there is the question of honor, and the potluck get-together or bring-your-own-bottle party is not generally popular in Rio.

Although Brazil is definitely a male-dominated society, machismo takes a milder and more subtle form than is generally found in neighboring Hispanic America. As could be expected in such a multicultural society, racial tolerance is widespread, though there are exceptions.

While they are at all other times a polite, decent people, something happens when Brazilians get behind the steering wheel. Be extremely cautious if driving or crossing streets, and be prepared to make a dash. Drivers expect pedestrians to get out of the way.

Expect schedules to be very flexible. It is not considered rude to show up half an hour to an hour late for a social engagement. Even the timing of business appointments can be flexible when compared with the US or Europe. Don't try to include too many in one day, as you may well find your schedule badly disrupted by unexpected delays.

Gay & Lesbian Travelers

Rio is one of the sexiest cities in the world, and all flavors are welcome in this cultural mixed salad. The gay community will have no problems networking with like-minded people in Rio, a city that has always been a magnet for the daring, outspoken, and proudly different. With an ever-evolving gay scene, it is difficult to pinpoint a special source of information, but there are several to choose from on the internet.

Back on earth and starting with the beach, the stretch in front of Rua Farme de Amoedo in Ipanema would be a great place to get to know people, and Le Boy club, at Rua Raul Pompéia 102 in Copacabana, is a good introduction to the gay scene by night, provided you don't get there before midnight. Transvestite prostitution is widely practiced in Rio, so either be cautious or prepared for surprises. Taking a stranger of any sex back to your room could be an invitation to disaster, as well as result in your eviction from your hotel; that's what motels are for.

Health

Vaccination or health certificates are not normally required for entry to Brazil. However, if within three months of traveling to

Brazil you have been to any of the countries listed below, you will need to show proof of vaccination against yellow fever: Angola, Benin, Bolivia, Burkina Faso, Burundi, Cameroon, Central African Republic, Colombia, Côte d'Ivoire, Democratic Republic of Congo, Ecuador, Equatorial Guinea, Ethiopia, French Guyana, Gabon, Gambia, Ghana, Guinea, Guinea Bissau, Guyana, Kenya, Liberia, Mali, Mauritania, Niger, Nigeria, Panama, Peru, Rwanda, São Tome and Principe, Senegal, Sierra Leone, Somalia, Sudan, Suriname, Tanzania, Togo, Trinidad and Tobago, Uganda, Venezuela.

Children between the ages of three months and six years may be required to show proof of vaccination against polio.

All these regulations may change from time to time, so it is essential that you check this prior to departure.

If you plan to travel from Rio into the Amazon region or in the Pantanal in Mato Grosso, you must have a yellow-fever shot: this protects you for 10 years, but is only effective after 10 days, so don't leave it until the last minute. As a last resort you can get a yellow-fever shot in Rio at the Health Ministry vaccination post located at Praça Marechal Ancora (near the ferryboat station), tel: 2240-3568. Visitors to jungle areas should consult their own doctor about the advisability of taking anti-malaria drugs.

Aids: The incidence of Aids in Rio and Brazil is very high: good sense is the only protection against infection.

Dengue fever: a health hazard specific to the Rio area is dengue fever, especially during the summer months. There are two main types of dengue fever. One leaves you feeling very low and aching all over, and usually runs its course in three days. The other variety, hemorrhagic dengue, is much more dangerous but fortunately occurs much less frequently. Do not take

aspirin if you think you may have dengue, as this will only complicate matters. No specific protection exists against dengue, but as it is transmitted by mosquito, insect repellents should be part of your travel kit.

Sun protection: Don't underestimate the tropical sun! Often, there is a pleasant but deceptive breeze as you loll on the beach and soak up too much sun. Use an appropriate sunscreen, start out with short sessions in the sun, and avoid the hottest part of the day. After the beach, use plenty of moisturizer. Drink plenty of fluids: coconut milk, fruit juice or mineral water are all excellent ways to replace lost minerals and fluids.

Drinking water: Although tap water in Rio is safe by international standards, you will do better not to drink it. This advice is made easier to follow by the fact that it doesn't taste very nice, so you will not be tempted. It is fine for brushing your teeth. The ubiquitous blue bottles of water can be bought inexpensively from any supermarket or drugstore, or from bars or kiosks.

Diarrhea: While this can technically be prevented by following food and water precautions, it is

BELOW: always wear a sun hat.

a vacation-ruining condition that may still strike despite the visitor's best vigilance. Antibiotics and anti-diarrheal drugs and a note regarding dosages should be an essential part of your travel kit if you are prone. If struck, avoid the sun and drink plenty of fluids, to avoid making things worse through dehydration. If the condition persists beyond a couple of days of ultra-sensible behavior, seek medical attention.

Medical Services

Should you need a doctor during your stay in Rio de Janeiro, your hotel should be able to recommend a reliable practitioner. Your consulate will also be able to supply you with a list of physicians who speak your language. Check with your health insurance company or travel agent before traveling to make sure your insurance plan covers any medical service necessary while abroad.

Emergency Hospitals

If you are involved in an accident and attended by the local emergency services, they are obliged, by law, to take you to a public hospital. This need not be the nightmare it sounds; the trauma facilities at the Hospital Miguel Couto (see below) are among the best in South America. If your condition requires a longer stay in hospital, check with your insurance company and with your consulate to see where you should be transferred.

Public Hospitals

These hospitals provide free treatment of any number of ailments, chronic and acute. They may seem very basic by North American standards.
Leblon: Hospital Miguel Couto, Rua Bartolomeu Mitre 1108, tel: 274-2121 or 2274-6050.
Botafogo: Hospital Rocha Maia, Rua General Severiano 91, tel: 2295-2121 or 2295-2295.
Centro: Hospital Souza Aguiar, Praça da República 111, tel: 2296-4114 or 2221-2121.

Barra: Hospital Lourenço Jorge, Avenida Ayrton Senna 2000, tel: 2431-1818 or 2431-1244.

Private Hospitals

If you have proper insurance cover, you would do better to go straight to a private hospital. If you need to be admitted for an overnight or longer stay, be prepared to part with a hefty sum on arrival as a refundable deposit.

Hospital Samaritano
Rua Bambina 98, Botafogo, tel: 2537-9722.

Clínica São Vicente
Rua João Borges 204, Gávea, tel: 2529-4422.

Copa D'Or
Rua Figueiredo de Magalhães 875, Copacabana, tel: 2545-3600.

Barra D'Or
Avenida Ayrton Senna 2541, Barra, tel: 2430-3600.

Drugs and Drugstores

There seems to be at least one drugstore on every block in Rio. New legislation has made it difficult to buy widely obtainable drugs without a prescription from a local doctor. The law requires each drugstore to have a pharmacist on duty at all times; this can be quite helpful if you do not know what you are looking for. Non-brand, generic drugs are available at often half the price of the original product; always ask if there is a generic drug *(tem generico?)* for whatever it is you have been prescribed.

Drugs, Other

Brazil is very much on the international drug route, and a fine way to end your vacation before it starts is to attempt to bring in illegal or recreational drugs with you. If you are caught, you will be in serious trouble.

I nternet

Brazil is one of the most internet- and web-savvy countries on the planet, and Portuguese is the second most used language on the web after English. Broadband connections should be available from most upmarket hotel rooms; hotel business centers also provide this service, but often at a high cost. There seem to be as many cyber cafés in Rio as there are drugstores, and you will not have to wander far to find one. Some are pretty basic, others are in charming bookstores with freshly made coffee and snacks available. Keeping in touch will not be a problem while you are in Rio.

A few useful addresses are: Letras e Expressões, a favorite newsagent and bookseller, which offers internet use at its two stores: Avenida Ataulfo de Paiva 1292, Leblon, tel: 2511-5085; and Rua Visconde de Pirajá 276, Ipanema, tel: 2521-6110. Most branches of McDonald's also have internet facilities.

L ost Property

This is, sadly, often just that: lost property. Cab drivers, however, have a good reputation for returning belongings left in their cars, and the Post Office runs a service whereby you can check if your lost passport has been handed in at one of their agencies by calling tel: 0800-570-0100. Otherwise, there's little to be done.

M aps

If you plan to travel much by road in Brazil, buy the *Quatro Rodas (Four Wheels)* Brazil road guide, complete with road maps and itineraries, available at most newsstands.

Media

Newspapers/Magazines

Most international newspapers are available in Rio, either on the day of publication or the day after. The biggest circulation daily in Rio is the broadsheet *O Globo*. Even if you know no Portuguese, the entertainment section is not difficult to understand, and *O Globo*'s *Rio Show* magazine insert, published on a Friday, is a useful source of information. *Veja* is a national glossy weekly news magazine, and it, too, publishes a Friday entertainment insert, called *Vejinha*. The advantage of *Veja*'s entertainment insert is that it is available all week, not just on Friday.

Newsstands are quite a feature of life in Rio, and can be

BELOW: Rio newsstand.

found on many street corners. They are kept on their commercial toes by intense competition, and are full of publications, many in English, on the widest possible variety of subjects. They also stock postcards, phonecards, batteries, lottery cards, and other travelers' essentials.

Television

Brazilians are television addicts, especially when it comes to the soaps. Shown during prime time, they attract huge audiences who get so caught up in the continuing drama that they schedule social and even professional activities so as not to clash with crucial episodes. The soaps not only reflect customs but set trends in fashion, speech, and social habits. You might like to glimpse an episode or two simply because millions of Brazilians will be doing the same thing. Brazil's giant TV Globo is the fourth-largest commercial network in the world. With more than 40 stations in a country with a fairly high illiteracy rate, it has great influence over the information received by huge numbers of people.

Most hotels in the city receive cable or satellite TV offering close to 100 channels, including most of the global favorites such as CNN and BBC World.

Radio

The radio will be of little use to the foreign visitor, but is very much a feature of life for many Brazilians. Many of the stations are controlled by Evangelical pastors, which, in part, accounts for the vast numbers of converts to evangelism and related variants of religion *(see page 40)*.

Money Matters

The real is the currency in Brazil, and there are 100 centavos to one real. The plural is reais. While nowhere near as volatile as it was during the days of galloping inflation, the real is pegged to the US dollar on a daily basis.

Rates are marginally less for travelers' checks. For ease of calculation, consider US$1 to be worth just over R$2.

BRANCHES OF INTERNATIONAL BANKS INCLUDE:

BANKBOSTON: AVENIDA RIO BRANCO 26A, CENTRO; AND RUA VISCONDE DE PIRAJÁ 338, IPANEMA.

CITIBANK: RUA DA ASSEMBLÉIA 100, CENTRO; AND RUA VISCONDE DE PIRAJÁ 459, IPANEMA.

hsbc: Rua da Assembléia 66, Centro; and Rua Visconde de Pirajá 259, Ipanema.

The Banco do Brasil maintains a 24-hour exchange facility in an office on the third floor of the international airport.

If you lose your credit card, it is much easier to get it canceled in your home country. Here are the local numbers to call if this is not possible:

American Express: tel: 0800-78-5050; Credicard, Mastercard, and Visa: tel: 4001-4411.

Cash Machines

Technically, you should be able to withdraw local currency from a cash machine on your credit card. There are ATMs all over Rio, but do be discreet while using them, and favor the ones inside shopping malls rather than those on the street. As glitches in cash withdrawals are not unknown, it makes sense to test your card before you actually run out of cash.

Visitors with disabilities may use the Banco do Brasil ATM at Rua Joana Angélica 124A in Ipanema, Avenida Nossa Senhora de Copacabana 594, Copacabana, or at their massive Cultural Centre at Rua Primeiro de Março 66 in downtown.

Travelers' checks

Most hotels will accept payment in travelers' checks, although they have somewhat fallen into disuse with the improvement of ATMs. Furthermore, you will get an inferior rate for traveler's checks. You can exchange dollars, yen, pounds, and other currencies at accredited banks.

O rientation

Squeezed between mountains and the sea, Rio lies just north of the Tropic of Capricorn, at latitude 22.5°. Misleadingly, the western part of the city, comprising Leblon, Ipanema, and Copacabana, most frequented by visitors, is known as the south zone (zona sul), while the eastern part of the city, where the airport is located is known as the north zone (zona norte). Rio is not a difficult place to keep your bearings, as the beach and other landmarks such as the Sugar Loaf and Corcovado mountains are constant points of reference. The major attractions are relatively well signposted; other parts of the city are not.

P ostal services

The Brazilian postal service goes through good patches and bad patches. If sending postcards to friends and family is seriously important to you, consider posting your cards when you get back home. Major branches of the post office are located at Avenida Almirante Barroso 63, Centro; Avenida Nossa Senhora de Copacabana 1298, Copacabana; and Rua Prudente de Morais 147, Ipanema.

Public Holidays

The number of public holidays observed in Brazil produces potentially long weekends, as a "bridge" is often built between the holiday and the nearest weekend. Carnival, of course, is a case apart, with people already preparing either to party and parade or to flee the folly on the Friday preceding. Although normal activities are meant to resume on the Wednesday, in practice the whole week is written off, and normality only resumes the following Monday.

TRANSPORT

ACCOMMODATION

ACTIVITIES

A – Z

LANGUAGE

Here is a list of the major holidays observed in Rio:

January

| 1 | New Year's Day |
| 20 | St Sebastian's Day (Patron Saint of Rio) |

February/March *(see separate selection below for Carnival dates to 2010)*

April

| 21 | Tiradentes Day |
| 23 | St George's Day |

May

| 1 | Labor Day |

June

*Corpus Christi

September

| 7 | Declaration of Independence |

October

| 12 | Our Lady of Aparecida (Patron Saint of Brazil) |

Commerce Day (shops closed)

November

2	All Souls' Day
15	Proclamation of the Republic
20	Black Consciousness Day

December

24	Christmas Eve
25	Christmas Day
31	New Year's Eve

Holidays marked with an asterisk (*) are movable. Corpus Christi is observed on the second Thursday after Pentecost, which is usually mid-June. Commerce Day is observed on the third Monday in October.

To help with forward planning, it may be useful to know that Carnival dates until 2010 are:

2007	February 18
2008	February 3
2009	February 22
2010	February 14

R eligious Services

Services in English are conducted at the following churches. Phone ahead to check on times.

Anglican: Christ Church, Rua Real Grandeza 99, Botafogo, tel: 2226-7332.

Roman Catholic: Our Lady of Mercy, Rua Visconde de Caravelas 48, Botafogo, tel: 2537-9065.

Evangelical: Union Church, Ava Prefeito Dulcídio Cardoso 4351, Barra, tel: 3325-8601.

Baptist: International Baptist Church, Rua Desembargador Alfredo Russel 146, Leblon, tel: 2239-8848.

Jewish: Associação Religiosa Israelita, Rua General Severiano 170, Botafogo, tel: 2543-6320.

S tudent Travelers

Students don't make up a big part of Rio's tourist trade, and few special concessions are made for them. Student discounts are not a familiar concept.

T elecoms

Payphones are blue and bulbous, and called *orelhões*: big ears. They accept phonecards, which can be bought at news-stands. To make an international call you must select an international service provider, whose number you insert between the 00 and the area code of the country you are dialing. Service-provider numbers are 21 for Embratel and 23 for Intelig. If staying in touch is imperative, you can rent a cellphone (mobile) before leaving home and pick it up at the airport on arrival. You will be given the number before you leave home. To rent a mobile, try Press Cell (www.presscell.com).

In an emergency you can use your own mobile, but it will be very expensive.

Time Zone

GMT minus 3 hours, Eastern Standard Time plus 2 hours.

Tipping

Restaurant bills include a tip, which is usually 10 percent, unless otherwise noted. Technically, this tip is optional, but in practice it is hard to get out of paying it. If you are paying with a credit card and feel you have been exceptionally well served, consider leaving the tip in reais-so the service staff will not have to wait for the transaction to clear before receiving it. Cab drivers are pleasantly surprised by a tip, even if you merely round up the fare shown to the nearest real.

Toilets

Public toilets are rare in Rio, but there is not usually a problem with walking into a bar or restaurant to use the facilities. If there's an attendant, a tip is expected. Ladies is *Senhoras* or *Damas*, Gentlemen is *Homens* or sometimes *Cavalheiros*. Signs are often abbreviated to "S" and "H".

Tourist Information

Riotur is the city's tourism authority, and deserves the excellent reputation it enjoys. Their bi-lingual *Rio Guide* is published six times a year, and is packed with reliable information about forthcoming events. Riotur's shopfront is at Avenida Princesa Isabel 183, Copacabana, on the road that separates Leme from Copacabana. It runs an efficient over-the-phone information service, called **Alô Rio**, tel: 2542-8080 or 0800-7071808.

Rio state's tourist authority (which deals with everything outside the city limits of Rio) is **TurisRio**. Its headquarters are at Rua da Ajuda 5, 6th floor, in the downtown area, tel: 2215-0011. They also have an office, where the staff speak English, in Rio Sul shopping centre (toll free tel: 0800-282-2007).

W ebsites

www.rio.rj.gov.br is the official Riotur tourist information site. It's in English, and very useful. www.riodejaneiroguide.com is good for information on accommodation, restaurants, entertainment, and general helpful hints.

LANGUAGE

UNDERSTANDING PORTUGUESE

Familiarization

Portuguese, not Spanish, is the language of Brazil. If you have any knowledge of Spanish, it will come in handy – you will recognize many similar words, and most Brazilians understand some Spanish. Be warned, though, that words that look almost identical when written may sound completely different when spoken. Although many educated Brazilians know at least some English or French and are eager to practice on the foreign visitor, don't expect the person on the street to speak your language.

You can easily get by in English at large hotels and smart restaurants. However, if you like to wander around on your own, a pocket dictionary would be helpful. First names are used a great deal in Brazil. In many situations in which English speakers would use a title and surname, Brazilians often use a first name with the title of respect. Senhor for men (written Sr) and Senhora (written Sra) or Dona (used only with first name) for women. If João Oliveira or Maria da Silva calls you Sr John, rather than Mr Jones, then you should address them as Sr João and Dona Maria.

If you are staying longer and

are serious about learning the language, there are Portuguese courses for non-native speakers.

A foreigner's effort to learn the local language is always appreciated. Meanwhile, here are some essential words and phrases.

Addresses

Alameda (abbreviated Al.) **lane**
Andar **floor, story**
Av. or Avenida **avenue**
Centro **the central downtown business district**, also frequently referred to as **cidade** or the **city**
Cj. or Conjunto **a suite of rooms or sometimes a group of buildings**
Estrada (abbreviated Estr.) **road or highway**
Largo (Lgo) **square or plaza**
Praça (Pça) **square or plaza**
Praia **beach**
Rodovia (Rod.) **highway**
Rua (abbreviated R.) **street**
Sala **room**
Sobreloja **mezzanine**

Ordinal numbers are written with a ° sign after the numeral, so that *3° andar* means **3rd floor**. The federal interstate highways are always written with a BR immediately in front of the number – for example, BR101, which follows the Atlantic coast.

Greetings/Generalities

Tudo Bem (all's well) is one of the most common forms of greeting: a person asks, "*Tudo bem?*" and the other replies, "*Tudo bem.*" This can also mean "OK," "all right," "will do," or as a response when someone apologizes, indicating, "That's all right, it doesn't matter."
Good morning *Bom dia*
Good afternoon *Boa tarde*
Good evening/night *Boa noite*
How are you? *Como vai?*
Well, thank you *Bem, obrigado*
Hello (to answer the phone) *Alô*
Hello *Bom dia, boa tarde*
Hi, hey! *Oi* (informal greeting)
Goodbye *Adeus;* **(casual)** *Tchau;*
(see you soon) *Até*
My name is... *Meu nome é...*
I am... *Eu sou...*
What is your name? *Como é seu nome?*
It's a pleasure (when introduced) *É um prazeri* (or frequently) *prazer*
Good! Great! *Que bom!*
Health! (common toast) *Saúde!*
Do you speak English? *Você fala inglês?*
I don't understand *Não entendo*
Do you understand? *Você entende?*
Please repeat more slowly *Por favor repete, mais devagar*

What do you call this (that)?
Como se chama isto (aquilo)?
How do you say...? *Como se diz...?*

Nouns/Pronouns

Who? *Quem?*
I *Eu*
We *Nós*
You (sing.) *Você* **(plural)** *Vocês*
He, She, They *Ele, Ela, Eles, Elas*
My, Mine (depending on gender of object) *Meu, Minha*
Our, Ours (depending on gender of object) *Nosso, Nossa*
Your, Yours (depending on gender of object) *Seu, Sua*
His or Her, Hers, Their or Theirs *Dele, Dela, Deles* (also *Seu, Sua* in all three cases)

Getting Around

Where is the...? *Onde é...?*
beach *a praia*
bathroom *o banheiro*
bus station *a rodoviária*
airport *o aeroporto*
train station *a estação de trem*
post office *o correio*
police station *a delegacia de polícia*
ticket office *a bilheteria*
marketplace *o mercado/a feira*
embassy *a embaixada*
consulate *o consulado*
Where is there a...? *Onde é que tem...?*
currency exchange *uma casa de câmbio*
bank *um banco*
pharmacy *uma farmácia*
(good) hotel *um (bom) hotel*
(good) restaurant *um (bom) restaurante*
snack bar *uma lanchonete*
bus stop *um ponto de ônibus*
taxi stand *um ponto de taxi*
subway station *uma estação de metrô*
service station *um posto de gasolina*
public telephone *um telefone público*
supermarket *um supermercado*
shopping center *um shopping center*

department store *uma loja de departamentos*
hairdresser *um cabeleireiro*
barber *um barbeiro*
laundry *uma lavanderia*
hospital *um hospital*
Do you have...? *Tem...?*
I want... please. *Eu quero... por favor.*
I don't want... *Eu não quero...*
I want to buy... *Eu quero comprar...*
Where can I buy...? *Onde posso comprar...?*
film *filme*
a ticket for... *uma entrada para...*
a reserved seat *um lugar marcado*
another (the same) *um outro igual*
another (different) *um outro diferente*
this, that *isto, aquilo*
something less expensive *algo mais barato*
postcards *cartões postais*
paper *papel*
envelopes *envelopes*
a pen *uma caneta*
a pencil *um lápis*
soap *sabonete*
shampoo *xampu*
toothpaste *pasta de dente*
sunscreen *filtro solar*
aspirin *aspirina*
I need... *Eu preciso de...*
a doctor *um médico*
a mechanic *um mecânico*
help *ajuda*
How much? *Quanto?*
How many? *Quantos?*
How much does it cost? *Quanto custa?, Quanto é?*
That's very expensive *É muito caro*
A lot, many *muito, muitos*
A little, few *Um pouco, um pouquinho, poucos*

Numbers

1 *um*
2 *dois*
3 *três*
4 *quatro*
5 *cinco*
6 *seis* (or often *meia*, meaning "half" for half-dozen)

7 *sete*
8 *oito*
9 *nove*
10 *dez*
11 *onze*
12 *doze*
13 *treze*
14 *quatorze*
15 *quinze*
16 *dezesseis*
17 *dezessete*
18 *dezoito*
19 *dezenove*
20 *vinte*
21 *vinte e um*
30 *trinta*
40 *quarenta*
50 *cinqüenta*
60 *sessenta*
70 *setenta*
80 *oitenta*
90 *noventa*
100 *cem*
101 *cento e um*
200 *duzentos*
300 *trezentos*
400 *quatrocentos*
500 *quinhentos*
600 *seiscentos*
700 *setecentos*
800 *oitocentos*
900 *novecentos*
1,000 *mil*

Opposites, etc.

yes, no *sim, não*
more, less *mais, menos*
large, small *grande, pequeno*
larger, smaller *maior, menor*
expensive, cheap *caro, barato*
warm, cool *morno, frio*
hot, cold *quente, gelado*
with, without *com, sem*
first, last *primeiro, ultimo*
far, near *longe, perto*
fast, slow *rápido, devagar*
right, left *direita, esquerda*
here, there *aqui, lá*
now, later *agora, depois*
good/well *bom/bem*
better/best *melhor/o melhor*
bad/worse *ruim/pior*

Transportation

taxi, bus, car *taxi, ônibus, carro*
plane, train, boat *avião, trem, barco*

A ticket to... *Uma passagem para...*
I want to go to... *Quero ir para...*
How can I get to...? *Como posso ir para...?*
Please take me to... *Por favor, me leve para...*
Please call a taxi for me. *Por favor, chame um taxi para mim.*
What is this place called? *Como se chama este lugar?*
How long will it take to get there? *Leva quanto tempo para chegar lá?*
Please stop here. Stop! *Por favor pare aqui. Pare!*
Please wait. *Por favor, espere*
I want to rent a car. *Quero alugar um carro.*
What time does the... leave? *A que horas sai o...?*
Where does this bus go? *Este ônibus vai para onde?*
Does it go via...? *Passa em...?*
Departure tax *Taxa de embarque*
I want to check my luggage. *Quero despachar minha bagagem.*
I want to store my luggage. *Quero guardar minha bagagem.*

At the Hotel

I have a reservation. *Tenho uma reserva.*
I want to make a reservation. *Quero fazer uma reserva.*
A single room *Um quarto de solteiro*
A double room *Um quarto de casal*
With air conditioning *Com ar condicionado*
I want to see the room. *Quero ver o quarto.*
suitcase *mala*
bag, purse *bolsa*
room service *serviço de quarto*
key *chave*
the manager *o gerente*

Money

cash *dinheiro*
Do you accept credit cards? *Aceita cartão de crédito?*

Can you cash a travelers' check? *Pode trocar um travelers' check? (cheque de viagem)*
I want to exchange money. *Quero trocar dinheiro.*
What is the exchange rate? *Qual é o câmbio?*
The bill, please. *A conta, por favor.*
I want my change, please. *Eu quero meu troco, por favor.*
I want a receipt. *Eu quero um recibo.*

At the Restaurant

waiter *garçon*
maître d' *maitre*
I didn't order this. *Eu não pedi isto.*
Is service Included? *Está incluido o serviço?*
the menu *o cardápio*
the wine list *a carte de vinhos*
breakfast *café da manhã*
lunch *almoço*
supper *jantar*
the house specialty *a especialidade da casa*
mineral water (carbonated/still) *água mineral com gás/sem gás*
coffee *café*
tea *chá*
beer *cerveja*
white wine *vinho branco*
red wine *vinho tinto*
a soft drink, juice *um refrigerante, suco*

an alcoholic drink, a cocktail *um drink/um cocktail*
ice *gelo*
an appetizer, a snack *um tiragosto, um lanche*
beef *carne*
pork *porco*
chicken *frango*
fish *peixe*
shrimp *camarão*
well done *bem passado*
medium rare *ao ponto*
rare *mal passado*
vegetables *verduras*
salad *salada*
fruit *fruta*
rice *arroz*
potatoes (french fries) *batatas (fritas)*
beans *feijão*
soup *sopa*
bread *pão*
butter *manteiga*
toast *torradas*
eggs *ovos*
sandwich *sanduiche*
pizza *pizza*
dessert *sombremesa*
sweets *doces*
a plate *um prato*
a glass *um copo*
a cup *uma xícara*
a napkin *um guardanapo*
salt *sal*
pepper *pimenta*
sugar *açucar*

TIME

Hours of the day are numbered from zero to 24, but can also be referred to as being in the morning *(da manhã)*, in the afternoon *(da tarde)* or at night *(da noite)*, so that 8pm could be referred to as *vinte horas* (20 hours) or as *oito* (eight) *horas da noite*.
When? *Quando?*
What time is it? *Que horas são?*
Hour, day *Hora, dia*
Week, month *Semana, mês*
At what time? *A que horas?*
At 1, at 2, at 3 *A uma hora, as duas horas, as três horas*
An hour from now *Daqui a uma*

hora
Which day? *Que dia?*
Yesterday *Ontem*
Today *Hoje*
Tomorrow *Amanhã*
This week *Esta semana*
Last week *A semana passada*
Next week *A semana que vem*
Monday *Segunda-feira* (often written 2a)
Tuesday *Terca-feira*, 3a
Wednesday *Quarta-feira*, 4a
Thursday *Quinta-feira*, 5a
Friday *Sexta-feira*, 6a
Saturday *Sábado*
Sunday *Domingo*
The weekend *O fim de semana*

FURTHER READING

General Reading

Brazil: Poetic Portraits (photographs and poems). Editora Escrituras, 1998.
The Brazilians, by Joseph A Page. Addison-Wesley Publishing, 1995.

History & Travel

Brazil: Five Centuries of Change, Thomas E. Skidmore (pbk), 1999. Accessible history of the country.
Brazilian Adventure, by Peter Fleming. Norwood. PA: Norwood Editions, 1978 reprint of 1933 edition.
Rebellion in the Backlands, by Euclides da Cunha, translated from Portuguese by Os Sertões. University of Chicago Press, 1957. An account of the 1890s War of Canudos.
Travels in the Interior of Brazil, by George Gardner. Wolfeboro, NH: Longwood Publishing Group, Inc., 1977 reprint of 1846 edition.

Black Culture

Brazil: Anthropological Perspectives, edited by Maxine L. Margolis and William E. Carter. Columbia University Press, 1979.
Freedom and Prejudice: The Legacy of Slavery in the United States of Brazil, by R. B. Toplin. Westport, CT: Greenwood, 1981.

Fiction

Dona Flor and Her Two Husbands, by Jorge Amado. New York, 1993.
Sixty-four Stories (64 Contos) by Rubem Fonseca. An anthology of stories by an author, who writes about the gritty side of urban life. 2004
Soulstorm, by Clarice Lispector, translated by Alexis Levitin. Short stories by popular feminist writer, New Directions, New York, 1989.
The War of the End of the World, by Mario Vargas Llosa, translated from Spanish. Penguin, 1997. A fictionalised account of the Canudos uprising in Bahia.
The War of the Saints, by Jorge Amado. New York, 1993.

FEEDBACK

We do our best to ensure the information in our books is as accurate and up-to-date as possible. The books are updated on a regular basis, using local contacts, who painstakingly add, amend and correct as required. However, some mistakes and omissions are inevitable and we are ultimately reliant on our readers to put us in the picture.
We would welcome your feedback on any details related to your experience of using the book "on the road". Maybe you recommended a hotel that you liked (or another that you didn't), or you have discovered interesting new attractions or facts and figures about the country itself. The more details you can give us (particularly with regard to addresses, e-mails and telephone numbers), the better. We will acknowledge all contributions, and we'll offer an Insight Guide to the best letters received.

Please write to us at:
Insight Guides
PO Box 7910
London SE1 1WE
United Kingdom
Or send e-mail to:
insight@apaguide.co.uk

Other Insight Guides

Of the 200 titles in the *Insight Guides* series, the books which highlight destinations in this region include: *Insight Guides* to *Brazil, Chile, Ecuador, Peru, Argentina, Buenos Aires* and *Venezuela*. There is also an overall guide to the world's most surprising continent, *Insight Guide: South America* and an *Insight Guide: Amazon Wildlife*, which vividly captures in text and photography the flora and fauna of the region.

Insight also publishes Insight Pocket Guides, which come with a pull-out map in the back. Written by local hosts, these are itinerary-based guides that prioritise the must-see sights, helping users make the best use of limited time. South American destinations in the series include *Rio de Janeiro* and *Ecuador*.

Lastly, Insight FlexiMaps, hardwearing laminated fold-out maps include *Ecuador and Galápagos* and *Rio de Janeiro*.

RIO DE JANEIRO STREET ATLAS

The key map shows the area of Rio de Janeiro covered by the atlas section. An index of street names and places of interest shown on the maps can be found on the following pages. For each entry there is a page number and grid reference

Map Legend

══╍══	Auto-estrada with Junction
╍ ╍ ╍ ╍	Auto-estrada (under construction)
═══	Dual Carriageway
─────	Main Road
╍╍╍╍	Secondary Road
╍═╍═	Minor Road
─────	Track
■─ ∙ ─	International Boundary
─ ╍ ─ ─	State Boundary
╍ ∙ ╍	National Park/Reserve
─ ─ ─ ─	Ferry Route
✈	Airport
♰	Church (ruins)
✝	Monastery
🏰	Castle (ruins)
∴	Archaeological Site
∩	Cave
★	Place of Interest
⚜	Viewpoint
⟑	Beach
═══	Auto-estrada
────	Dual Carriageway
───	Main Roads
───	Minor Roads
════	Footpath
╍╍╍	Railway
	Pedestrian Area
	Important Building
	Park
Ⓜ	Metro
🚌	Bus Station
❶	Tourist Information
✉	Post Office
✛	Cathedral/Church
☾	Mosque
✡	Synagogue
⚱	Statue/Monument

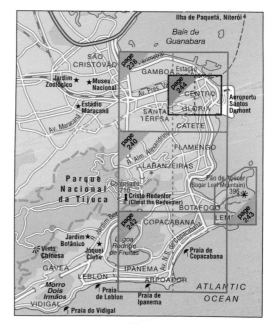

Baía de Guanabara

Morro
da Saúde

ZONA
PORTUÁRIA

Avenida Rio de Janeiro

R. Silvino

Rua do Propósito

Rua Pedro Ernesto

Avenida Rodrigues Alve

R. Rivadávia Correia

Rua do Livramento

R. do Fa

Avenida Prof. Pereira Reis

R. Cordeiro da Graça

Rua Equador

Av. Cidade de Lima

SANTO
CRISTO

Terminal
Rodoviária
Novo Rio

Pça.
Marechal
Hermes

Rua Santo Cristo

Pça.
Santo
Cristo

Santo
Cristo

R. Santo Cristo

Túnel
João Ricardo

Ld. do Faria

CEMITÉRIO
DOS INGLESES

GAMBOA

page
244

Avenida Pedro II

Avenida Francisco Bicalho

R. Gen. Luis M. Morais

R. Maia e Souza

R. Golemburgo

Alves

Pedro

R. Sara

R. Atila

R. Carlos Gomes

PARQUE VILA
FORMOSA

R. Vidal Negreiros

R. da América

R. Carioca

R. de Santo Gamboa

N.S. da
Penha

R. Ebroino Urugauai

Bento

Ribeiro

Pompeu

Estação Dom
Pedro II

Central

R. Moreira Pinto

R. do Pinto

N.S. Monte
Serrat

R. Nabuco de Freitas

R. Senador

Rua Senador

Rua da América

Quinta da
Boa Vista

R. Br. de Angra

R. Pereira Franco

Pça. 11
de Junho

R. Gen. Caldwell

Praça da

R. Moncorvo Filho

Estação
Barão
de Mauá

Hipólito

Hospi
Estad
Souza A

Estação Lauro
Müller

Avenida Presidente Vargas

Praça
Onze

R. Benedito

R. Júlio Carmo

R. Marquês do Sapucaí

Avenida 31 de Março

Rua

Frei Caneca

R. de Santana

R. Joaquim

R. Pereira de Almeida

R. A. Cavalcanti

R. Machado Coelho

R. Rodrigues Santos

R. Neri Pinheiro

R. Correa Vasques

R. Sta. Maria

R. Pres. Barroso

CIDADE NOVA

Riachuelo

R. do Matoso

R. Barão de Uba

Palhares

São
Joaquim

Estácio

Av. Salvador Sá

Rua Frei Caneca

Sambódromo

N.S. de Fátima

R. Paula

Av.

Medalha
Milagrosa
N.S. das Graças

R. J. Paulo

Rua J. Paulo

R. Haddock Lobo

ESTÁCIO

R. de Lacerda

Penitenciária
Lemos de Brito

Penitenc. Milton
Dias Moreira

R. do Catumbi

R. Carolina Reyder

R. do Paraíso

CATUMB

Largo das
Neves

Rua Dr. Satamini

Avenida Engenheiro Freyssinet

Rua Barão de Itapagipe

Rua

R. Japeri

Maia

R. São Roberto

R. Major Freitas

São Carlos

R. Ambire Cavalcanti

Morro de
Santos Rodrigues

Van

Ervan

CEMITÉRIO
DO CATUMBI

Rua

R. Elione de Almeida

R. Gonçalves

R. Miguel

Resende

Rua Aarão Reis

Itapiru

R. Dr. Agra

Rua

R. Queirós Lima

Rua Navarro

RIO
COMPRIDO

0   600 m

0   600 yards

A   B

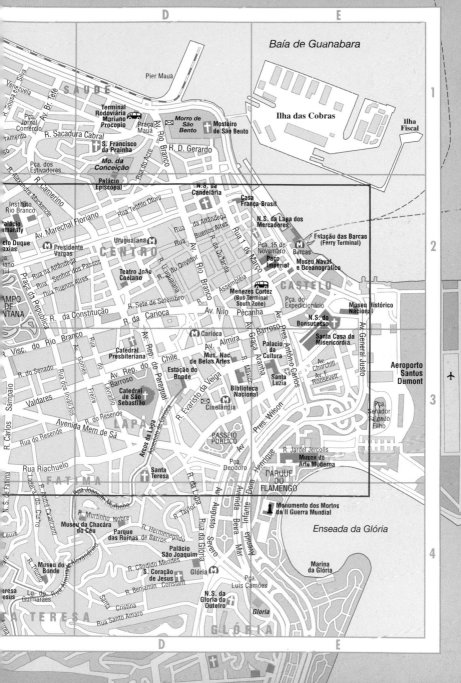

Baía de Guanabara

Ilha das Cobras

Ilha Fiscal

Pier Maúa

SAÚDE

R. Br. Tefé

Venezuela

Silva

Sousa

Pça. Jornal Comércio

ramento

R. Sacadura Cabral

Terminal Rodoviária Mariano Procópio

Praça Maúa

Av. Rio Branco

Rua do Acre

Morro de São Bento

Mostéiro de São Bento

Mo. da Conceição

S. Francisco da Prainha

R. D. Gerardo

so

Pça. dos Estivadores

R. Alexandre Mackenzie

R. Camerino

Palácio Episcopal

N.S. da Candelária

Casa França-Brasil

Instituto Rio Branco

alácio amaraty

Av. Marechal Floriano

Rua Teófilo Otoni

da Alfândega

N.S. da Lapa dos Mercadores

Rua Buenos Aires

Rua 1 de Março

Pça. 15 de Novembro

Estação das Barcas (Ferry Terminal)

cio Duque axias

ja. iano ul

Presidente Vargas

CENTRO

Uruguaiana

Rua

Rua

Av. da Quitanda

Paço Imperial

Barcas

Museu Naval e Oceanográfico

Praça da República

Rua da Alfândega

Rua Senhor dos Passos

Rua Buenos Aires

Teatro João Caetano

Rua do Ouvidor

Av. Rio Branco

Av. Uruguaiana

Assembléia

Menezes Cortez (Bus Terminal South Zone)

CASTELO

AMPO DE NTANA

R. Sete de Setembro

R. da Constituição

R. da Carioca

Av. Nilo Peçanha

Pça. do Expedicionário

N.S. do Bonsucesso

Museu Histórico Nacional

R. Visc. do Rio Branco

Av. Rep. do Paraguai

Carioca

Av. Almira

Av. Graça Aranha

Barroso

Pres. Antônio Carlos

Santa Casa da Misericórdia

R. Gomes

Rua

Catedral Presbiteriana

Chile

Mus. Nac. de Belas Artes

Palacio da Cultura

Av. General Justo

Aeroporto Santos Dumont

R. do Senado

Freire

Lavradio

Av. Rep. do

Estação do Bonde

México

Santa Luzia

Av. Churchill

Av. F. Roosevelt

Valdares

R. dos Invalidos

Catedral de São Sebastião

R. Evaristo da Veiga

Biblioteca Nacional

Pres. Wilson

R. Carlos

Sampaio

R. do Resende

LAPA

Arcos da Lapa

Cinelândia

PASSEIO PÚBLICO

Pça. Sénador Saldauho Filho

Rua Riachuelo

Avenida Mem de Sá

R. da Lapa

Av.

Pça. Deodoro

Av.

Dom Henrique

PARQUE DO FLAMENGO

R. Jardel Jercolis

Museu de Arte Moderna

FÁTIMA

N.S. da Fatima

Santa Teresa

R. Joaquim Murtinho

R. Taylor

Rua Augusto Severo

Avenida Beira Mar

Av. Infante

Monumento dos Mortos da II Guerra Mundial

Ladeira do Castro

R. André Cavalcanti

R. Murtinho Nobre

Museu da Chacára do Céu

Parque das Ruínas

R. Hermenegildo de Barros

Rua da Glória

Enseada da Glória

Leme

Rua Joaquim Murtinho

Palácio São Joaquim

R. Cândido Mendes

S. Coração de Jesus

Glória

Pça. Luis Camões

Marina da Glória

Museu do Bonde

R. Ave Almir.

R. Alexandrino

R. Benjamin Constant

N.S. da Gloria do Outeiro

eresa esus

Lg. do Guimarães

Santa

Cristina

Rua Santo Amaro

Gloria

A TERESA

GLÓRIA

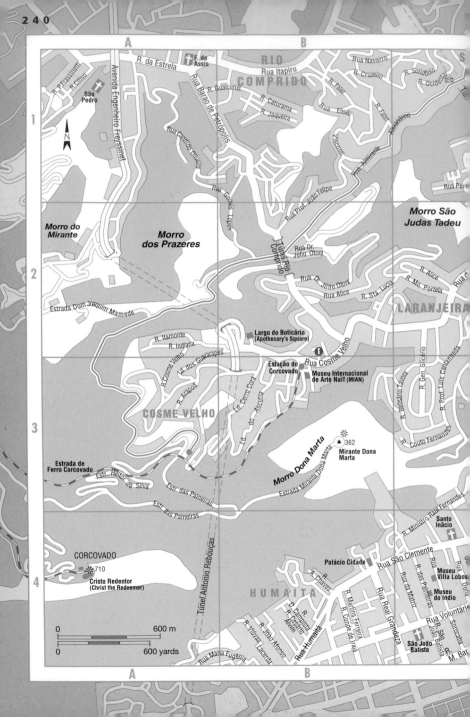

A

B

R. P. Frassinetti

R. Critiso

São Pedro

R. da Estrela

F. de Assis

RIO COMPRIDO

Rua Navarro

R. Cruzeiro

R. Solidade

R. Ocidezal

Rua Itapiru

Rua Barão de Petrópolis

R. Gualcurus

R. Caturama

R. Jaqueira

Rua Itapiru

R. Falei

R. Falei

Rua Elisae

Visconti

Pen. Aquideate

Neves linho

Avenida Engenheiro Freyssinet

Rua Catrudo Oliveira

Rua Gomes Lopes

Rua Prof. João Felipe

Rua Pén

1

Morro do Mirante

Morro dos Prazeres

Túnel Rio Comprido

Rua Dr. Júlio Otoni

Morro São Judas Tadeu

Estrada Dom Joaquim Mamede

Rua Dr. Júlio Otoni

Rua Alice

R. Sta. Lúcia

R. Alice

R. Mo. Portela

Rua

LARANJEIRA

2

R. Itamonte

R. Indiana

Ld. dos Guararapes

R. Cosme Velho

R. Arapoã

Largo do Boticário
(Apothecary's Square)

Rua Cosme Velho

Estação do Corcovado

Museu Internacional de Arte Naïf (MIAN)

R. Belisário Tavora

R. Gen. Glicério

R. Prof. Luis Cantinhata

R. Couto Fernandes

COSME VELHO

Ld. do Carro Cora

Ld. da Ascurra

Morro Dona Marta

362

Mirante Dona Marta

3

Estrada de Ferro Corcovado

Estr. Heitor da Silva

Estr. das Palmeiras

Estr. Mirante Dona Marta

Estrada Mirante Dona Marta

R. Ministro Raul Fernandes

Santo Inácio

Estr. das Palmeiras

CORCOVADO

710

Cristo Redentor
(Christ the Redeemer)

Túnel Antônio Rebouças

Palácio Cidade

Rua São Clemente

R. das Palmeiras

Rua da Matriz

Museu Villa Lobos

Museu do Índio

4

HUMAITÁ

R. A. Chaves

R. Campista

R. Cesário Alvim

R. Vinued Lacerda

R. João Afonso

Rua Humaitá

R. Martins Ferreira

R. Conde de Iraja

Rua Real Grandeza

Rua Voluntária

R. São João Batista

Sorocaba

São João Batista

M. Bar

0   600 m

0   600 yards

Rua Maria Eugenia

A

B

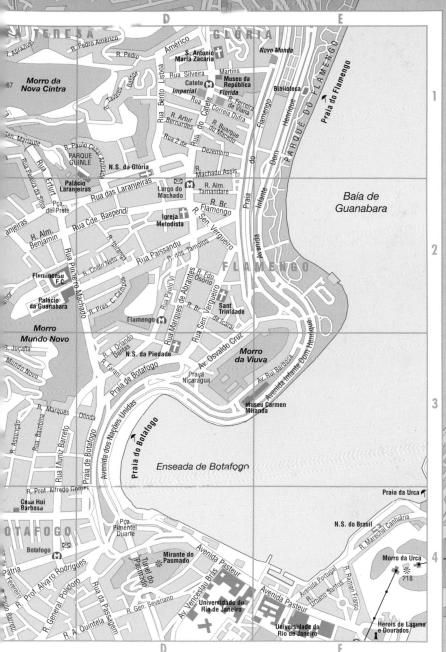

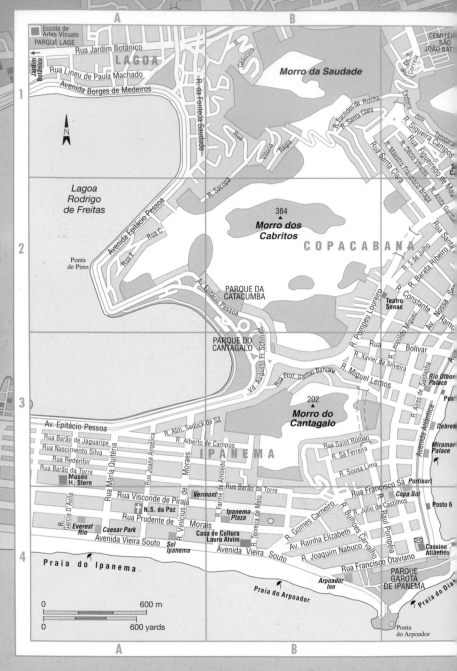

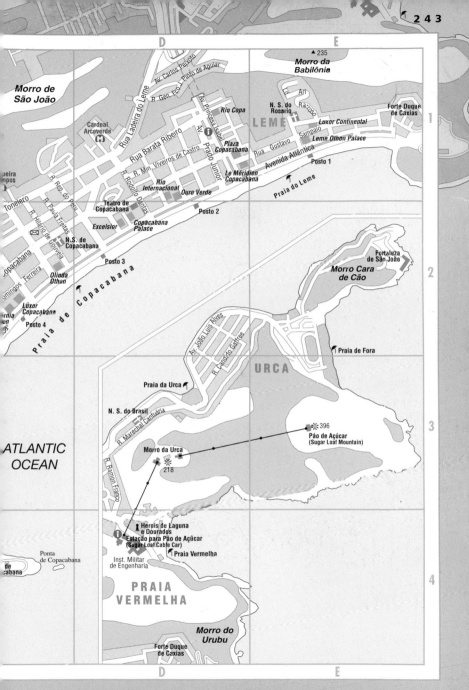

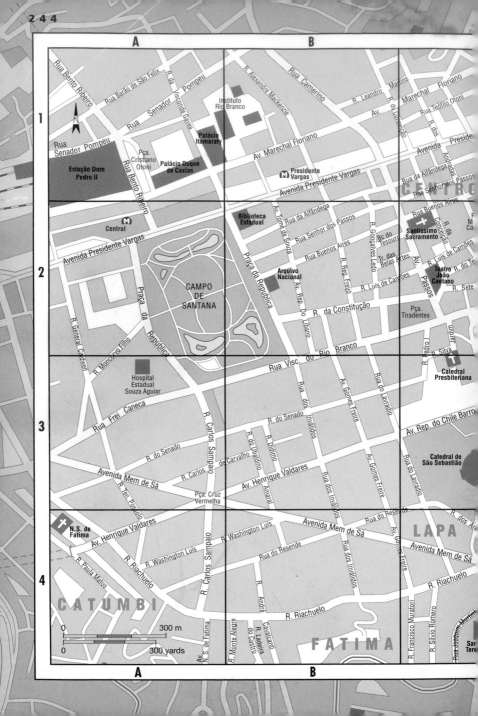

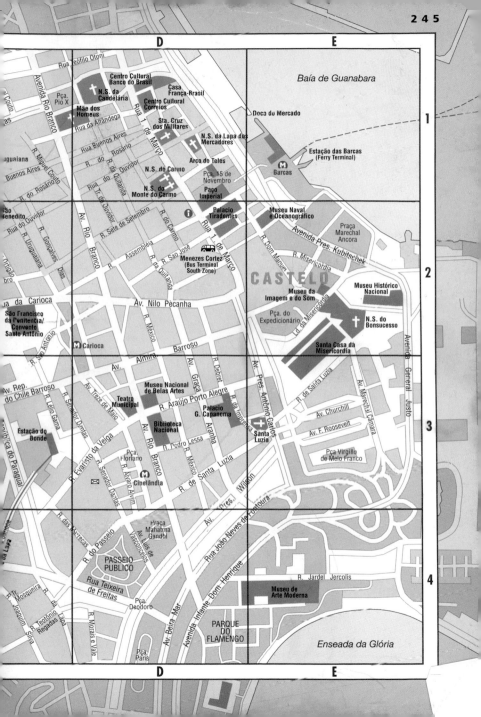

Baía de Guanabara

D

Rua Teófilo Otoni

Centro Cultural
Banco do Brasil

N.S. da
Candelária

Pça.
Pio X

Casa
França-Brasil

Mãe dos
Homens

Centro Cultural
Correios

Rua da Alfândega

Sta. Cruz
dos Militares

Doca du Mercado

Rua Buenos Aires

Rua 1 de Março

Rosário

N.S. da Lapa dos
Mercadores

R. do Ouvidor

R. da Quitanda

1

Estação das Barcas
(Ferry Terminal)

Arco do Teles

N.S. do Carmo

Pça. 15 de
Novembro

Barcas

N.S. do
Monte do Carmo

Paço
Imperial

E

R. do Rosário

R. do Ouvidor

Rua do Ouvidor

R. Tr. do Ouvidor

Av. Rio Branco

R. Sete de Setembro

R. do Carmo

Palacio
Tiradentes

Museu Naval
e Oceanográfico

Praça
Marechal
Ancora

Avenida Pres. Kubitschek

2

Assembleia

R. São José

R. Dom Manuel

R. Miséricordia

Menezes Cortez
(Bus Terminal
South Zone)

CASTELO

R. da Quitanda

Museu da
Imagem e do Som

Museu Histórico
Nacional

Av. Nilo Peçanha

R. México

Pça. do
Expedicionário

Ld. da Miséricordia

N.S. do
Bonsucesso

São Francisco
da Penitência/
Convento
Santo Antônio

Barroso

Santa Casa da
Misericordia

Carioca

R. São Antônio

Almira

R. Debret

Av. Pres. Antônio Carlos

Av. Marechal Câmara

Av. General Justo

Av. Graça

R. de Santa Luzia

Av. Rep.
do Chile Barroso

Av. Treze de Maio

Museu Nacional
de Belas Artes

Teatro
Municipal

R. Araújo Porto Alegre

Palacio
G. Capanema

R. da Imprensa

Av. Churchill

R. Senador Dantas

R. Lélio Gama

R. Evaristo da Veiga

Biblioteca
Nacional

R. Pedro Lessa

R. México

R. da Aranha

Santa
Luzia

Av. F. Roosevelt

3

Estação do
Bonde

Pça.
Floriano

R. Álvaro Alvim

R. de Santa Luzia

Av. Pres. Wilson

Pça Virgilio
de Melo Franco

Cinelândia

R. Senador Dantas

Av. Pres. Wilson

Praça
Mahatma
Gandhi

Av. Luis de Vasconcelos

Rua João Nieves de Fontoura

Av. Beira Mar

R. das Marrecas

R. do Passeio

PASSEIO
PUBLICO

R. Jardel Jercolis

4

Rua Teixeira
de Freitas

Pça.
Deodoro

Museu de
Arte Moderna

Avenida Infante Dom Henrique

R. Morais e Vale

Pça.
Paris

PARQUE
DO
FLAMENGO

Enseada da Glória

D

E

STREET INDEX

ART & PHOTO CREDITS

4Corners' Images 16, 80, 90, 131
Jenny Acheson/Axiom 53
akg-imagesLondon 28
**Pedro Armestre/AFP/Getty
Images** 74
Ricardo Azoury/Corbis 40
Campos & Davis/Apa 1, 5T, 9T,
10/11, 30, 32, 41, 50R, 56, 61,
65, 66, 67, 68, 69, 70, 75, 88,
88T, 89, 89T, 91T, 95T, 98, 98T,
111, 116, 117, 119, 123T, 124T,
129, 130T, 135T, 136, 146, 147,
152, 153, 156T, 157T, 158, 162,
207, 211, 212, 221, 226
Corbis 19
Vanor Correia/LATINPHOTO 44R
Douglas Engle/LATINPHOTO 4T,
35, 36, 45, 60, 64, 73, 99, 128
Mary Evans Picture Library 18, 20,
21, 22, 23, 24, 25, 26, 38, 39
Eric Carl Font/Apa 4C, 5B, 6T,
6B, 7TR, 7CL, 7B, 8TL, 8B, 9CL,
9CR, 42, 43, 44L, 49, 50L, 51,
52, 54, 55, 57, 59, 78/79, 91,
92, 92T, 93, 93T, 94, 95L, 95R,
96, 96T, 103, 104, 104T, 106,
107, 108, 109, 109T, 110, 111T,
112, 112T, 113, 117T, 118,
119T, 121, 123, 125, 125T, 130,
132, 133, 134, 134T, 135, 137,
141, 142, 143T, 144, 145, 145T,
148, 149, 149T, 151, 151T, 154,
155, 160, 160T, 161, 163, 163T,
166/167, 170, 171, 172, 172T,
173, 173T, 174T, 176, 176T,
177, 177T, 178, 178T, 183, 184,
184T, 185, 185T, 186, 187, 187T,

188, 188T, 189, 192, 193, 194,
195, 196L, 196R, 196T, 197,
197T, 198, 199T, 200, 201, 202,
203T, 208, 209, 223, 229, 230
Fototeca9x12 14/15, 126
Getty Images 2/3, 63, 143
**Christian Heeb/Laif/Camera
Press** 86
Hemis/Alamy 168
Jon Lusk/Redferns 72
John H. Maier Jr. 3BR, 33, 58,
71, 102, 159, 179, 180, 182
The Estate of Margaret Mee 150
Richard T. Nowitz 48, 97
Photolibrary 12/13
**Conrad Piepenburg/Laif/Camera
Press** 87
Ingolf Pompe 76/77, 120, 140,
204/205
Brian Rasic/Rex Features 124
Ronald Grant Archive 62
Sipa Press/Rex Features 29
**South American Pictures/Tony
Morrison** 37
Srdjan Suki/epa/Corbis 34
Time Life Pictures/Getty Images
27, 31

PICTURE SPREADS

Pages 46/47: ABACA/EMPICS
47CL; akg-images 46/47;
akg-images/IMS 47BL; Campos
& Davis/Apa 46C; Corbis 47TR;
Getty Images 46BR, 47CR, 47BR;
Time Life Pictures/Getty Images
46BL

Pages 100/101: Steve J.
Benbow/Axiom 100BR; Jil
Douglas/ArenaPAL 101BL; Getty
Images 100BL; Russell Monk/
Masterfile 100/101; Hilary
Shedel/ArenaPAL 101CR, 101BR
Pages 114/115: Eric Carl
Font/Apa 114/115, 114BR;
Kadu Niemeyer/Arcaid 114BL,
115CL, 115BL, 115BR; Alan
Weintraub/Arcaid 114CR, 115TR
Pages 138/139: Campos &
Davis/Apa 138BR, 139BR; Eric
Carl Font/Apa 138/139, 138BL,
138CR, 139CL, 139CR, 139BL
Pages 164/165: Bongarts/
Getty Images 165BL; Douglas
Engle/LATINPHOTO 165TR; EMPICS
164/165, 164BL; Eric Carl
Font/Apa 164CR, 164BR, 165BR
Pages 190/191: All photos
Eric Carl FontApa

Cover: front cover **James
May/SuperStock**, back cover left
Stauffenberg Müller/Fototeca9x12,
back cover centre and **inside
back flap** Eric Carl Font/Apa

Cartographic Editor: Zoë Goodwin
Map Production: Dave Priestley,
Stephen Ramsey, Mike Adams
and James Macdonald

©2006 Apa Publications GmbH & Co.
Verlag KG, Singapore Branch

Production: Linton Donaldson

GENERAL INDEX

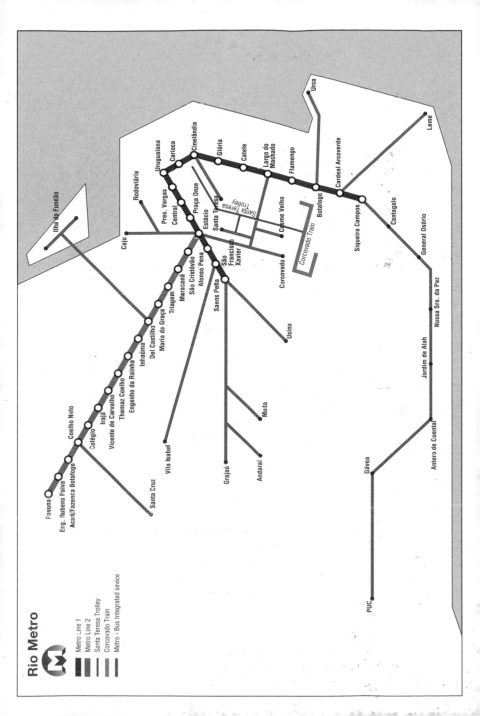